Betsy
Bonaparte

The Belle of Baltimore

Claude Bourguignon-Frasseto

Betsy Bonaparte

The Belle of Baltimore

CLAUDE BOURGUIGNON-FRASSETO

Translated from the French by Elborg Forster

MARYLAND HISTORICAL SOCIETY
Baltimore

© Claude Bourguignon-Frasseto, 1988, 2003
Published by the Maryland Historical Society
201 W. Monument Street
Baltimore, Maryland 21201

Library of Congress Cataloging-in-Publication Data

Bourguignon-Frasseto, Claude.
  [Betsy Bonaparte, ou, La belle de Baltimore. English]
  Besty Bonaparte : the belle of Baltimore / Claude Bourguignon-
Frasseto ; translated by Elborg Forster.
  p. cm.
  Includes index.
  ISBN 0-938420-82-8 (pbk. : alk. paper)
  1. Bonaparte, Elizabeth Patterson, 1785–1879—Family. 2. Jârâme
Bonaparte, King of Westphalia, 1784–1860—Family. 3. Bonaparte
family. 4. Napoleon I, Emperor of the French, 1769–1821—Family.
I. Title.

DC216.95.B629 B6813 2001
944.05'0922—dc21

                                                          2001052145

Manufactured in the United States of America.
The paper used in this publication meets the minimum requirements
of the American National Standard for Information Sciences Perma-
nence of Paper for Printed Library Materials ANSI Z39.48-1984.

For my grandfather, Sylvestre Frasseto
and my friends in Baltimore

Contents

Introduction

I HAVE BEEN IMMERSED IN NAPOLEONIC HISTORY
since my childhood, in that my Corsican mother imbued me with it.
Even if I did not share entirely her enthusiasm for that great organizer
who also was a great warrior, I always was interested in that fascinating
period of our history, which so greatly shaped the history of Europe.

And I was even more fascinated in that a faraway ancestor of my
mother's family had been a close friend of the Bonapartes in Ajaccio, the
present administrative capital of Corsica. Later on, in 1806, he even
was invited to the imperial court at the Tuileries, in Paris.

More recently, I learned about a very beautiful American girl who
married a Bonaparte. Which Bonaparte, I did not know. I did not know
then of the earlier biographies of Betsy written in America. Through
my research, at the Foreign Office archives in Paris, I found letters written from Baltimore by an "Elisa." At that time, Elisa, Napoléon's sister,
was grand-duchess of Tuscany and residing in Italy. It could not be the
same person. And that was how I discovered the existence of Elizabeth
Patterson, called "Betsy" by her American family, and "Elisa" by Jérôme
Bonaparte, her husband.

Alas! It was a short-lived marriage, as Napoleon obliged his younger
brother to divorce. But a son, Jérôme-Napoléon, was born from that
union.

I was fascinated by this story of a failed love in an international
context and followed beautiful Betsy—alias "Elisa"—throughout Europe, through her difficult relationships with the imperial family, and
her life after the divorce. This is the story I wanted to tell.

I owe to the Maryland Historical Society and to my friends in
Baltimore many thanks for having allowed me to go deeper into my
research about Elizabeth Patterson. First of all, the society's staff, amiable and competent, allowed me to consult in pleasant surroundings

documents very useful for my research, begun in France at the Foreign Affairs Archives, the National Library, and the Historical Service of the Navy. Very soon, it appeared that a stay in Baltimore would be essential, and there I must particularly thank William and Sona Johnston, curators at the Walters Art Gallery and Baltimore Museum of Art respectively, for their hospitality and their advice. Through them, I met Geoffrey and Claudia Fielding (the grand-daughter of Eugene Didier, author of the 1879 volume *Life and Letters of Madame Bonaparte*), also learned friends, who in their turn invited me twice to Baltimore to finish my research, centered this time on Betsy's two grandsons, each of them brilliant in their own fields. Many thanks to them, too.

Here I must recall my meeting with Mr. Guy Wildenstein, president (among other illustrious appointments) of the American Society of the French Legion of Honor. That meeting was suggested by my sister, Mme Isabelle du Pasquier (former curator of the Musée de la Légion d'Honneur herself). Mr. Wildenstein was particularly interested in the career of Charles Joseph Bonaparte, and warmly encouraged me to take up my research around him and his brother. Of course, all this led to the consideration of having the book translated and published in the United States, for which I am very grateful.

In Paris — and around Paris — I was greatly aided, too, in consulting documents and the Bonaparte images by the director of the Château de Malmaison (formerly owned by Napoléon and Josephine), Mr. Bernard Chevallier. As for the Bibliothèque Marmottan in Boulogne-Billancourt, which owns an important collection of works relative to the Napoleonic era, I warmly thank for their friendly and efficient help Mr. Bruno Foucart, Mme Nicole Ambourg, Mr. Jean-Michel Pianelli, and Miss Claire Poirion.

To conclude, I shall say with gratitude that the present publication was made possible thanks to the interest taken in my book by Dr. Robert I. Cottom, Publisher for the Maryland Historical Society, a fine translation from the original French made by Elborg Forster, and the skills of my editor, Donna Shear.

Claude Bourguignon
Clamart, July 16, 2003

Foreword

$\mathcal{A}$S PRESIDENT OF THE AMERICAN SOCIETY OF the French Legion of Honor, I was invited, in October 1998, to speak at a symposium in Paris, France, on the importance in the United States of the French decoration, created by Emperor Napoleon some two hundred years ago, which today still is one of the foremost distinctions in the world.

At that event I met Mrs. Isabelle du Pasquier, an old friend and former curator of the Museum of the Legion of Honor in Paris. She told me about her sister Claude Bourguignon-Frasseto, who was researching the life of a certain Betsy Patterson. Later that month, I had the pleasure of making Mrs. Bourguignon's acquaintance. We talked about the members of the Bonaparte family who had settled in the United States and, in particular, the extraordinary course of events that compelled the French Emperor's youngest brother, Jérôme, an officer in the French navy, to disobey orders, abandon his post in the Caribbean island of Martinique, run off to America, and fall in love with a beautiful young girl from Baltimore.

Mrs. Bourguignon, who is of Corsican descent, has understandably always been fascinated by the epopee of this extraordinary family, whose son rose to legendary power and left an indelible mark all over Europe and even, as we will see, on the United States. She noticed my interest in the Bonaparte-Patterson love story and offered me the book she had written on that little-known chronicle.

It is in Mrs. Bourguignon's book that I discovered that Jérôme Bonaparte originally wanted to settle in the New World. Had he been allowed to do so by his brother, he could have been the Emperor's personal representative on this side of the Atlantic, establishing close ties between the two nations. One can only wonder about the various scenarios that might have been . . . such as American soldiers joining the

"Great Army" and turning Waterloo into a French victory, or Napoleon being allowed to go into exile in America.

I was truly fascinated by this apparently simple love affair that could have changed history and Napoleon's fate had he not forced his brother to renege on his marriage and return to Europe. Jérôme's American marriage produced a son and two grandsons. Charles Joseph Bonaparte, the youngest, befriended Theodore Roosevelt at Harvard University. As civil service commissioner, Roosevelt called extensively on his friend's help. In fact, Roosevelt used to tell Charles: "you represent the principles for which I hope to stand." It is therefore not surprising that President Roosevelt asked Bonaparte to serve in his cabinet, successively as secretary of the navy and as attorney general.

Mrs. Bourguignon's remarkable talent as a storyteller brings to life the principal actors of the times, through Betsy's eyes. We meet Napoleon's family and, in particular his mother Laetizia and sister Pauline, who both appeared to be genuinely fond of Betsy, and especially of her son. We also meet many intellectuals who shaped public opinion and who advised Betsy, some surely with ulterior motives, through her trials and tribulations as she strived to obtain recognition for her son as a Bonaparte in his own right.

After reading her book, I exchanged many letters, phone calls, and faxes with Mrs. Bourguignon, in which I emphasized how important I thought an American edition would be. She decided to follow my advice, and, very much a perfectionist, traveled to Baltimore to research some additional details she wished to include in her new edition. I am indeed very proud to have been involved in a small way in persuading Claude Bourguignon to make this revised American edition, and I wish to thank her for inviting me to write this Foreword.

Finally, I believe a few words are in order about the Emperor, who seems to have pulled all the strings and who so fascinated Betsy. Those who would portray Napoleon as a shallow power-thirsty tyrant have a totally wrong idea of the man. He was a true statesman who created a judicial system so modern for the times that Napoleon's Code is still in effect today, and a Legion of Honor based on personal merit, not birthright, a concept so democratic that it has allowed the French Order to endure into the twenty-first century. Certainly he was a dictator, not very different from the autocrats that ruled at the time. He knew that, in order for his regime to survive, he had to establish a dynasty, thus his obsession with putting his siblings on the vacant thrones of the territories he had conquered.

Among the descendants of Napoleon I, two inherited his flair for statesmanship: one of his nephews, the son of Louis, who became Napoleon III, Emperor of France; and a great-nephew, the American grandson of Jérôme, who became attorney general of the United States.

Guy Wildenstein
New York

Part I

A Corsican on the Shores of the Chesapeake

I

*T*HE WIND, THE WIND! IT RUSHES THROUGH ROWS
of red brick houses lined up along South Street, catches in shop signs,
and climbs up the hill where stands the proud mansion of wealthy
Charles Carroll, carrying the smell of spices from the East Indies and the
shouts of sailors unloading their ships on the nearby wharf.

In 1793, Baltimore is still a small town of fifteen thousand inhabitants, the fourth largest of the United States after Boston, New York,
and Philadelphia. But it will double its population over the next ten
years and experience a fabulous boom, thanks to its privileged position
at the upper end of the Chesapeake Bay and the growth of its maritime
trade with Europe and the Antilles during the French Revolution and
the Napoleonic wars.

As early as 1729, its exceptional site in the heart of Maryland, named
in honor of Henrietta Maria by King Charles I, had appealed to the
commissioners in Annapolis charged with laying the foundations for a
new port, for this port was also close to the Philadelphia Road, to the
Patapsco River, and to the rushing waters of the Jones Falls, which
could furnish energy to the mills along its banks.

The rich soil of the region allowed for vast wheat and tobacco plantations, and the port of Baltimore would serve to export these products.
A few stakes driven into the ground, a duly executed contract of sale
stipulating forty shillings per hectare from Mssrs. Carroll (who had themselves been given this land by Lord Baltimore), and Baltimore was born.

In Baltimore, at number 20 South Street, in a large Georgian-style house of red brick with white shutters, a little girl tosses in her bed, unable to find sleep. She is very pretty, with her hazel eyes and her chestnut hair; she is eight years old and her name is Elizabeth.

Her father, William Patterson, is a wealthy local merchant. The son of a poor Scots-Irish farmer, he arrived in Philadelphia in 1766 to seek his fortune. His beginnings as a lowly employee of a shipping magnate of Irish origin, to whom he had been recommended, were modest. But by the age of twenty-one he already had his own business, able to outfit two ships with his savings and go into maritime trade. It was the time when revolt began to seethe in America.

General Washington appealed for help. The France of Louis XVI would soon send reinforcements: La Fayette, Rochambeau, d'Estaing, de Grasse. Meanwhile he asked all American citizens who desired their independence — and not all of them did, for many still had great respect for the British Crown — to rise to the occasion. William Patterson heeded that call. He was an energetic and intelligent young man. He embarked for France on one of his ships, sailed to Nantes, and returned with weapons. For all his intrepid courage, however, he was not quite a hero. On the return voyage, he asked the captain of the brig that carried him to let him off on the island of Saint-Eustache, a Dutch possession near Guadeloupe. Service to his country was one thing, business another.

He spent two years on that island, where he skillfully wove a network of commercial relations that were to be useful to him when he returned to the United States in 1778. Saint Eustache also served him as a basis from which to provision Washington's army. Soon, however, the Dutch became concerned about this and refused to back his efforts on behalf of the "rebels." He sought refuge in Martinique, a French possession whose authorities were only too glad to shelter him.

In 1778, when he returned to Philadelphia, he was rich and enjoyed great favor with the Congress and with the commanding general. He bought some real estate in the developing market town of Baltimore and elsewhere in Maryland and then decided to get married: his bride was pretty Dorcas Spear, daughter of a local notable. They settled in Baltimore.

He was devoted to duty, Mr. Patterson. Tall, solidly built, with a high forehead and penetrating eyes under his powdered wig, sober in his dress, he was the very image of a *pater familias* of the old school. "I have always considered it my duty," he was to write in his will, "to watch over my family. . . . I have not sought honors" — which did not prevent him from accepting the presidency of the first bank in Baltimore — "but consider that every citizen should contribute more or less to the good of society when he can do so and when it is not too much to his disadvantage." What a characteristic remark! It is certainly a far cry from this sober and earnest man to the muddle-headed ideological exaltation that is shaking up the peoples of faraway Europe!

That evening little Elizabeth, curled up in the linen sheets of her little four-poster bed, hears his confident steps as he climbs the stairs of his house, candle in hand. He stops by the door of each of his sleeping children, makes sure that the windows are properly shut and that all fires are banked, and then prepares for his well-deserved rest.

Elizabeth admires this intelligent and authoritarian father. And yet she is as stubborn as he is and has often shed floods of tears when he has denied her one of her whims. More than anything, she loves to visit him in his offices on Gay Street, next door to the Patterson warehouses. Accompanied by her Aunt Nancy, her mother's sister, or one of her older brothers, she watches the unloading of ships in the harbor: brigs, schooners, and store ships have arrived from the Antilles filled with molasses and cane sugar, others have brought manufactured goods from England or French silk cloth, and there are also vegetables from the Eastern Shore. Once it has been unloaded from the ships by the stevedores, the merchandise is transported to the hinterland, toward Philadelphia or Virginia, in covered wagons drawn by four or six horses with bells around their necks.

Right next to the pier, near the warehouses, are chandler shops that sell sails and sailing supplies. Workmen are engaged in building small boats of mulberry wood, oak, Carolina or Georgia cedar. And of course, there is no lack of taverns — The Golden Horse or The White Swan, where beer and whiskey flow in abundance.

Mr. Patterson does not particularly like to have his children wander about in this neighborhood. When he sees them there, he makes them come up to his office. There he instructs Elizabeth and her two older brothers, John and Robert, in the rudiments of bookkeeping and the shipping business. Later Robert would become his father's business associate. But Elizabeth herself, "Betsy," as her father affectionately calls her, also enjoys juggling figures. That is why her Aunt Nancy, a shrewd businesswoman, is giving her a few arithmetic lessons.

Often when the day is clear, Mr. Patterson has a carriage harnessed and drives his children up to Federal Hill, which overlooks the city. In the distance he can see, with the help of a telescope, his ships as they make their way up the Chesapeake Bay, returning from Europe or the Antilles. Each of the children wants to be the first to identify one of their father's brigs, the *Intrepid* or the *East Wind*.

The Chesapeake, a large estuary almost as vast as a sea, is also crisscrossed by private boats belonging to owners of property close to the shore who prefer traveling by sea or river to using the bad local roads.

From the top of Federal Hill one can also see far into the surrounding countryside with its large fields of wheat and grain, a very pretty sight when it is in bloom, the Hooper Islands, a bird paradise, the fifty mills driven by the Jones Falls, and the roads leading to the city: Frederick Road and Yorktown Road. These thoroughfares are crowded with long lines of wagons or flat carts drawn by oxen, as well as with the herds of rich German farmers driven in from Pennsylvania or western Maryland.

Twenty miles from Baltimore, along the Patapsco River (an Indian name meaning "where the snow stops") is the Pattersons' country place, Springfield, where they go during the hottest part of the summer to escape the malignant fevers that are rife in the towns at that time. One year five hundred persons died in Philadelphia alone! The quality of the food no doubt has something to do with this, for the newcomers do not eat fresh meat; for the most part the basis of their diet is salt pork and potatoes . . . with plenty of alcohol to wash it down.

At the Pattersons', of course, as in most well-to-do urban families, fresh food is eaten. There is fish from the Chesapeake — shad, herring, gudgeon, mussels, and crabs — and there is an abundance of vegetables. Betsy has rosy cheeks and is in excellent health, as are her brothers.

In 1793 the Pattersons have seven children. Six more are to be born. Only seven will survive.

Betsy not only acquires notions of arithmetic from her Aunt Nancy, she also attends a school run by French nuns.

Many French people live in Baltimore. Some are royalists who have fled the Terror, for instance the Pascaut de Poléon family, whose oldest daughter, Henriette, is one of Betsy's best friends, while others are Acadians. Others still are rich planters from Saint-Domingue, who are beginning to flee that island. The finest French possession of the era, the "pearl of the Antilles," Saint Dominque plays a major role in France's commerce by providing it with sugar, indigo, and coffee. For some years now, revolt has been smoldering among the black residents, and the wind of the French Revolution has only served to fan the agitation. "Poor whites" and mulattoes have tried to seize leadership in the sedition, but they have gradually been swamped by the masses of blacks. What could they do against five hundred thousand black slaves, exasperated by terrible mistreatment and inspired by a resolute leader, Toussaint L'Ouverture?

Some had left the island as one would leave a sinking ship and had gone to Cuba, Jamaica, or the hospitable shores of America. Many had settled in Baltimore, where they worked as hairdressers, hatters, teachers of French or the arts. They are people like Madame Lacombe, headmistress of the school to which Mr. Patterson has decided to send his daughter.

Betsy is fascinated by the refined manners of the French, even those who work in modest occupations and have little money. Listening to their nostalgic stories, she dreams of discovering France for herself. But of course, it would be an aristocratic France filled with counts and marquis, not that of the *sans-culottes*. When she visits her friends the Pascaut de Poléons, she loves to hear the marquis play his flute, accompanied on the harpsichord by his wife. When M. de Poléon has finished playing, he reaches into the pocket of his velvet waistcoat for a superb gold snuff box, from which he extracts a pinch of snuff in an elegant gesture that makes his alençon lace cuffs quiver ever so slightly.

What a contrast with Mr. Patterson and the other merchants of her town, who are sitting in their functional counting houses dressed in sober dark suits! Dreams are one thing — and reality another. Betsy admires her father, takes an interest in his business, and has a taste for mathematics, but her dream is all about chateaux, jewels, and aristocracy.

In 1793 Baltimore still talks about Lafayette and of the day in 1781 when the French general arrived at the head of his expeditionary corps, limping and in rags; some of his soldiers were barefoot. Washington, with whom he was allied, had sent him to Virginia to rendezvous with Greene's army in order to stop the advance of the British. The French troops had forded the Susquehanna River, but the wind had been so fierce and the river so rain-swollen that they had to leave their baggage carts and their supplies behind on the other shore. Demoralized and stripped of everything, some of the troops had balked at going to fight in the South. And it is safe to say that without Baltimore, without the town's ladies and girls who went to work, each of them sewing something, be it a pair of trousers, a jumper, a hunting shirt, or a hat, and that without the local merchants who had taken the best bolts of cloth from their warehouses, the soldiers would not have gone on. Lafayette had pledged himself to reimburse the entire sum — more than two thousand guineas! — and did so two years later, when the war was over. Motivated by his deep gratitude to Baltimore's inhabitants, he had insisted that Congress pass a special resolution commending the town for its civic virtue. In the course of a triumphal voyage to the United States in 1785, the French general returned to Baltimore, spending considerable time at the Patterson home, where he was received as a friend.

One day Elizabeth's milk sister, Jessie, the daughter of Mummy Lou, little Betsy's black wetnurse, wearing an air of mystery, comes to pick her up in her room for a walk down to the harbor. As they walk along, the little black girl explains that the night before her grandfather had talked in her presence of an old black sorceress who lives by the docks near the White Swan Tavern and who can predict the future by looking at the lines of one's hand.

Before long the little girls find themselves in a smoke-filled room where black folks are gathered singing in low voices. Mummy July sits near the fire smoking a long pipe. She is a big woman, her white hair is pulled back into a bun, and she is wearing a long flowered dress of dubious color. Betsy flinches for a moment when she sees her, but then her curiosity gets the better of her fear. She holds out her hand. For a long moment the old woman does not speak, just rocks back and forth in her rocking chair, her pipe between her lips.

"Well, how about that?" she finally grumbles.

Betsy feels more and more ill at ease.

"Yes . . . yes, I do see something odd here. There is one line that cuts the other . . . and over here it almost looks like a crown."

The two little girls have stopped breathing. In the half-darkness, Jessie's wide-open eyes shine like two agates.

"You will be the most beautiful girl in Baltimore, Miz Betsy. . . . You will marry a foreigner with a famous name. . . . Maybe a king. . . ."

"Will I be a queen, then?" asks Betsy, delightedly.

"That I don't know. . . . But you'll be very close to the crown."

Betsy's heart pounds as hard as the spritsail of the *Intrepid* in a stiff breeze. She has always dreamt of princes, castles, and shimmering dresses while ensconced in her rich but austere home, where she is raised by parents who, despite their wealth, are staunch republicans. What she has heard is enough to turn the head of a little girl attracted by the unusual and the marvelous.

Jessie also holds out her hand. A few minutes later the little girls leave the old woman's den, glassy-eyed and with hesitating steps. Betsy takes deep breaths of the sea air. She adjusts the hood of her cape and pulls her milk sister to the military port, where two frigates flying the French flag are riding at anchor, the *Hercule* and the *Triomphant*.

Farther down on the bay are three English brigs bobbing on the waters of the Chesapeake with all their sails taken in; like watchful birds of prey, they are on the lookout for everything that approaches the American coast. A foreign prince, perhaps? English or French?

A fresh breeze springs up. Betsy keeps her face turned to the sea.

2

$\mathcal{I}$N AJACCIO, ON THE WESTERN COAST OF CORSICA, the wind blows from the land as the *libecciu,* and from the sea, but people much prefer the latter, for the wind from the interior is not only cold in winter and very hot in the summer, but also carries the emanations of the nearby marshes.

A little boy with black eyes and curly hair is playing by the harbor in the south of this island in the middle of Mediterranean Sea, a harbor that is very different from the port of Baltimore. The Bonaparte family, like the Pattersons, has many children, and the house on the rue Malerba often resounds with joyous shouts. The building has an ochre-colored façade; without a balcony, it is a bit austere and looks out over a square shaded by a few trees where Jérôme, the little boy, often plays with his young friends. Sometimes they run down the next little street, the Strada Dritta[1], to reach the sea, which can be seen at the end of tight rows of pink or pale yellow houses with laundry strung across the streets. One also has to be careful not to be hit by a bucketful of greasy water if someone misses the fayence funnel which, attached to the outside of each house, leads to the cesspool ducts.

But Jérôme does not care, all he wants is to get away from the somewhat tense atmosphere of the *Casa* Bonaparte, from all these bearded faces of conspirators who have lately been coming and going to the upstairs drawing room where the younger children are not allowed to go.

[1] Today rue Bonaparte

In this year 1793, two important events have happened in the Bonaparte family. First, one of Jérôme's older brothers, Napoleon, at the time an artillery lieutenant in the French army who has repeatedly distinguished himself on the continent, has returned to his native island and seems determined to stay there. And the little boy admires this brother with his sharp features, the eyes that sparkle with intelligence, and the determined chin.

"Lend me your sword and your pistol," he sometimes begs.

This amuses the big brother, and he lets him parade around and fire blank shots.

The other event has been the death of the children's grand-uncle, archdeacon Lucien, the uncle of their father Charles Bonaparte. Ever since his nephew's death — which occurred not long after Jérôme's birth — the archdeacon had advised Signora Letizia, left a widow with many children.

From his sickbed, which he had not left for some time, the archdeacon had autocratically directed the finances of the *casa*. This man of the Church was above all an excellent man of business. For him, feelings did not count, except when it came to defending the little clan to which he had attached himself. Intent on preserving and increasing his nephews' patrimony, he had litigated for years on end against the Bozzi family in order to renovate a part of the Bonaparte house and thereby add a few rooms to house the numerous progeny of his nephew Charles. He had actually gone so far as to drag his brother's widow Saveria into court, as well as the Ramolino family, whom he pressured to pay the remaining portion of beautiful Letizia's dowry. As a result, his hapless cousin Jean had found himself sleeping on straw, after his furniture and other possessions were sold at auction on the piazza del Olmo.[2]

No, Uncle Lucien did not trifle when it came to the family's business, but his niece and his great nephews adored him. While Charles, the young lawyer who had died too young and had once been the friend of the Corsican nationalist Paoli, had been of an impetuous, fickle, and careless character, Uncle Lucien was all seriousness and temperance, possessed of a sense of economy that came close to stinginess.

---

[2] Today Place des Palmiers.

And since he had not been able to move for some time, his bed served as a safe. Under his mattress he kept money accrued from various sources of revenue. Thanks to Lucien, the family owned vineyards on the outskirts of Ajaccio and olive trees that yielded oil. The uncle also had talents as a broker and engaged in horse trading. All of this helped the household make ends meet. In the cellar, where Jérôme sometimes liked to take his little friends, stood the press and the mill that served to make the oil, and the boys could smell the strong odor of the olives when they were brought in from the Milelli farm.

Uncle Lucien, then, had not moved from his bed in the last years of his life, and Jérôme, who was only eight and a half, did not remember ever seeing him standing on his legs. When it became necessary to redo his bed and freshen it up a little, it was impossible to turn the mattress, so that his attendants had to undo its seams under him in order to fluff up the wool and the feathers with which it was stuffed. At such times an acrid smell would fill the room, but only Madame Letizia and her servant-girls were present.

Only two months after Napoleon's return to the old homestead, Uncle Lucien had died, surrounded by all of his grand-nephews. His will was very much in keeping with his tightly run financial management and it resuscitated several statutes of the old Genoese law, which at the time had no equivalent in French law. Later, Napoleon was to incorporate these into his law code, particularly the prohibition for children to marry before the age of twenty-five without the consent of the head of the family, under penalty of losing their rights to the patrimony. This proviso would eventually cause bitter resentment among some of them.

Another personality who frequented the *casa* at the time was young Joseph Fesch, half-brother of Madame Letizia, whose mother had married a Swiss gentleman after she was widowed. Archdeacon Lucien had taken care of him as well. He had made him take holy orders, not without inculcating in him a great realism. Indeed it was at his instigation that Fesch, who had become a priest by 1790, had taken the loyalty oath to the new regime in 1790. These two prelates were ardently pro-revolutionary!

Now it is the end of May 1793, and little Jérôme Bonaparte is most interested in joining his friends of the Borgo. Entering through the gate that can close the access to the citadel, he finds himself on the piazza del Olmo. Before him lies the Borgo, the part of town[3] where most of the Corsicans who have come down from their outlying villages have settled, sometimes generations ago. It is a very picturesque though rather insalubrious place, dotted with tanneries, granaries, and storehouses for salt; the gibbet too stands here.

Jérôme has several friends in this area and always hopes to go playing by the nearby harbor with them. With a bit of luck, perhaps Gian-Battista, a fisherman he knows well, will take them out to sea when he puts out his nets. But today no boat leaves the shore. Here and there along the pier, little groups of men converse in grave tones. As for Gian-Battista, he demonstratively turns his back on Jérôme when he sees him coming.

The little boy is intrigued. "What is going on here?" he wonders. The Revolution has spread so much hatred, here as elsewhere, that he has become used to fierce expressions, to voices lowered when curious strangers approach, and to raised fists. But today the gondolas of the coral fishers are gently bobbing at anchor in the harbor. "What are they all doing, stopping work like this?" little Jérôme says to himself, beginning to worry ever so slightly. He remembers that two years earlier he had experienced the same suspicion-filled and threatening atmosphere when his brother was elected lieutenant-colonel of the national guard.

This was a much sought-after position. Napoleon, having conducted a brilliant election campaign, had been elected by a strong majority over his neighbor of the same age, Mathieu Pozzo di Borgo. That night, family and supporters had gathered in the rue Malerba for a great celebration. Was it this episode that would seal forever the hatred of the Pozzo di Borgo family for all Bonapartes and eventually turn Mathieu's brother Charles-André into Napoleon's most dangerous enemy? Or was it just the chamber pot accidentally emptied by Mme Pozzo di Borgo on Charles Bonaparte's best suit?

But right now Jérôme does not think of this story. All he is interested in is meeting up with the children of the citadel and the little

[3] Today rue Fesch

13

Borghiani with whom he wants to fight, even if these boys outnumber him and often have the upper hand. He is just filling his pockets with stones in preparation for the coming battles when a bearded man appears, dressed in one of the heavy capes called *pelone,* his head covered with the pointed hat of the shepherds.

"Gerolamo," he shouts, "don't you know that it is dangerous to run around in the street? Come on, let's go home, Signora Letizia is looking for you."

This man is Peretti, a partisan of the Bonaparte family, who has arrived a few days earlier from his village of Bocognano. He and several other villagers are camping out day and night at the family house. Mattresses have been thrown down everywhere, in the drawing room, on the landing of the staircase. All these sinister-looking characters sleep with their guns at the ready, with stilettoes stuck in their belts.

Jérôme is not afraid. These mysteries are exciting. In the evening, before he is sent to the rustic wooden bed he shares with his brother Louis, he opens his black, shiny eyes as wide as he can and tries to catch a few scraps of the conversation.

On the doorstep the nursemaid Camilla Ilari is waiting for him. She has crossed her hands over her black apron, and the face looking out from her *mezzaro* is severe.

"*Che ragazzo!*" she cries. "Worse than his brother Nabulione! Just where have you been?"

"I hope I'm not in for the strap," Jérôme thinks with a shiver, for Madame Letizia is not shy about spankings.

But he is safe, for this evening Madame Letizia has other worries. The trumpet sound has been heard throughout the island. When the call came from Pascal Paoli, the Corsicans of the mountains have risen up against the domination of France and its blood-stained Revolution, which has not gone down well in the country, where inequalities had not existed. The Bonapartes, having first been allied with Paoli, have decided to cast their lot with France and the Republic. They count Saliceti, Barras, and Maximilien-Francoise Marie Isidore Robespierre among their friends. While they have few supporters in Ajaccio, they are more popular in Bastelica, Bocognano, and other neighboring villages.

In the *casa* the atmosphere is even more tense than usual, and people look serious. Today the good smell of soup cooked over bacon that ordinarily rejoices Jérôme's heart does not meet him in the entrance-way, and the kitchen is empty. Madame Letizia is sitting in the drawing room. She is surrounded by her mother, her half-brother Joseph Fesch, and the family's confidential adviser, the faithful François Braccini.

Suddenly, someone beats violently against the flap door to the court-yard. The signora turns pale and clutches her throat. Jérôme and his young sister Annunciata (the future Caroline) are still standing by the doorstep and watch as the gate opens and a troop of armed men climbs up the small wooden staircase. They are led by a young man with an open face who, pushing the children aside, rushes into the drawing room and cries, "Signora Letizia, you must flee with all your family!"

The speaker is Costa, an old friend of the family, escorted by his clan from Bastelica.

"Paoli," he continues, "has given orders to arrest you and to bring you to him, dead or alive. His men will soon be at the town gates."

"I am ready to sustain a siege, if need be," the signora replies in a firm voice.

Jérôme and Annunciata, the two youngest children, are placed in the charge of their grandmother, whereas the others quickly dress and go elsewhere with Madame Letizia and her half-brother.

Jérôme will always remember this nocturnal flight through the narrow streets of the old town. His grandmother takes him to the Pietrasanta home, to her own family. But the very next morning the children will be united with their brothers and sisters at Milelli, the Bonaparte family's country house located on the road to Alata not far above the city. There, in the peaceful garden shaded by olive trees, the children feel safe.

It is but a fleeting illusion. Muffled noises rise from the city below, and frightening flashes of fire dance above the citadel when another friend of the family, Abbé Coti, appears on the path riding on a donkey.

"Paoli's men are looting and burning your house," he says, "and soon they will come up here looking for you. You can't stay!"

The safest thing to do, according to the faithful Costa, who, along with a few of his men from Bastelica, is ready to stay with Madame Letizia and her children, will be to cross the maquis — the dense trees and shrubs — to reach Capitello Point. There Napoleon — who is on his way from Calvi with the Revolutionary representatives — will join them by a small boat called *chebec*. Some of the men from Bastelica will return to Ajaccio and claim that they have accompanied the Bonaparte family to Sagone, that is, in the opposite direction.

The little group immediately sets out on its headlong flight through the maquis. It is the end of May and the rock rose, the myrtle, and the hawthorne are in bloom and spread their sweet smell. But their thorns scratch the children's cheeks, and especially the youngest ones are whining. "Look at me and suffer in silence," their mother tells them in a firm tone.

It is twelve miles to the tower of Capitello, and the paths are steep. Having crossed the marshes of Campo d'ell 'Oro with their noxious vapors, the little troop reaches the banks of the Prunelli. Rain has swelled the river so much that the mother and the children cannot ford it, as the men do. Fortunately, Costa has been able to find a horse somewhere so that he can, one by one, ferry over Letizia, Marianna (the future Elisa), Louis, Jérôme, and Annunciata.

They have barely reached the other side when they hear the sound of voices. They are those of the inhabitants of Zevaco, Paolists one and all. Costa pushes his charges behind some bushes, and they all hold their breath. They really look frightening, these Corsican mountain men with their *baretti* looking like Phrygean caps, their heavy capes, and daggers in their belts!

Once that danger has passed, the flight continues. By evening the little troop arrives at Capitello. How calm it is here at the foot of this tower, one of many the Genoese have built all along the Corsican coast. The wind has completely died down. Around eleven o'clock a gondolier steps out of his boat, fills his barrels with water at the mouth of the Prunelli, and leaves without suspecting anything unusual. Jérôme and Nunciata are excited at the idea of sleeping outside under the stars! Their mother has trouble keeping them quiet.

When they wake up the next morning they find a basket filled with provisions by their side: a delicious goat cheese called *brocciu*, chestnuts, some *lonzu*, and a container of fresh water. Shepherds of the vicinity have brought them during the night.

Another long day passes, then another night. On the morning of

30 May, the Bonapartes are awakened by the sound of cannon fire: the Republican fleet is approaching Ajaccio and is beginning to bombard the citadel. From their observation point by the tower of Capitello on the other side of the gulf, right across from the city, they can see puffs of smoke and, after a short delay, hear the cannon blast.

Jérôme, who can't sit still and thinks only of having fun, is sorry that he does not have a good pair of binoculars like his brother Napoleon. It's really too bad! If he did, he could have followed the fighting. But apparently it is soon over anyway, for the brigs turn around and sail away from the coast. *Sangue di Sambiulino!* No one understands what has happened.

Madame Letizia is half-dead with anxiety. She knows that they cannot stay forever in this area, where they are bound to be found sooner or later. The story has it that Jérôme is the first to see a boat making for Capitello Point. It is a *chebec,* he is sure of it, for he has recognized its rigging!

And indeed, a squat and bluff-bowed boat soon moors in a nearby inlet. A canoe is launched and a lean young man jumps into it.

"Nabulione, Nabulione," Madame Letizia tearfully sighs a few moments later, as she holds her son in her arms. But there is no time for outbursts of emotion. The family must sail immediately and make for Girolata, where they will be better protected. The next morning they will travel from there to Calvi, where the fugitives will be taken in by friends, and where Joseph will also join them.

Then, on 11 June, they really depart for France, that unknown country where the Revolution is still raging. The crossing takes two days. Two days in which Jérôme, who has good sea-legs, happily drinks in the sea breezes. Having left the *libecciu,* he encounters the mistral in Toulon. Along the Corsican coast the scents of the maquis still tickle his nose. Perhaps he thinks, as his brother Napoleon was to put it, that he would "recognize his native Corsica with closed eyes." But for the moment he looks to the future. "When I grow up, I will be a sailor," he thinks.

YEARS HAVE PASSED. HAVING FOUND A REFUGE FIRST AT TOULOUN, AND AT Marseille, where he lived in a narrow alley near the Old Port and finally in the rue Paradis, Jérôme and his family have known dire poverty. But he is carefree by temperament, and so, barefoot or not, he goes to play by the port with his friends, just as he used to do in Ajaccio. His mother and his sisters must work to make a living, and no one has much time to watch him. He does go, sometimes, to learn a bit of French, arithmetic, and history from a nice lady who lives in the neighborhood, but what he really likes is the school of the street, which he attends diligently.

Eventually, as Napoleon rises through the ranks, as Lucien becomes an important figure in politics, and as Joseph is appointed to the military supply corps, the financial situation of the Bonaparte family improves. So Jérôme has to leave Marseille. Napoleon has decided to take charge of the youngest brother's education. He would send him first to the Irish school at Saint-Germain-en-Laye, together with his stepson Eugène de Beauharnais — an excellent student, that Eugène, who is always held up as an example to Jérôme — and then to the Oratorians of Juilly. During his vacations he spends time at his sister Elisa's, now the wife of Félix Bacciochi, who lives in the rue du Rocher or at Madame Permon's, whose daughter Laure, the future Duchesse d'Abrantès, is about his age.

But for Jérôme the best memory of those years will be his stay at the château of Mombello, near Milan, during the Italian campaign. He would always be dazzled by the memory of these vast halls with their sculpted ceilings and the crowd of generals in colorful uniforms bowing to his brother. How self-assured this brother has already become, and how respectfully everyone listens to him! Jérôme feels that he shares in some of this fraternal glory. This is where he first acquired the taste for luxury and ostentation that he would never lose. He probably feels that he is living in a fairy tale: having been desperately poor as a child, here he is, treated like a prince. He feels like a prince, and he will be a prince as long as he lives. What a wonderful destiny! And what a bore to go back to school after such a vacation!

Two years later, when Napoleon has become First Consul, he brings his brother to the Tuileries. Jérôme is lodged on the mezzanine floor, below his older brother's apartments. Present at all the parties, the adolescent is the darling of the ladies who frequent the salons of the small consular court. The company includes *incroyables* in English riding-coats, Jacobins sporting red collars and short hair. and *merveilleuses* in Greek tunics. Napoleon's conquests have borne fruit even in the world of fashion. Italy and the discovery of the ruins of Pompei led to great enthusiasm for the long fluid muslin gowns that mold women's shapes, even if they leave something to be desired, as well as for an architecture inspired by antique temples. As for the Egyptian campaign, it has begun to make lotus blossoms, scarabs, and sphinxes' heads sprout from the feet of tables and chairs.

Jérôme already struts about with great confidence at such gatherings, where all eyes are on his sister-in-law Josephine, the Creole "made entirely of lace and gauze." He also loves to walk about in Paris, a Paris that gradually recovers its festive air, and where the theaters are never empty. There is the Théatre de l'Egalité (Comédie Française), the Theatre de la République (les Variétés) and the informal theater (Vaudeville), which sometimes performs plays that celebrate his brother's victories, such as *Hope Reborn* or *The Hero's Return from Egypt*. But he also enjoys walking in the gardens, of which there are many: Tivoli, Mouceau (the future Parc Monceau), the Italian garden, and of course the famous gardens of the Palais Royal, where public speeches are sometimes given and where there is an abundance of cafés and restaurants — as well as of prostitutes who offer their charms for sale under the arches of the galleries.

In the streets the boutiques are brightly lit. The most enticing street by far is the rue Saint Honoré, where luxury goods are for sale in many stores. Jérôme can't resist. One day Bourienne, the steward at the Palace, is greatly surprised to receive a bill for 16,000 francs from a luxury goods store at the sign of the "Purple Monkey." It is for a magnificent crystal and vermeil toiletry set. Who can have ordered these shaving bowls, these scent bottles, these razors? It is not Bonaparte, nor his wife, nor any of the dignitaries in their entourage. After further investigation it turns out that the purchaser is a young boy of fifteen, Citizen Jérôme, whose only explanation is, "What can I say, I just love beautiful things."

So he loves travel toiletry sets? Well, he will certainly be in for a good bit of traveling.

3

*C*ITIZEN GENERAL, I AM SENDING YOU CITIZEN Jérôme Bonaparte, who is to be apprenticed to the navy. You know that he must be held to severe discipline and must make up for lost time. You are to demand that he be conscientious in carrying out the duties of his chosen profession."

Sent on his way bearing this message, Jérôme Bonaparte, at the age of sixteen, takes his first steps in his new career. Not that he is too happy about it, for he would much rather have become an aide-de-camp to his brother and continued to receive some smattering of his glory. But he has no choice. His first voyage takes him to the Mediterranean and to Egypt, and in 1801 he sets out for Haiti.

Actually, he has no reason to complain, for he advances rapidly. Within a few years, he will climb the ladder: a mere "aspirant second class" in November 1800, he is to reach the grade of vice admiral in September 1806, having done real service for no more than six months in those six years. But it is, and always will be, quite natural for this easygoing young man not to be surprised at anything. After all, is he not the brother of Napoleon? The Napoleon who by this time is determined to play the naval card against England, the mistress of the seas. One Bonaparte reigning as master over all of Europe and another reigning over the seas — what a magnificent dream!

Saint-Domingue, "the pearl of the Antilles," is in very bad shape at this time. Toussaint Louverture, who had briefly rallied to France, is now playing his own game and setting up a dictatorship. Napoleon, who wants to put him down, sends an expedition headed by his brother-in-law Leclerc (husband of Paolina, now Pauline). A fleet of thirty ships is levied under the command of Admiral Villaret de Joyeuse. Jérôme embarks on the *Foudroyant* commanded by Admiral Latouche Tréville.

At Port-au-Prince and at Cap-François the arrival of the French troops triggers the resistance of generals Dessalines and Christophe, who instigate a veritable carnage among the white population.

Jérôme experiences all of this and fights courageously, but his frivolous and fanciful side never flags. When he visits his sister and brother-in-law Leclerc at the Estaing residence on the heights above Cap-François, those around him are flabbergasted one evening to see him parade around in the blue, silver-braided uniform of a captain in the hussars. The uniform of a naval ensign just seems too modest! As plantations are burning all around him, happy-go-lucky Jérôme feels free to indulge his every whim.

Meanwhile, in addition to the war, yellow fever is wreaking havoc. Leclerc, who already feels contaminated by this disease, which will carry him off a few months later, decides to send his young brother back to France, carrying dispatches for Napoleon. This is a great disappointment to Pauline, who had been very happy at the idea of enjoying the company of this entertaining brother for a while.

"Garrison life does not seem to agree with you," the First Consul remarks after a few weeks, having gotten wind of his youngest brother's indiscretions.

Jérôme has to bow to the inevitable. Before long he sails for the Antilles on the brig *L'Epervier* commanded by his friend Halgan. As bad luck would have it, Halgan falls ill, so that Jérôme has to take his place. But then he in turn does not feel well, not well at all. And to top it off, he catches cold while visiting the Soufrière volcano. He spends several days shaking with bouts of fever.

Two months of enforced rest will change the course of his future life, or at least his immediate future, for one day while he is convalescing he receives word of the death of his brother-in-law Leclerc, who has fallen victim to the *vomito negro,* the dreaded yellow fever that has ravaged the Europeans of the Antilles and the ranks of his own crew.

The idea of patrolling the Caribbean has lost its appeal. But, since every misfortune has its good side too, his illness brings him the acquaintance of a charming Creole by the name of Alexandre Lecamus, a young fellow who, just as easygoing as himself, shares his pranks and one day suggests to him a little side-trip to the United States.

"Great idea," cries Jérôme, delighted. "But I can't leave my command just like that. . . ."

"We'll wait for a proper opportunity," Lecamus says in his soft, singing voice.

The opportunity is not long in coming, and it is brought about by a blunder on Jérôme's part. While patrolling the channel of Domenica, the young man, always the brave soldier, has one day been careless enough to mistake a merchant vessel flying the British flag for a British warship and decided to board it. This kind of blunder is easy to make, for on long voyages merchant vessels are outfitted with several cannon to defend themselves against privateers of every stripe. But whenever this happens, it is liable to trigger a diplomatic incident with the English, now that the truce under the Treaty of Amiens has become a mere piece of paper.

"I am informed of your impulsive act," the admiral writes to him in high dudgeon. "You must be gone from Martinique by the time I receive the protest. You will therefore set sail immediately in order to join the First Consul."

"My dear admiral," Jérôme replies, "our opinions differ, but I shall be glad to subordinate my way of seeing the matter to yours."

At this point he remembers Lecamus's suggestion. After all, why should he take a chance on being intercepted by the English, who are patrolling the Atlantic and all around the Antilles, when a trip to the United States would be most educational and also help his problem blow over?

Jérôme does not hesitate. Together with Alexandre Lecamus and Meyronnet, his former first mate on the *Epervier* who has also become his boon companion, he decides to sail up the Chesapeake. There is even a fourth musketeer: he is Jean-Jacques Rewbell, son of one of the former members of the Directory. Having handed over the command of the *Epervier* to another officer, Jérôme takes a small boat piloted by an indigenous sailor. This craft is to take him and his "attendants" —

rounded out by a physician, a young Creole, and a few domestic servants — to the shores of America.

ON 20 JULY 1803, JÉRÔME LANDS AT NORFOLK, A SMALL TOWN LOCATED at the mouth of the Chesapeake. Since his entourage does not have any money, he decides to go to Washington, where the French legation has been moved. Meanwhile Meyronnet will proceed to Philadelphia for the purpose of chartering an American vessel that will safely convey them back to France.

Having crossed Virgina in two days on horseback, they reach Washington, still a small town with houses scattered in an insalubrious plain along the Potomac. In 1800 the decision to move the seat of government to this deserted place had been settled, but was not universally supported. The presidential mansion, referred to as "the Palace," is not completed; the Capitol, where the Congress is to meet, consists of two unconnected wings, and the famous colonnade is still lying on the ground. A single street runs through the little town; it is bordered by red brick houses and a few log cabins where black people live.

Scattered throughout the countryside are a few modest inns and boarding houses, where the members of Congress stay during the session and where they live like hermits. The most prominent of these places is Gray's Inn. But Washington has no fine stores, no market, no theater, nor any distractions. What a difference with the activity and the liveliness of New York, Philadelphia, or Baltimore!

A short distance away arises the outline of Georgetown, an older agglomeration equipped with a commercial river port on the Potomac. Among the imposing Georgian houses, some more modest though charming cottages have found their place. One of these is the residence of the French legation.

Louis-André Pichon, the consul-general, has no inkling of the troubles that are about to be unleashed on him. He is a man in his thirties, active, ambitious, and hard-working, who has been living in America for several years but has assumed his important position only recently. Married to an American, by whom he has one child, he loves the democratic institutions of this young country with as much enthusiasm as he had brought to the French Revolution. It makes him rather uneasy to see that the Consulate is moving France toward a regime of personal power. In every disagreement he is always quick to adopt the views of the Americans. Fortunately for him, Thomas Jefferson, who is president of the United States at this time, happens to be a faithful friend of France.

Pichon, who only fills in as chargé d'affaires until a minister plenipotentiary is appointed, has to deal with all kinds of urgent matters. Among other things, he must arrange for repatriation and subsidies for French settlers who have escaped the massacres at Saint-Domingue, many of whom are in desperate straits.

The trouble is that the coffers of the consulate are not very well-filled at this time, and the young consul bitterly complains about this state of affairs to Talleyrand. "How do you expect France to cut a decent figure abroad with such meager resources?"

He himself certainly does not rack up excessive expenses, if only because Washington does not present any temptations in that direction.

Another thorny problem for Pichon is Louisiana. France had received it back from Spain in 1800 and is now negotiating its sale to the United States. Who is delighted by this prospect? The American government, of course. "It's really too bad," Pichon says to himself. "Such a beautiful colony, where France is still so popular. . . . But no one can go against the First Consul's will; why, even his brothers did not agree with him on this. And he certainly was not about to consult the nation."

It seems that in the wake of the revolt at Saint-Domingue Napoleon has lost interest in Louisiana, which had to be provisioned from the Antilles, and that he wants to concentrate on his European wars. "The only good part," Pichon muses, "is that this strengthens our friendship with M. Jefferson."

The consul is therefore very busy dealing with budgetary problems, with territorial borders (for the United States also wants to obtain a piece of Florida, a territory bordering on Louisiana that belongs to Spain), and with American ships that the French navy has boarded as they blithely continued to trade with the rebels of Saint-Domingue, whom they sometimes even supplied with arms.

Pichon is at his desk when he is told that a young man with an odd

Creole accent wishes to see him. "Another colonist at the end of his rope," he grumbles.

It is Alexandre Lecamus. The diplomat is dumbfounded to hear that Jérôme Bonaparte, the youngest brother of the First Consul, has arrived from Norfolk and wishes Pichon to call on him at his inn. Pichon, displeased by this request, which he considers contrary to normal usage, but impressed by such a surname just the same, drives Lecamus back to town in his cabriolet.

He finds Jérôme installed at the home of a certain Joshua Barney. Despite young Bonaparte's warm greeting, the diplomat finds it difficult to hide his disgruntlement. For Commodore Barney has a bad reputation in Washington. It is said that he has amassed a considerable fortune through smuggling and piracy. Nonetheless, this florid, jovial, and roundish man with his turned-up nose has fought in the French army, where he has earned his stripes and has distinguished himself brilliantly in the American War of Independence. Pennsylvania has awarded him a golden sword with a damascene blade. A colorful personality, he has been the subject of many songs.

He has already had time to tell Jérôme about some of his adventures, for instance about the time he was presented at the court of France, when Marie Antoinette kissed him!

Jérôme seems delighted with this new acquaintance. He pays little attention to Pichon's questions and simply tells him that he needs $5,000 for the incidental expenses of himself and his entourage, and $10,000 more for chartering the *Clothier,* a ship that Meyronnet has found for him in Philadelphia and on which he plans to return to France.

The consul, initially worried at having to disburse such a large sum, takes comfort in the thought that this will help this undesirable guest depart as soon as possible. "You cannot stay here long," he says, "for the English will soon get wind of your arrival; they have spies everywhere. They are cruising up and down the East Coast and don't hesitate to sail up the Hudson or the Chesapeake. They think they are Masters of the Sea (which in fact they are!) and their arrogance is without equal."

A few days later he learns that the young man and his retinue have changed their minds. Joshua Barney has offered to take his guests to Philadelphia, York, and his home town Baltimore, where he has a great many friends. Jérôme accepts with alacrity. He decides to send Meyronnet on the *Clothier* to receive his brother's orders.

BALTIMORE! OVER THE LAST TEN YEARS THE CITY HAS GROWN AND DOUBLED its population. It is gay and spruce, full of elegant stores that carry copies of French and English fashions. A tower has been built on Federal Hill, from where one can easily watch the arrival of merchant ships in any weather. On Lexington Square there is a market where farmers from the surrounding countryside bring their produce. Intense activity reigns on the piers, where black slaves ceaselessly discharge merchandise. For a moment, in a vision that flits by as quickly as the passing of a butterfly, Jérôme sees before him the port of Ajaccio, with its ocher and pink houses, the Borgo, and the citadel. How far he is from Corsica! But his agile mind, accustomed from childhood to adapting to all circumstances, however unusual, quickly turns away from the past and jumps into this joyous and exciting present.

"You'll see," Barney tells him. "There is a lot going on here. It's not like Washington. There are balls, concerts, plays, and hunts for the gray or red fox. And in September there are the Havre de Grace and Govanstown races. Everyone who belongs to good society goes to these. I have a stable myself. I'll take you."

Jérôme would have liked to stay at the Fountain Inn, the most famous hotel in Baltimore, where Lafayette and Jefferson have lodged, but the commodore won't hear of it: he wants the three young men to stay at his house. He is friends with many of the town's notables and the son-in-law of Samuel Chase, one of the signers of the Declaration of Independence.

Within a few days, everyone in town has learned that a Bonaparte has arrived. Despite Pichon's warning, Jérôme has done little to remain incognito. Actually, many a Baltimorean has seen him and his ample entourage arrive in his rented coach with its yellow wheels. His name is already on everyone's lips.

Soon it is the end of August, and the town's fancy families — the Catons, Pattersons, and Smiths — return from their summer residences, where they have fled the heat and the miasmas of the harbor's water. The first races at Havre de Grace, at the mouth of the Susquehanna, take place in early September. From early in the morning, the road is filled with cabriolets, landaus, whiskies, charabancs and simple horseback riders. It is a regular competition for elegance. Everyone tries to outshine all the others. Jérôme, Jean-Jacques Rewbell, and Joshua Barney are in naval uniforms. The commodore is wearing that of the American navy, blue faced with red.

Barney, who knows everyone, gives the names of people as they arrive: "Here comes the Caton family," he says. From the back of a smart coach drawn by four white horses jump two footmen who open the doors for a respectable-looking couple and a trio of fresh and merry girls. "And these are Mary, Eliza, and Louisa, known as "the Three Graces."

The Pascaut de Poléons, who are not as wealthy, have a more modest coach, from which emerges the Marquis de Poléon — powdered wig, lace jabot, and aristocratic bearing. Jean-Jacques Rewbell's heart beats faster as he sees a slender and timid young lady alight; it is Henriette, the marquis's eldest daughter. "And over there are also the Murphies, the Yardleys, and the Wedgewoods."

A little distance away they see two young men riding bay horses. Between them, on a smaller dappled-gray mount, a very slender and elegant young girl dressed in a spencer and brown skirt, with an ostrich feather on her hat, is riding side-saddle.

Jérôme and his friends would not have paid particular attention to her if just then her horse had not reared. She brings it under control with a firm hand, but it continues to chomp at the bit and toss its head. Impressed by her beauty, Jérôme learns that the girl's name is Elizabeth Patterson, that she is the daughter of one of the town's richest merchants, and that she has been nicknamed "the Belle of Baltimore."

Whenever there is talk of a pretty woman, Jérôme becomes very excited. Young as he is, he already has several conquests to his name. Training his field glass on the group of three riders, he attentively observes the young woman. "*Santo Dio, che meraviglia,*" he mutters. "Never have I seen such bearing, such a fine profile, and such harmonious proportions."

This being the case, he no longer pays much attention to the small red silhouettes that are racing by down there on their thoroughbred horses. Is that Thunderstorm or Whisky at the head of the bunch? But who cares, anyway?

Betsy, of course, is aware that the young French officer is watching her, and when she learns that he is the brother of the First Consul she becomes quite flustered. From time to time she surreptitiously observes him. He is not very tall, to be sure, but his uniform admirably molds his slender waist. His profile is imperious, like his brother's. In fact, he seems to resemble the First Consul, judging by the portraits of Napoleon Betsy has seen in the gazettes, except that there is something gentler, more effeminate about his face. For just a moment, she remembers the prophecy she received from Mummy July ten years earlier. But no, that's really quite impossible . . .

Besides, at the end of the race, Betsy is quite upset to see that the young man has walked over to the Chase family. Bowing to old Samuel Chase, he has said, "It is a great honor for me to shake the hand of one of the famous signers of the Declaration of Independence." And his sunny smile has taken in the rest of the family as well, Mrs. Chase and their young daughter Mary, who looks very fragile in her white cotton dress.

Elizabeth angrily bites her lips and then quickly turns her head, so that no one will see that all her attention is riveted on a single person.

But the next morning she receives a note from her friend Mary Chase: she and her two older brothers are invited to a ball Samuel Chase is to give two days hence in honor of the First Consul's brother. Her chaperone will be Nancy Spear, her favorite aunt. This lady, who has never married, lavishes all of her affections on the Patterson children. She is also a highly intelligent woman, who every year attends all public meetings of the Congress while it is in session. A suffragist before the movement was born! Mr. Patterson sometimes teases her about it: "Nancy, I won't put you in my will unless you give up this dreadful habit."

Betsy, for her part, is most anxious to look her very best at Samuel Chase's ball. "I have to be the most beautiful," she thinks to herself.

And the most beautiful she will be in that assembly, even though there will be no dearth of pretty girls. No need for a jewel to enhance the delicate line of her neck or the perfection of her oval face. As for the extreme slenderness of her waist, her dress of pink Indian cotton shows it off most delightfully. From the moment she enters, Elizabeth is besieged on all sides: William Johnson wants to dance the quadrille with her, George Wedgewood asks for the country dance, and John Yardley for the polka. Just as she is about to write the third name on her dance card, she sees a slender silhouette making its way through the crowd of her admirers and hears a decisive voice with a foreign intonation saying in an imperious tone: "I think the polka will be for me, if Mademoiselle Patterson is agreed, of course."

Wearing a magnificent light blue hussar uniform with silver braiding — his favorite outfit — Jérôme Bonaparte bows before her. Betsy blushes, stammers a few words of assent and, under the rueful glances of John Yardley, who walks away, notes on her dance card the name Bonaparte, the world-famous name that makes all of Europe's sovereigns tremble. She is positively dizzy. Is it the fault of the polka, or is it the voice that softly speaks to her, pronouncing the r's in such a funny way? Or is it just the magic of her cavalier's name?

Even after the last strains of the polka have faded, Elizabeth feels as if she were still floating in a dream. And then, just as Jérôme, smiling rather wistfully, steps away from her and takes her hand to lead her back to her place, a little incident occurs: the gold chain she is wearing around her neck becomes entangled in the braids of the young man's uniform, and he has a difficult time disentangling it.

"You see," he says with a smile, "we are not meant to separate."

TIME SOMETIMES CREEPS ALONG AS SLOWLY AS THE CARTS THAT RUMBLE UP Rolling Road. Betsy would like to push it, compress it, hurry it along. Her history, math, and French classes and her piano lessons have become positively dull. And oh, those long afternoons spent embroidering in the garden with Mrs. Patterson and her sister Peggy — what a bore!

These days the only pleasant moment comes at bedtime, for this is when, tucked away under the coverlet of her four-poster bed, she has the leisure to conjure up in her memory all the vicissitudes of her encounter with Jérôme Bonaparte. There is no use trying to chase away the image of those black curls, that proud face with the lively eyes, that laughing and sensuous mouth. He has become part of her life and her Maryland admirers — John Yardley, Jack Lewis, and William, the young lawyer from Annapolis — have been relegated to the shadows.

Days go by without any news. Then, one afternoon, Henriette Pascaud comes to call. Betsy hastily closes the book of poems by Young over which she had been yawning and rushes to the drawing room. Henriette has news for her: she is about to become engaged to a French officer. The news takes Elizabeth's breath away. All at once her dreams are crumbling. So, what about the laughing face and the caressing voice in her ear?

But she learns that the future bridegroom is Jean-Jacques Rewbell, Jérôme Bonaparte's friend. And also that M. Pascaud de Poléon, despite his royalist opinions, has not voiced any objections, even though Jean-Jacques is the son of a former member of the Directory. The wedding will take place soon, for he must return to France and wishes to take his young wife with him.

Does this mean that the French will leave soon? But Henriette continues: her parents are planning to give an engagement dinner tomorrow evening. The Pattersons are invited, of course, as are Barney and all his young friends. Thus it comes about that Elizabeth sees Jérôme the next evening, and every day after that, for the young man is increasingly attracted to her.

Commodore Barney, in whom Jérôme has confided, and who is quite amused about this intrigue, does his best to set up encounters by organizing a fox hunt in the countryside, inviting Betsy and her Aunt Nancy to his box at the theater, or even accompanying Jérôme to the Pattersons in his cabriolet in person.

Jérôme is obviously more and more in love with Betsy, finding her cheerful, witty, and more cultivated than many of his own female compatriots. She speaks French fluently and knows the works of the eighteenth-century philosophes by heart. But her favorite author, she says, is a man of the previous century, the Duc de La Rochefoucauld, whose maxims have become her bedside reading. Is this, Jérôme asks her, what has given her her sparkling looks, her art of the witty rejoinder? He is fascinated by her vivacity.

William Patterson and his wife soon become concerned about this turn of events. Mr. Patterson is angry: "This relationship will not lead to anything good," he grumbles. Dorcas, his wife, who can see how much her daughter is in love and who knows how stubborn she can be, is afraid that Betsy will become altogether unmanageable if she is forbidden to frequent young Bonaparte. As for General Smith, his brother-in-law, a United States Senator, he would not be displeased to see a budding union between his niece and her young swain. His knowledge of French and his close friendship with Jefferson justify his hopes for an ambassadorship to France. This position would surely be his if he were to enjoy such a close connection with the First Consul's family.

WHILE SUCH PLANS ARE TAKING SHAPE IN THE GENTLE LIGHT OF AN INDIAN summer along the banks of the Patapsco River, where Jérôme often goes riding in the company of the Belle of Baltimore, what has become of Louis André Pichon? The French consul and his family have been on vacation in the nearby countryside, where they could escape the pestilential vapors that arise from the marshes around Washington during the month of August. But now he is back in the little porticoed house in Georgetown where his living quarters and the offices of the French legation are located. Goodness! A whole stack of dispatches awaits him. The *Clothier,* he learns, the boat that Meyronnet had chartered in Philadelphia and on which young Bonaparte was to sail for France, has left without him. Jérôme, realizing that the English captains who patrol the length of the East Coast have found out about his projected voyage and are getting ready to capture him, has preferred to send his adjutant Meyronnet under an assumed name, expecting him to bring back the First Consul's orders. Meanwhile he is having a wonderful time in Baltimore, where he is spending money like water, and therefore asks Pichon for additional funds.

An unfortunate return from vacation! More trouble is ahead. Pichon's coffers are empty, and he already faces a $10,000 bill for the useless chartering of the four-hundred-ton brig *Clothier!* Not to mention all the refugees flooding in from Saint-Domingue, people who must be given some financial help. What a thoughtless fellow, this Jérôme!

In his best hand, Pichon does not deny himself the satisfaction of asking this young scatterbrain a few pointed questions: When is he planning to return to France? Does he realize that, as far as the French navy is concerned, he is a deserter? And is this Barney with whom is constantly partying really proper company for the First Consul's brother?

By return mail, Jérôme replies sharply that "he holds quite a different view of the events surrounding his departure." And as for the discreet allusion to his socializing with Joshua Barney, he asserts that he is perfectly capable of choosing the company that is befitting for him. But Pichon does not give up. He learns that a French frigate under the command of the head of the Willaumetz division, the *Poursuivante,* will very shortly drop anchor in Baltimore. This will be the perfect opportunity for Jérôme's honorable return to France. Moreover, the staff of this squadron is to be received by the American president. Pichon offers to present young Bonaparte at the same time.

The president, Thomas Jefferson, author of the Declaration of Independence, has founded the Republican Party. He is an elegant and cultivated man who, having served as minister plenipotentiary in France during the Revolution, has conceived a great affection for that country and remained its friend ever since. He is in correspondence with such French philosophes and writers as Volney, Cabanis, and Dupont de Nemours.

The son of wealthy Virginia landowners, he is a man of simple tastes who dresses modestly and has decided shortly after his inauguration that he would do away with all etiquette. Henceforth, he has declared, no one would have precedence over anyone else. This policy, as we shall see, could at times lead to rather unfortunate incidents.

On the appointed evening, Jérôme and the French officers are received by a tall and robust man with a kindly smile on his freckled face. His outward appearance seems a bit neglected: brown coat, red vest, knee breeches of threadbare corduroy, heelless slippers. Jérôme, who is young enough to dread overly formal receptions, very soon feels at ease. After a few moments it seems to him that he and Jefferson are real friends. Nor does it hurt that the president has a competent cook and a good cellar of French wines. Warmed by the drinks, the conversation flows easily; the main topic is Louisiana, whose sale is under way, and also, of course, the omnipresence on the seas of the "British Leviathan," as Jefferson puts it.

No, he does not like the English, a stance that exposes him to the acerbic criticism of the Federalist opposition. He fears the British maritime power, considering it more dangerous than the growing appetites of Napoleon, of which he disapproves; but after all, they are confined to Europe. The important thing is that they share a common enemy.

Thanks to the unexpected purchase of Louisiana, the United States will be able to expand toward the West. Jefferson's dream of a country stretching from one ocean to another is beginning to come true: has he not just sent two young explorers, Lewis and Clark, to the Pacific coast?

In short, the atmosphere in the presidential "palace" is idyllic on that evening of 26 October 1806: the wine is flowing, tongues are loosened, and everyone is in good spirits.

Poor Pichon! Another setback is in store for him. For as he drives Jérôme back to his inn, he learns that the young man is planning to get married. "The ceremony will take place on 11 November," Jérôme declares matter-of-factly, as if he were planning to buy a new pair of shoes, "and you, Citizen Consul, will of course be invited." When Pichon points out that he has promised to sail on the *Poursuivante* — Captain Willaumez has ordered him to do so, and he is his superior — Jérôme, without batting an eyelash, replies that this is quite out of the question now and that furthermore he does not have to take orders from anyone. Pichon asks whether he realizes that he is not yet nineteen years old. "I soon will be," Jérôme rejoins, "and besides my ensign's commission gives me twenty-one, which is the age required for marriage both in France and in America. In any case, my demand has been made and accepted by Mr. Patterson. The Marquis d'Yrujo served as my spokesman."

This really upsets the consul. Why is the Spanish ambassador mixed up in this business? At this point his country is not on the best of terms with France because of disagreements over the borders of Louisiana. Jérôme explains that d'Yrujo just happened to pass through Baltimore. The Spanish ambassador is a cheerful, elegant, and clever young man to whom he has simply taken a liking. The Spaniard understands him particularly well because he too has married an American, the daughter of the governor of Pennsylvania.

The consul is downcast. "I know about that," he sighs. "Why did you ask a foreigner whose country is hostile to ours to serve as your intermediary? We are allied with Spain, to be sure, but the Spanish are angry with us for selling Louisiana, which we had just recovered by treaty, to the Americans, whom they consider dangerous neighbors for their possessions on this continent. Moreover, M. d'Yrujo hates your brother. I really don't understand what could have made him do such a thing."

"Actually, I understand him only too well," the disgruntled diplomat says to himself as he mulls all this over, huddled in the darkness of the carriage that bumps along over the rutted Georgetown streets. To begin with, Yrujo, that Spanish aristocrat all puffed up with pride, whose antics had sometimes brought a touch of hilarity to the diplomatic life of Washington, hates Citizen Pichon, a plebeian lawyer propelled to his post by the Revolution, a day laborer in the diplomatic field, as it were. Why, he does not even have the grade of minister, being a mere chargé d'affaires.

Yrujo is suspicious of Napoleon, whose ambitions are beginning to worry the Spanish court. And then there is the question of Spanish Florida: the Americans would like to annex a part of it, but its frontiers with Louisiana have never been clearly delineated. "This is such a muddle," Pichon thinks, "that young Bonaparte's marriage is bound to create even more confusion. And that is precisely the reason why Yrujo is pushing this union: he knows that Napoleon will be displeased, and he secretly enjoys that idea. This is pure machiavellianism."

That evening, by the light of a candle, Pichon works late in his office. He writes to Talleyrand, the French minister of foreign affairs, to inform him of what he has just learned. Then he plunges into a study of the French laws and discovers that only six months earlier, in March 1803, a special decree reinstating an ancient law, possibly derived from the laws of Genoa (shades of Grand-uncle Lucien!), has been inserted into the Civil Code. It stipulates that the minimum age required for marrying without the consent of the parents is twenty-five years.

That night Pichon has trouble falling asleep. The very next morning he writes to his consular agent in Baltimore, M. Débécourt, instructing him to use all available means to oppose this marriage, for he can foresee that it will result in terrible trouble for the two of them. He also posts another warning to Jérôme, making it even stronger than the last one. "You cannot," he tells him, "without causing harm to the person you have chosen and to the respectable family to which she belongs, disregard the legal obstacles that stand in the way of this alliance."

And finally, he calls on the Marquis Yrujo at the Spanish embassy, threatening him with breaking off diplomatic relations with Spain if he attends the wedding. M. d'Yrujo usually does not mince words, but in this particular circumstance he prefers not to push the point.

A few days later, the representative of France believes that he has needlessly upset himself. No one talks about these marriage plans any longer, and Jérôme calls on him to tell him that he has decided to go to New York. It has been a close call!

4

A FEW DAYS LATER, MR. PATTERSON TELLS HIS
daughter that he has decided to remove her from Baltimore for a time.
She will leave the very next morning to stay with relatives in Virginia. No
amount of begging and sobbing does any good. Her father is adamant.

Elizabeth has set out in a charabanc with Jessie and Mummy Lou,
who sits bolt upright in a blue dress with a big starched white collar, a
white bonnet on her head. She tenderly watches Elizabeth, who for the
first time finds the trip very long. In a gloomy mood, she sulks by
herself, rejecting Jessie's friendly attempts to distract her and keeping
her eyes fixed on the wooded valleys of Maryland as they fade from her
view.

The night before she has received a note from Jérôme telling her
that he will take advantage of her absence to visit New York as part of
his "mission." This note was not reassuring to Betsy. In New York there
will be temptations, pretty women in showy clothes, for it is a more
luxurious and pleasure-loving city than Baltimore, Boston, or Philadelphia. Money is flowing freely there, and distractions abound. And all
that time, she will bury herself here at a plantation called Three Oaks,
amidst farmers and slaves! What a miserable compensation!

And yet it is beautiful in Virginia. The late autumn is magnificent.
The woods are filled with red maples, oaks, and white walnut trees.
Dahlias, roses, and chrysanthemums are blooming all around the long
and low-slung house with its surrounding gallery. Behind it are the
outbuildings, the slave quarters with their chicken coops and their veg-

etable patches, as well as the dairy, the drying shed for the tobacco, and the carpenter shop — a whole miniature world. In front of the house, fields stretch as far as the eye can see.

If her heart were not so heavy, Betsy would fill her eyes with all that beauty. She would watch the wild geese that rise in large flocks from the lakes, she would pick bayberries along the paths, and she would listen to the songs of cardinals and mockingbirds. But her head is filled with one single image: Jérôme, Gerolamo, who is no longer just the young Bonaparte, but has eyes, hands, a slightly hooked nose, and an insinuating voice with a curious accent. His face relegates to total obscurity all the Johns, Jacks, or Lewises of Baltimore who have courted her. Now she is truly in love: this is the man she must have, and no one else. Fortunately, the post chaise does bring her his letters from New York; they take longer than she would like, but she replies immediately.

She tries to imagine the young man in New York, the largest city in the United States. Less staid than Philadelphia, it is a study in contrasts, for it already has a certain grandeur, with elegant neighborhoods where majestic residences stand next to pretty villas surrounded by gardens, with cafés, theaters, and an opera where ostentatious luxury is displayed. All of this is offset by slums along the Hudson River, where blacks and poor immigrants are living, and by smelly workshops where fur is being tanned. It is a noisy city, resounding with the cries of chimney-sweeps, rag-pickers, knife-grinders and hucksters selling water, newspapers, and even oysters, which they cart around in big wheelbarrows. It is also dirty, populated with wild pigs that freely roam among the feet of pedestrians, gobbling up odd pieces of refuse here and there and thereby performing a kind of rudimentary street-cleaning. Wild pigs, just like in Corsica. . . . "I suppose Jérôme will feel right at home," thinks Betsy, quite amused. "I can't wait to see him so he can tell me about his trip."

After two weeks the young girl simply cannot stand the boredom and the impatience any longer and decides to return to Baltimore without letting her parents know. She will find some kind of pretext: the need to resume studying at Mme Lacombe's, preparations for the holiday season. Or, better yet, Henriette Pascaud's wedding, for Henriette, unlike herself, is getting married, and no one is trying to stop her!

At the house on South Street, her parents give her a cool reception, but her young brothers and sisters, especially Edward, her favorite, won't let go of her when she has alighted from the charabanc. That evening, despite the cool season, she has opened her window half-way, hoping to enjoy the sea breeze. She hears a slight sound in the garden and soon sees a slender silhouette emerge from behind a dogwood tree. "Elisa," he softly calls. It is he, yes, for only he calls her thus, having chosen this Italian-sounding first name for her because, he says, it reminds him of one of his sisters.

Betsy hastily puts on a big cape and creeps down the stairs, hoping no one will notice her. And then she is in the arms of Jérôme, who presses her to his heart, kisses her, caresses her. "We must get married," he whispers; I know I can find the words I need to convince your father. I would rather die than be separated from you. I may be a little young, but is that a flaw? And my family — when they see you they are bound to approve of my choice. Napoleon himself, the man you call the "stewart of the universe," has married for love. And yet, his wife was older than he, and divorced, too. Our mother actually can't stand her. But you, my Elisa, I am sure she will take to you right away.

Meanwhile Mr. Patterson is worried sick. He has received a solemn letter of warning from M. Pichon, the representative of France. M. Débécourt, his agent in Baltimore, has come to see him, to lay out for him, just to make sure, all the obstacles that stand in the way of this marriage. He has also received two anonymous letters.

When Elizabeth hears of this, she is indignant. It's just pure jealousy, she asserts. And, even if there were some slight risk, she would be a hundred times happier to be married to a Bonaparte for an hour than to another man for a lifetime!

Poor Betsy, she does not know how cruelly ironic fate can be sometimes. The resistance of Dorcas and William Patterson is weakened by so much steadfastness. Samuel Smith, the general and senator who is married to one of Dorcas's sisters, and his brother Nicolas, who is Secretary of the Navy, once again try to persuade them, pointing out the more general benefits of such a union. If it came to pass, Mr. Jefferson might well appoint General Smith to minister plenipotentiary in France, a post he has coveted for so long. He has learned that Robert Livingston, who holds this position now, is about to return. And this might well go both ways: being France's minister to the United States would be quite the thing for Jérôme, who seems to be learning English rapidly and has already given proof of his great ease in social situations when he was received at the presidential palace. And what an honor it would be for the United States to receive as its representative of France the First Consul's own brother! Surely, this would be a guaranty of lasting peace!

And since this is the United States, the land of democracy and liberty, why not unite these two young people, who are so much in love with each other?

So the marriage is decided upon. And since Jérôme is Catholic, it will be celebrated by the bishop of Baltimore, Msgr. Carroll. All the best society of Maryland will be invited. Only the Marquis Yrujo, though approached, will refuse to attend, scared off by the perspective of a diplomatic incident with France.

As for Louis-André Pichon. . . . Well, he just has to bow to a *fait accompli*. Having been led to believe, for a time, that the project had been abandoned, he had gone about his business, thinking that he had more important things to attend to than the marriage of that giddy young fellow Jérôme. Yet that scapegrace is not all bad either; has he not recognized that Mr. Barney really is not proper company for him, and that "Citizen Pichon has shown as much zeal in working against [Barney] as others have exhibited falseness and self-interest in supporting him?"

While Louis-André thus sleeps the slumber of the just, and while Elizabeth and her mother hastily assemble her trousseau, William Patterson, good businessman that he is, has had a marriage contract drawn up. Designed to protect his daughter against all eventualities, it is, he thinks, "in conformity with the regular laws of the State of Maryland and the Republic of France." "In case it were nonetheless to come to a separation (God forbid!), Elizabeth Patterson is to have the full and entire use of all her own property, whether real, personal, or mixed, both present or future."

On the 25th of December of that year, Louis-André Pichon, who has celebrated Christmas Eve with his family the night before, receives the visit of a snow-covered rider who jumps off his horse and knocks at the door of the French legation. He carries a message that the young consul opens with a frown.

"Monsieur," Alexandre Lecamus writes to him, " I herewith inform you on behalf of M. Jérôme Bonaparte that his marriage to Mlle Patterson has been celebrated last night. He has also asked me to tell you that he is impatiently awaiting the arrival of the $4,000 you are supposed to remit to him. His engagements are becoming pressing, and his household will soon have to meet additional needs. He therefore asks you to be kind enough to send that sum as soon as possible."

Without a word, the hapless diplomat drops the paper on the table. What is there to do and to say in the face of such thoughtlessness and duplicity?

Two days later he will learn that the consular agent in Baltimore, M. Sotin, has been present at the ceremony and signed as a witness. This brand-new consul has just arrived to replace M. Débencourt, who has died of an accident in December. Persuaded that his absence would not have prevented anything, M. Sotin had not wanted to affront the Patterson family, who had insisted that he be present. He is rather sheepish as he outlines the details:

> Let's see, he writes, which will have been the most outstanding event of this year 1803? There is the sale of Louisiana; there is the fall of Saint-Domingue, where Cap-François is coming under the full control of the armies of Christophe and Dessalines as we speak; there is also our break with England — and then there is the marriage of Citizen Jérôme. Well, so far as I am concerned, I wonder whether this last event, minor as it is by comparison with the others, will not sound the death-knell to my diplomatic career.

Pichon immediately sits down to write a couple of letters: One to Sotin to disapprove of his conduct, the other to the French foreign minister, Talleyrand, to report the events and to try to exculpate himself. And then, realizing that he must let matters take their course, he shrugs his shoulders, fills his pipe with good Virginia tobacco, and goes back to his papers.

5

A WEEK LATER PICHON WATCHES THE YOUNG couple's arrival in Washington, after a very short honeymoon. The two young people seem so happy and so much in love with each other that the consul's attitude softens. Now that the matter is settled, he will have to entertain the Bonapartes, and so he invites them to dinner.

It is a joyous evening indeed, spirited enough to break the monotony of a consul's life. Jérôme is flighty and frivolous, to be sure, but he is also cheerful and affable. Don't people usually have the virtues of their flaws? As for Elizabeth: "This young woman is really pretty . . . and witty," he writes to Talleyrand.

So the dour diplomat begins to relax somewhat, ready to look at the good side of things. It is also helpful that certain recent incidents at the "presidential palace" — the White House — have been balm for his nerves. A new British ambassador, Mr. Merry, has come to present his credentials to the American president. Attired in full court dress, he had his first shock when he encountered a man wearing country clothes and heelless slippers; he could hardly believe that this was the President of the United States. But this was nothing compared to the dinner to which he and his wife were invited two days later.

To his great surprise, Mr. Jefferson had insisted that in addition to the Spanish ambassador, M. d'Yrujo, and the American cabinet ministers, M. and Mme Pichon should also be present at this occasion. Mr. Merry, a big, red-faced, and apoplectic man, choked with fury. "What is this? He invites the representative of a hostile nation? This will never do!" he thinks.

As the guests sipped a glass of Madeira, Thomas Jefferson displayed his usual good humor. But when the time came to go to the table, he took the hand of Mrs. Madison, wife of his Secretary of State, and led her to the place of honor. When Mr. Merry tried to sit down next to the Marquise d'Yrujo, he was thwarted by a young American congressman who, lightening quick and unimpeded by an excess of politeness, had snatched this place from him.

A few days later, the same scenario had been enacted at the dinner given by the Secretary of State. Indeed, it had been even worse, for this time Mrs. Merry, her face red to the roots of her hair, had found herself left standing alone in the middle of the drawing room, since no one had offered his arm to lead her to the dining room. Her husband was indignant and had finally rectified this breach of manners, whereupon the two of them had ended up in some undistinguished seats at the lower end of the table. "This is really too much," the English ambassador had whispered into his wife's ear. "From now on, my dear, you will no longer accept invitations of this kind. I prefer to spare you such affronts. We will simply say that you are ill, even if you are in perfect health."

Needless to say, all of this is no help in resolving the serious problems that are outstanding between the United States and Great Britain. Louis-André Pichon is delighted. The Marquis d'Yrujo, offended in his aristocratic soul by the look of triumph on the Frenchman's face, will now listen to the recriminations of the English couple with a sympathetic ear and espouse their cause.

In the wake of a few incidents of this kind, Mr. Merry ("a good and competent man," Jefferson calls him, "but unfortunately saddled with an ill-tempered wife") will ask to be recalled to England for health reasons and in fact does suffer a stroke a few months later.

As the year 1804 begins, Pichon therefore feels rather more optimistic about things. He is particularly pleased that as soon as the young Bonapartes have arrived, President Jefferson has expressed the wish to invite them to an intimate gathering, together with the Pichons, the two Smith brothers, and the Marquis d'Yrujo.

Years ago, Thomas Jefferson had been on friendly terms with William Patterson, who rendered most useful services to the army during the French Revolution, when he supplied it from his base on Saint-Eustache. But more than that, Jefferson, like so many others (among them Yrujo) has been charmed by young Betsy. At this reception, he laughingly offers her his arm to lead her to the table. Duly reported to Merry and his wife, this detail gives rise to more resentment.

Truth to tell, the President is not displeased to see the union between his young compatriot and the brother of the First Consul. As soon as he has heard the news, he has written to his ambassador in Paris, Mr. Livingston, instructing him to let it be known in high places that the Patterson family is most respectable and very wealthy.

What a pleasant and relaxed evening! The turtle soup, the roast bear, and the wines are delectable. Emilie Pichon amicably chats with Betsy. From where he is sitting, Louis-André Pichon attentively watches Jérôme. "It is true that he has a lively mind and a good bit of judgment," he thinks. "Too bad that at his age he leads such an idle life. For a young fellow like him, that is very bad. He'll soon have to find another post in the navy."

Over the following weeks he does his best to achieve just that. Jérôme must be sent back to France as soon as possible, he thinks. The life of pleasure he leads with his young wife and her friends is not doing him any good. It is true that in Washington, thanks to the presence of the inevitable Joshua Barney and to the wealthy relations of the Patterson family, Betsy and her husband are invited everywhere. Jérôme has presented his wife with expensive Parisian clothes from Leroy's. The fashion right now is Greek muslin: flowing, high-waisted gowns that leave neck and arms exposed, and under which Betsy, who has a perfect figure, does not wear so much as a shift. In Washington, where European fashions arrive only after several Atlantic crossings, she is a sensation. "Lady Eve," she has been dubbed. The women outdo each other in criticizing her: "She makes no secret of her anatomy," they say spitefully. The men crowd around her to see better and smilingly admire her.

"I am sure," says Aaron Burr, the vice president, "that I could stuff all of her dresses together into my pocket and mistake them for my handkerchiefs."

Betsy's aunts talk sternly to her: What would her father say if he heard of this? "But look here, that's what Jérôme likes!" the young woman exclaims. "In these clothes I remind him of the First Consul's court. And above all, it seems that I look a lot like his sister Pauline!"

WILLIAM PATTERSON, FOR HIS PART, CONTINUES TO WORRY ABOUT HIS daughter's marriage, despite the assurances of Mr. Livingston, who will plead her cause in Paris. Moreover, Robert, the Pattersons' second son, has agreed to go to Europe. What better advocate could Betsy have? He adores his sister.

Robert is an intelligent and competent young man, who is actively involved in running the business with his father. He is supposed to sail for Amsterdam in February anyway to take care of some business matters, and plans to go on to Paris, where he will meet Mr. Livingston. The latter will try to put him in touch with the Bonaparte family. Jérôme has of course written to his family before the marriage. But the mails are so slow . . .

It was perfectly true that one often had to wait until someone went to Europe to send along a letter, or until a frigate had loaded enough freight to make the voyage to Europe worthwhile. Moreover, given the constant activity of the privateers and the British warships in the Atlantic, one could never be sure that a ship would arrive safely. "Packetboats" that were exclusively used for regular mail service were not yet in existence; they would begin operating from New York in 1812.

Robert is in love with Mary Caton, but he has gladly taken ship to serve his sister's concerns. He writes home from time to time. And when his missives arrive, every word is closely picked over, analyzed, and weighed. Whenever possible, the recipients try to read between the lines. This was actually to become the rule a year later, when Robert, fearing that his correspondence might fall into the hands of the English or the French police, decides to write coded and unsigned letters.

Robert, then, having taken care of some regular business, finds himself in Paris, where an old Baltimore friend, Paul Bentalou, serves as his interpreter. Immediately after his arrival he has called on Mr. Livingston, the minister plenipotentiary of the United States. "The best thing to do," Livingston has told him after a moment of silence, "would be for your sister and brother-in-law to stay in the United States for a long enough time, to allow everyone here to calm down. For I cannot hide from you the fact that the First Consul is highly displeased. His first reaction when hearing of his brother's sentimental plans, was to recall him immediately. But now that the marriage has been concluded . . ."[1]

Robert observes the ambassador's delicate hands, which are playing with a paper-cutter. "Would Jérôme be granted an annual income?" he asks. "Good question. I have spoken about this to Joseph, who has offered to invest a thousand crowns in American funds. I pointed out to him that this would be insufficient, considering that the young people will have to buy a house in town and a secondary residence in the country, which is necessary because of the threat of yellow fever. They would therefore need an income of $25,000 to $30,000 per year, but Joseph threw up his hands in horror. . . . I hope we can get him to compromise at $20,000!"

Robert has done more than calling on the ambassador. Miss Monroe, the daughter of the American envoy to Great Britain, has also given him a letter of introduction for Hortense, the wife of Louis Bonaparte and her former schoolmate at Madame Campan's establishment.

But the best news is that one fine morning he receives a note from Lucien Bonaparte, informing him that he and his wife expect him at their home. Robert and Paul Bentalou do not need to be told twice. An hour later, they are in the rue Saint-Dominique to call on Lucien and his second wife Alexandrine. And Robert can't believe his ears as his friend translates the words of their host: "Please tell Mr. Patterson that our mother, myself, and the whole family unanimously approve of this union. It is true that the First Consul does not share this opinion for the moment, but he must be considered isolated within the family."

Robert attentively watches this slender man, who looks so intelligent and energetic and is known to have braved the wrath of his brother when he married the woman he loves. Will Jérôme be able to do likewise, without letting anyone change his mind?

"Our brother Napoleon is aiming very high," Lucien continues, "but this has nothing to do with the rest of us, simple citizens that we

---

[1] Letter of Robert to his family, March 1804, and letter of Paul Bentalou to Wm. Patterson.

are. When we marry, all we have to consider is our own happiness. Lucky Jérôme, he can become an American citizen!" When Robert points out that he will have to wait seven years until he can take the oath of citizenship and that he will have to renounce all titles of nobility, all honors or benefits in his country of origin, Lucien rejoins without hesitation: "Excellent; such a 'novitiate' can only be salutary for him. And the honor of becoming an American citizen certainly warrants it. His situation will be much preferable to ours."

Lucien falls silent. He cannot reveal that at this very moment he is applying for passports for himself and his family. He has succeeded in enlisting support for this step from his sister Elisa and even from his mother, who is beginning to be frightened by the too rapid rise and the growing ambition of Napoleon.

For the last three years an "American conspiracy" had been taking shape at Malmaison, behind the backs of the First Consul and Joséphine. If the whole Bonaparte family, except for Napoleon, had gone to America in search of fresh air by 1805, it is likely that many European sovereigns would have breathed easier . . .

6

OUR CITY, ESPECIALLY MARKET STREET, ex-
hibited a lively scene yesterday and to-day, from the incessant passing
and repassing of *sleighs and four !!!! sleighs and two!! * and *sleighs and one!*
The younger part of our city patriots were, as customary on such occasions, troublesome and dangerous with their snowballs. Madame
Bonaparte, we understand, was thrown at and struck by a ball; for the
perpetrator of which, it is said, her husband offered a reward of *five
hundred dollars. . . .*[1] Mr. and Mrs. Bonaparte went to Washington yesterday. Their journey was attended by a mishap, but Mrs. Bonaparte
was saved thanks to her presence of mind. When the coachman was
thrown from his seat, Mrs. Bonaparte reached out to seize the reins, but
was unable to stop the horses. Seeing that they were becoming entangled, Mrs. Bonaparte opened the carriage door and jumped out into
the snow with both feet, thereby escaping the danger. She was not
injured."

Clearly, the young Bonapartes continued to be in the news. The
gazettes find them a more agreeable subject to write about than the
polemics between Federalists and Republicans or the international economic situation.

In March, Jérôme takes his wife to the most fashionable painter,
Gilbert Stuart, who has painted the portraits of all the celebrities of the
period, among them Washington, Jefferson, and John Adams. So dazzled

[1] Quoted in W. T. R. Saffell, *The Bonaparte-Patterson Marriage in 1803* (Philadelphia:
Published by the Proprietor, 1873).

is Stuart by the fresh beauty of his young client that he proposes to Jérôme to paint a three-fold portrait of his wife: full face, in profile, and in three-quarter face, unable to make up his mind which would be the most favorable angle.

Jérôme and Elizabeth take advantage of this renewed stay in Washington to see a few friends. Again there are balls, again there are parties — all of them watched with a jaundiced eye by the consul-general. "What frivolity!" he grumbles. "Madame certainly does not have it in her to lead Citizen Jérôme to serious matters. She is proud of her position and only interested in enjoying the éclat it lends her," he writes to Talleyrand.

Pichon just shrugs his shoulders when he reads in the gazettes about the fancy social events in which the young couple is involved. He has more serious things to worry about. Saint-Domingue, in particular, continues to cause him a great deal of work. American merchants have not stopped sending their ships to that island, where they amass fortunes supplying food and weapons to the black insurgents.

"Would you rather see the English playing this role?" Jefferson asks the representative of France when he presents his grievances. "They would like nothing better!" By way of reprisal, French privateers pursue the American merchant ships and board them; hence the frequent recriminations on both sides.

Eventually, however, some of the American captains will feel pity for the French families massacred by the blacks and hide some of the survivors on board their frigates; some of them simply hit people over the head before stuffing them into sacks which they stow away in the hold. Sooner or later these unfortunate fugitives come ashore in Norfolk, Baltimore, or New Orleans, and then the consul has to deal with these dramatic cases.

While the struggle for independence in Saint-Domingue pleases the northern states, it is extremely worrisome to those of the South, such as Virginia, which have large numbers of slaves imported from Africa. Suppose this wind from the Antilles were to spread the ferment of rebellion among our blacks?

At a different level, diplomatic intrigues are being spun. Betsy's uncle, General Smith, has still not given up his Parisian ambitions, but

Pichon thinks that if such a nomination were made, the Federalist — and rather pro-English — opposition would immediately accuse the government of being pro-French. The marriage of the young Patterson girl to a Bonaparte brother has already given rise to a good bit of grumbling among the Federalists. Jefferson constantly has to walk a tightrope and must not openly favor one side or the other.

"Citizen Bonaparte," Pichon writes, " I have received word from Annapolis that the Frigate *Poursuivante* will once again call on the port of Baltimore. You should seize this opportunity to sail. She is commanded by Admiral Willaumez."

"That is quite out of the question, Citizen Pichon," Jérôme replies. "I must continue to await my brother's orders. And Meyronnet has still not returned from France. Moreover, it would be most imprudent of me to sail on a warship with my wife."

Jérôme seems to be in no hurry to return to his country. And Mr. Patterson, justifiably concerned about the clouds that his daughter will encounter in the French sky, offers to charter a much more comfortable ship as soon as his son-in-law is ready to sail.

Admiral Willaumez has left Baltimore very angry with his subordinate. Then, a month later, Jérôme receives a letter from Décrès, the minister of the navy: "It is the intention of the First Consul that you are not, under any circumstances, to return to France by any other means than on a French warship. If any other opportunity for your return should present itself, you are expressly forbidden to make use of it."

"I should have gone back on the *Poursuivante,*" Jérôme says to himself. "Now everybody is after me." Meanwhile, he continues to live a life of ease. Nonetheless, doubts and regrets are beginning to assail him. By late March Meyronnet has returned from France, where the family had not yet learned of Jérôme's marriage (since it had not taken place when the young man left Baltimore). Meyronnet has brought back Napoleon's latest belligerent declarations, his renewed call to arms against England.

Soldiers, haughty England already groans under the yoke of her conquerors! London lies before you! Within twenty days, the tricolor flag will wave over the walls of its odious Tower.

How could anyone resist such patriotic sounds? If Jérôme hides out abroad much longer, there will be nothing for it, he will look like a deserter. He must flee the delights of Capua.

But how? "Two of our frigates, the *Didon* and the *Cybele,*" Pichon informs him, "will ride at anchor in the outer harbor of New York." By the time Jérôme has gathered up his belongings, taken leave of his friends, and hurried off to New York with Elizabeth, escorted by Mr. Patterson, it is too late. The English, who have their ears everywhere, have been alerted to this departure and two of their brigs, the *Cambrian* and the *Boston,* arrive to block the outer harbor just as the French vessels are ready to set sail.

Jérôme promptly disembarks — much to the relief of Betsy, although she does not dare admit it. As long as they are already in New York anyway, she suggests to him a little side trip toward the Great Lakes and a visit to the Niagara Falls. They are magnificent, and there at least they will be alone . . .

In 1804 it was quite an undertaking to visit the falls. Such a trip required two weeks of traveling under difficult conditions. Having sailed up the Hudson by sloop as far as Albany, Jérôme and Betsy take a crowded stage coach to Geneva. There the road ends. This region, which in the past had belonged to the Indians, who had eventually sold off the rights to it, is beginning to be populated by new settlers. Log cabins and freshly cleared land can be seen everywhere. As they travel a little farther, they see a new family arrive in a covered wagon. As soon as they have found a place that suits them, these people begin to cut down trees that will serve to build their own log cabin. Watching this, Jérôme feels a pioneer's soul stirring within him. Here at last is a place that reminds him of the harsh mountains of his native Corsica! Later, when he has come to know the pomp and circumstance of court life, he will perhaps remember this journey to the wild region of the American Great Lakes as if it had been a dream.

He and Betsy accomplish the last leg of their outing on horseback, sleeping under the stars on the shores of Lake Erie. Not a single inn is to be found nearby. There is only the Niagara River, "running as fast as a galloping horse," and the falls, whose deafening noise can be heard in the distance.

Back in Baltimore, the two young people briefly stop in Washington, where they learn that the French consul wishes to see them. He has just received new dispatches, with some delay, for an earlier batch had been intercepted by the English. Pichon looks troubled. He asks Jérôme into his office, and, after a moment of silence, tells him: "I have orders to cut off your allowance." Jérôme winces, swallows hard: "As soon as I return to the service, I will receive my pay." "Quite so. But your brother wishes you to return to France by yourself, and on a warship. He has forbidden all French captains to receive on board their ship 'the young person to whom you are united.' . . . In other words, he does not recognize your marriage."

This is serious, and Jérôme is stunned for a few moments. But he is an impenitent optimist. He raises his head and states firmly: "No, I will not leave Elisa behind. I must keep the promise I made to my father-in-law, and I am sure that when my brother sees her, he will succumb to her charm, just like everyone else."

Pichon does not say anything. He walks up and down in his office, torn between the satisfaction of seeing that a lesson has finally been administered to this callow youth who is so sure of everything and spends money like water, and the sympathy he cannot help but feel for this young couple whom he has come to love despite himself.

It is true, Elizabeth is very pretty, and her family is highly respected. But Louis-André Pichon, unlike Jérôme, is not given to optimism! Understandably so, for he has just learned that he has been recalled. He almost expected as much, but he did not think that it would come so quickly. A minister plenipotentiary has been appointed; it is General Turreau, and he will take up his post in late autumn. As for himself, he will move to Philadelphia as soon as he has explained the procedures to the new man.

What accounts for Pichon's sudden transfer, which looks very much like a fall from favor? Does it have to do with the complaints that young Bonaparte had earlier made against him, when he objected to being lectured to? Or, on the contrary, with the fact that the chargé d'affaires has been unable to prevent the marriage of that same Jérôme? Louis-André is inclined to accept the second hypothesis, and this makes him very sad.

In Baltimore, William Patterson has already heard the news, for he has received a letter from Robert: "The determination of the First Consul is only too clear," he writes, "and it is a lucky thing that Jérôme is in America. He must stay there until the marriage is recognized here. . . . At this point all we can count on is his honor."

Jérôme himself receives a threatening letter from the minister Décrès, which only confirms what Pichon has told him. The vise is closing. How to get out of it?

Some time later, Mr. Patterson learns from his brother-in-law Samuel Smith that in the end the post of ambassador to Paris he had coveted has gone to General Armstrong. He will depart shortly. Without paying attention to the recriminations of his brother-in-law, who does not appreciate being bested, William Patterson thinks to himself that this development may afford a satisfactory solution: How about asking Armstrong to take Betsy with him while Jérôme would sail on a French warship? It turns out, however, that after having agreed to this plan, the general, apprehensive no doubt that it would be unwise to offend the First Consul, changes his mind.

NEWS FROM EUROPE GRADUALLY TRICKLES IN. IT IS MIND-BOGGLING: Napoleon has been declared Emperor! And, what is more, this title will become hereditary in his family! His brothers and sisters have become Imperial Highnesses; Louis has been made a High Constable as a first step to being offered the crown of Holland, and Joseph, the future king of Naples, has become Great Elector. Both have been endowed with incomes of a million francs per year. Only Lucien and Jérôme, who have contracted unions contrary to the wishes of the Emperor, are excluded from the succession.

As for Jérôme's marriage, it has been annulled by a decree of the French Senate and is expected to be annulled likewise by the papal court. Jérôme is becoming seriously alarmed: he really must go back to France as soon as possible. If he does not, he will have to shut the book on his family forever, and that would be intolerable to him. Besides, he is beginning to fear that he is missing something. He must partake of the Bonaparte destiny. When he goes to throw himself at his brother's feet, accompanied by his "dear Elisa," Napoleon will forgive him. Betsy too is deeply convinced of this. Who would be able to resist her charm? But of course she isn't taking into consideration her brother-in-law's obstinacy. Has anyone ever seen him go back on a decision?

But there is also some better news. Madame Letizia sends word through some friends of the Pattersons advising Jérôme to send his wife to Holland and to hurry on to France as soon as he can, since a conciliation will no doubt be possible. And Joseph, the eldest son of the family, writes this: "I do not know your resources, but do not forget that everything I have is at your disposal, for I will be happy to share everything with you. . . . Please tell Madame Bonaparte that whenever she has arrived and been received by the head of the family, she will not have a more devoted brother than myself."

The young couple regains hope. Jérôme, in deepest secrecy, takes the necessary steps for fitting out a ship. Before long he announces that he has chartered a three-master, the *Philadelphia,* belonging to a certain M. Breuil. It is to depart the day after tomorrow from Philadelphia.

So, here they are, two days later, accompanied by Nancy Spear — she will finally see Europe! — and only two servants, so as not to attract attention. Not a single English frigate on the horizon! The boat sails down the Delaware without difficulty, but as it comes out of the bay a high wind begins to blow from the northeast. The pilot comes to speak to Jérôme: "What do you think? Should we go around the cape and try our luck?" "The storm will be worse in the open sea," Jérôme asserts. "We cannot expose the ladies present to that danger."

The boat turns back and seeks an anchoring place inside the bay. But during the night the wind has doubled its force and in the morning, when it is decided to weigh anchor, the hapless *Philadelphia* is caught in a whirlpool of opposing currents. There is no way to get out of the bay or to go back. Very soon the boat is breaking up and tossed ashore two hundred yards from a fishing village. "We should have gone out to sea last night," the captain thunders. "Too late for regrets," Jérôme shouts, "the best we can do now is to look out for our safety. . . ."

So they hurriedly throw lifeboats into the sea, which almost shatter against the rocky coast. But fortunately all the passengers and sailors arrive safe and sound in the village, where they are taken in by the fishermen.

Jérôme tries in vain to keep up his good humor and is beginning to realize that he has lost a great deal of money in this expedition, particularly since in order to preserve anonymity he has not taken out any insurance on the brig. He therefore owes the owner more than $6,000. A good thing that the helpful M. Pichon still hovers backstage!

William Patterson now decides to take matters in hand. This ballet of false departures has thoroughly irritated him. He cannot offer one of his own ships, for if it became known that he is the owner, it would attract attention. But his friend Stewart Brown can place his best brig, the *Erin,* at the young couple's disposition; it is a three-master with copper lining, and all the comforts desirable for a future mother. For when Elizabeth sails on 10 March, she is five months pregnant. This time Nancy Spear does not accompany her — she has been burned by the misadventure on the *Philadelphia* — but one of Betsy's friends, Eliza Anderson, is going along, as are the indispensable Lecamus, Dr. Garnier, and William Jr., the eldest of the Patterson siblings. There are also four or five domestics, but to Betsy's great disappointment Jessie has refused to follow her milk-sister.

Mr. Patterson has some urgent last-minute instructions for his daughter: "If you can't land in Lisbon," he tells her, "Captain Stephenson is prepared to take you to Bordeaux or to Amsterdam, where your brother Robert is."

One friend of the young Bonapartes who will not come to see them off (he does not even know they are leaving), is Consul Pichon, who has yielded his place in Washington to General Turreau, who has become France's new minister plenipotentiary to the United States even though he does not speak a word of English. For the last two months Louis-André Pichon has acquainted a very grumpy Turreau with the business at hand, for the general has trouble acclimatizing himself, as well as trouble with an ill-tempered wife — whom he will in fact send back to France six months later.

Pichon thus has to put up once again with a lot of grousing and grumbling. When all is said and done, he is rather glad to be leaving Washington, where he has lost his only daughter (fortunately his wife is pregnant again), and will soon thereafter go back to France. He needs a change of air, but he is quite worried about the fate that is in store for him on the other side of the Atlantic. Is he in disgrace? Interestingly enough, Jérôme Bonaparte, who at this very moment is sailing toward France, will one day come back into his life. When he has become king of Westphalia and his kingdom's finances are in a sorry state, he and Alexandre Lecamus (by then grand chamberlain and Count of Fürstenstein) will remember their old friend Pichon, whose ambitions on his return to France have not been quite fulfilled. He is a competent jurist of great integrity. Where would they find a better man to try to shore up this tottering edifice?

At the end of three years, however, Louis-André Pichon — initially delighted and touched to be reunited with the young rogue who had caused him so many headaches — would throw in the towel. Pichon would leave Westphalia, and this time for good. He was done with the Bonapartes.[2]

---

[2] Rallied to the Bourbons in 1815, he was ennobled and became a councilor of state under the Restoration. His two sons were named Jérôme and Théodore.

7

*T*HE BRIDGE OF THE *ERIN* RESOUNDS WITH PEALS of laughter. Betsy and Eliza Anderson are talking about their friends and acquaintances in Baltimore and tearing them to pieces. Goodbye, America! They are already thinking of their life in Europe and discussing the latest fashions. The Emperor, it seems, has forbidden muslins and the Greek style and ordered everyone to wear satin and silk in order to give a boost to the silk manufactures of Lyon. No lady dares present herself at the Tuileries dressed in muslin. Rumor has it that Josephine has been in tears over this!

Jérôme comes from time to time to check on his "two Elisas," and then rejoins Alexandre Lecamus and his other companions for a game of whist or chess. Off the Azores, slightly rough seas cause some passing discomfort among the travelers, but nothing serious happens. No sign of the "Leviathan of the seas." By 2 April, Lisbon is already in sight.

"We shall have to ride at anchor off the tower of Belém to comply with the quarantine," the captain announces after he has fired the twelve prescribed cannon salvoes. "The authorities of this country are very strict in this matter, so this will take eighteen days." Jérôme is greatly irritated and asks Stephenson to do everything he can to shorten the procedure, for he must join his brother as soon as possible.

Betsy and Eliza Anderson have borrowed the captain's field glasses and inspect the surrounding area. They are quite astonished at the number of ships flying different flags in the harbor. Is this because Portugal is at peace with all nations just then? The city of Lisbon is built on seven hills, like Rome. And here and there one can still see the rubble left by the earthquake that struck fifty years ago. To the left rises the convent of the Hieronymites.

It is early spring, and everything is in bloom. Bright red pomegranate trees, geraniums, orange and almond trees, rockroses. Aloes and datura bushes spread their sweet smells: it is enchanting. Betsy, who tries hard to not to think of anything but the present, drinks in these moments of happiness.

Quem nao viu Lisboa nao viu cousa boa . . .[1]

The captain has been able to obtain a shorter quarantine. Despite the pseudonyms behind which Jérôme and his wife are hiding — M. and Mme Albert — everyone knows the identity of the famous couple that has arrived in the Portuguese capital. The passengers have been allowed to go ashore and have taken lodgings in Sao Francisco de Paula Street, in one of the fine inns of the city, which they are eager to visit.

Betsy and Mrs. Anderson have a little trouble with their high heels on the steep and poorly paved streets of Lisbon, but they are delighted to be there. Betsy writes in a small notebook that she has visited the famous church of Saint-Roch. Accompanied by Jérôme and William, the young women also go shopping; Betsy's husband presents her with drop earrings, topazes and amethysts. Being newlyweds, they also buy household linens: embroidered sheets and tablecloths, as well as fine batiste handkerchiefs.

But that evening, Jérôme is visited in his hotel by the French chargé d'affaires, M. Sérurier, an austere figure, whose ceremonious demeanor makes Elizabeth want to giggle.

She will not giggle for long.

"The Emperor bids you join him immediately in Milan," he sternly tells Jérôme. "You are to go by yourself, for I have orders not to deliver a passport to *Mademoiselle Patterson*." Crimson-faced, her eyes blazing, Betsy immediately flashes back: "Tell your master that *Madame Bonaparte* is ambitious and that she demands her rights as a member of the imperial family!"

It's the old story of the earthen pot hitting the iron kettle . . .

---

[1] He who has not seen Lisbon has never seen anything beautiful.

The earthen vessel will have to take to the sea again on the *Erin,* which takes several weeks to make its way to Amsterdam. Meanwhile Jérôme speeds off on horseback toward Italy in the company of Alexandre Lecamus. They have to cross the whole breadth of Spain, reaching Madrid by way of Estremadura. They will have to pass Barcelona, Perpignan, Montpellier, Valence, and Grenoble, before they will arrive in Milan.

Jérôme and Alexandre are bent over a map. At their side, their horses are browsing in the sparse grass of the Alentejo. The smells here are almost the same as in the mountains of Corsica: masses of myrtle, lavender, and rosemary are growing here, as they do in the maquis, and there are also white, yellow, and red rockroses with flowers as big as garden roses. Whenever he comes to a turning point in his life, Jérôme cannot help but evoke his native isle. How far away it is, how his life has rushed by since he has left it . . . and how heavy his heart feels now!

His mind and body still filled with memories of his pretty wife, the young man pursues his long ride at his companion's side. Both are silent, contrary to their normal habits. That evening they dismount in an uncomfortable Portuguese *venda*, where the beds are full of bedbugs. Two days later, in a Spanish *posada* on the other side of the Portuguese border, Jérôme is greatly surprised to run into General Junot and his wife. The general and future Duc d'Abrantès and his wife (Laure Permon, a childhood friend of Jérôme) are on their way to Lisbon, where Junot has been appointed ambassador. How wonderful to meet up like this, quite by chance, with old friends from the past. The four decide to lunch together. Laure, who furtively watches Jérôme, finds that he looks more serious and thoughtful than she has ever seen him. As she observes him, she thinks of the games they played as children in the rue du Rocher and of all the silly pranks they made up together. Mme Permon was very fond of this boy and even tended to spoil him . . . Jérôme tells them in minute detail everything that has happened in his life over the last two years.

Laure and her husband are very eager to obtain more details about American life, which seems to them as exotic as that of the Persians. After lunch the four of them take a walk in the garden of the *posada*. When there is a moment of silence, Junot seizes the opportunity to hazard a piece of advice: "If I were in your place, Jérôme, I would not try to buck the Emperor's will." "You forget, Junot, that I have pledged my honor toward my in-laws. . . . Even supposing that I was wrong to marry Miss Patterson without the consent of Napoleon (even though my mother and Joseph had given theirs), is it fair that the punishment should fall upon my poor innocent wife? A woman as kindhearted as she is beautiful?"[2]

To prove his point, Jérôme shows the duly enchanted couple a miniature portrait of Elizabeth. Laure thinks that she looks like a more lively version of Pauline. "That is true," Jérôme agrees with a smile. "You are not the first one to point this out to me. And now judge for yourself whether I could possibly abandon a person like her. . . . I wish my brother would consent to seeing her, to listen to her for just one moment: I am sure that her triumph would be assured. As for me, I am firmly resolved not to yield. Knowing that I am right, I will not do anything that I might later regret."

Jérôme is still a long way from Milan. With a heavy heart he will soon have to say goodbye to the Junots.

He rides on through immense meadows where asphodels are in bloom, passing vineyards, olive trees, and live oaks, with the Sierra de Guadarama looming in the background.

"I HAVE ARRIVED HERE LAST NIGHT, MY DEAR BELOVED ELIZA," HE LATER writes from Madrid. "I hope everything will go well; for my part at least I will do everything I must do, and thereafter I will place my trust in God and we will bear our misfortune if things do not work out."

Barcelona, the Pyrenees, Perpignan, Montpellier, Valence. . . . What an interminable journey! When their horses are worn out, Jérôme and Alexandre stop at a relay station. And in the evening, by candlelight, Jérôme is still filled with longing and writes to his dear Eliza: "You can count on me to be with you by June 1 or 15 . . ."

Behind the Alps, the Emperor is waiting for his brother. And Lecamus, who furtively watches his friend's drawn face and his slender body as it bounces with the horse's bumping trot, says to himself that Jérôme reminds him of the frightened gazelle as it comes to drink at

---

[2] Memoirs of the Duchesse d'Abrantès, *Le Consulat et l'Empire*, vol. 5.

the river while the lion, comfortably ensconced in his lair, patiently awaits its coming.

Is it the fog that rises from the Tajo and engulfs the hills all around, the domes, the arsenal, the covered grain market, and the red and black silhouettes of the vegetable sellers, old women wearing white linen kerchiefs on their heads, or is it that Betsy's vision has become blurred from following the ever smaller forms of two riders dissolving in the distance, turning a corner, and then disappearing completely from her field of vision?

All of a sudden, she can no longer stand the early morning noises of the city: the cries of the hawkers, the jingling of the bells of goats and mules and the pealing of church bells give her a migraine. And then that all-pervasive smell of grilled sardines and fried cod . . .

"Let's go away from here," she murmurs. "How about visiting the convent of the Hieronymites in Belém?" Eliza Anderson suggests. Yes, that is a fine idea. Of course, it is seven miles to Belém, seven miles of being tossed about in a litter carried by two mules (one in front, one in back), but what a reward it will be to arrive in the monastery's gothic cloister and under the vaulted ceiling with its exuberant Manueline ornamentation!

The two women are walking in the gardens filled with the fragrance of jasmine. Betsy feels calm again. She also consoles herself by buying from the good sisters some embroidered linens for the baby she is expecting. All in all, however, she is getting impatient to leave here, to get to Amsterdam, and to have the child . . .

WHILE ELIZABETH IS KILLING TIME BY VISITING THE SITES AND WHILE JÉRÔME rides hell-bent for leather through Spain and France in pursuit of his brother, William Patterson and his wife are eating their hearts out with anxiety. Two letters from Robert in Paris have arrived. Given the seriousness of the revelations contained in them, they are written in code and unsigned: "Above all, Betsy must not go to France. If she did, she might consider herself lucky if she were simply sent back. Rumor has it that Lucien has been arrested in Milan and that he is now in irons."

According to Robert, his brother-in-law is risking the same treatment, as he reveals in his second missive. "If Jérôme arrives here, he will unquestionably be sequestered until he is released upon orders from the Emperor. . . . It is even whispered that Lucien may have been assassinated, although there is no confirmation for this."

Dorcas is overcome with sadness and blames herself for letting her daughter go. But her husband points out to her that they could not have let Jérôme sail by himself either. After all, he insists, this is the destiny Betsy has chosen for herself. Instead of leading a tranquil life in her own country, in the bosom of her family, she was determined to pursue a dangerous adventure.

8

*T*HE THREE WEEKS' CROSSING BETWEEN BALTIMORE and Lisbon may have seemed easy to Elizabeth, but this voyage to the Netherlands seems interminable. She suffers through twenty-six days on a rough sea, compounded by the constant fear of spotting English sails on the horizon.

Finally, on 10 May 1805, the *Erin* arrives at the mouth of the Zuiderzee, a few miles from Amsterdam. Ships here normally cannot proceed without being escorted by a pilot boat. Two, three days pass, and no such boat appears on the horizon. Captain Stephenson therefore decides to shorten sail and push on. When his ship is only a few cable lengths from Amsterdam, a pilot boat draws near. An elderly man climbs aboard the *Erin* and offers to guide her into port. The *Erin* has barely let down her anchor when a salvo is fired from a nearby ship. Intrigued, the captain asks the pilot what this can mean, but the pilot has no idea.

A sloop comes speeding toward the American ship and stops alongside. "Are you from Baltimore?" someone asks. "We are." "Are you arriving from Lisbon?" "We are," the captain replies again, much astonished. "Well then, you cannot come into the harbor." And the sloop sails away.

The captain flushes with anger. "After all, we are not at war with Holland, as far as I know," he thinks. As for the old Dutch pilot, he seems extremely agitated. "Damnation!" he mutters, "I sure made a hell of a mistake! My colleagues and I, we were all given orders to watch out for you. But for a moment, when I saw your brig making its way up the River Texel all alone, I forgot my instructions and only thought of how I could help you. Now I can look forward to the rope, or at least to prison, unless they make allowances for my advanced age."

When Betsy hears of this new blow she has suffered, she collapses in tears on her berth. Will every port in Europe be closed to her because of one man's implacable rancor? "This is dreadful," she sobs, "I will never see Jérôme again." Her brother William and Mrs. Anderson try to console her, but both of them are worried.

Up on his poop deck, the captain is furious. He has been made to fit his ship between a big sixty-four-gun frigate and a sloop, which are doing guard duty, as it were. As an extra precaution, two smaller boats constantly patrol around the *Erin* as well. "They really must be afraid of us," he mutters between clenched teeth.

A strong north wind has sprung up. The ship is pitching dangerously. Every time a sudden gust drives it a little too close to the frigate, threatening shapes appear behind the cannons. And to make matters even worse, the *Erin* has run out of fresh food: all that is left are a few biscuits and a little salt beef.

"We have nothing left to eat," Stephenson shouts into his speaking tube, "can you help us if we cannot get supplies ourselves?" "Yah, yah," the Dutch reply indifferently. Finally, after four days, William Patterson Jr., Dr. Garnier, and four sailors have become desperate enough to launch a rowboat and man the oars, bound and determined to break through the boom and bring in supplies. Disaster! The frigate is about to open fire. Already the cannoneers are stepping up to the breeches with burning matches. The rowboat turns around and the six men in it clamber up the rope ladder as fast as they can and tumble onto the deck. Fortunately the Dutch admiral, who has watched the whole scene from a neighboring vessel and is intrigued by this suicidal operation, sends a small craft to inquire. "What is the meaning of this *tintamarre?*"[1] he wants to know.

As soon as he learns of the desperate plight of the American brig, he decides to supply its needs. But, he adds, he has received orders from the Grand Pensioner of the Batavian Republic, a close friend of Napoleon, not to allow the *Erin* to land in any Dutch port. "His Majesty the Emperor," Talleyrand has written to him, "has been informed that a

---

[1] "Uproar."

woman by the name of Patterson has followed M. Jérôme Bonaparte to Europe and has landed with this officer in Lisbon. Immediately after her arrival in that city, this woman, who is using the name Mme Jérôme Bonaparte, has embarked on a vessel bound for Holland. . . . His Majesty has asked me to write you confidentially to bid you prevent her from staying in Holland and forcing her to return immediately to the United States."

"Where will we go?" the captain and the utterly crushed passengers are wondering. Given Betsy's advanced state of pregnancy, a return to America is out of the question. Should they anchor their ship in a Scandinavian or German harbor, Bremen for example? Let the young woman give birth in a place where she does not understand the language? In the end the winning argument is that of William Patterson Jr.: his sister, he says, must have her child in England. After all, the United States and Great Britain are not at war at this moment; the Pattersons have many connections there; and there will be no language difficulties. And also, it is not far to Dover . . .

The very next afternoon the boat docks in the English port. Finally, they all will be able to go ashore, much to the relief of Betsy, although she had not foreseen the huge crowd of curiosity seekers who had flocked to the port to witness her arrival. Why, she is being greeted like a queen!

Despite its other preoccupations, the English government has had to dispatch a military unit to escort the young woman as she disembarks. James Monroe — still the minister plenipotentiary in London — and his family have found her a hotel in Mayfair, the city's fanciest neighborhood. There too, crowds pursue her all the way into the vestibule. William and Dr. Garnier have to act as bodyguards.

Betsy, who had been very depressed when she was refused entry by the Dutch, perks up considerably. She has become a public figure. A victim of tyranny? Perhaps so, but pity is better than indifference. With her head held high and great dignity, she walks through the curious onlookers who line her path, flashing a little smile from time to time. The next morning's London papers, the *Courier* and the *Morning Chronicle,* resound with her name.

The English, to be sure, are quite ready to feel pity for this young victim of the abominable Bonaparte who at this very moment is planning to invade their island. But they also have a great curiosity about everything that has to do with France, and sometimes even friendly feelings, as they have shown by their warm reception of so many emigrés during the French Revolution.

A FEW DAYS LATER, MISS MONROE OFFERS TO INTRODUCE THE YOUNG WOMAN to London's high society. She can't very well remain cloistered in her apartments, she tells her, waiting for news from her husband that may or may not come. "I am in too advanced a state of pregnancy," Betsy replies, "and in fact I would prefer to move farther away from the center of London, find a house in the surrounding countryside, Surrey, for instance."

Then she talks about some walks she and Eliza Anderson have taken around London, where everything is new to her. They went to Marylebone and to Hyde Park, where they greatly enjoyed the eccentric behavior of certain young men called *dandies,* the most famous of whom is George Brummel, whom all London calls "le Beau."

Betsy soon persuades her friends that moving would be best, and they find her a little house in a small community near London, called Camberwell.

On 7 July 1805, she goes into labor. Dr. Garnier delivers her, assisted by a young English assistant. It is a boy! Who knows, Betsy thinks dreamily, perhaps he will be the instrument of a reconciliation between the Emperor and myself. For the fact is that the Emperor does not have an heir. Joseph is the father of two daughters; only Louis and Lucien have boys, but there is deadly enmity between Lucien and his brother. Whereas Jerôme has always been the benjamin, the favorite. Perhaps his son . . . "Your name will be Jérôme-Napoleon," she says as she places a kiss on the baby's little red hand.

After all these weeks of uncertainty and tension, she finally has a real feeling of well-being and is determined to enjoy herself. Nonetheless she has been shrewd enough to have the birth of little Jérôme-Napoleon certified by two foreign personalities, the Austrian ambassador and the Prussian envoy, whose signatures have been duly notarized. Come what may, she is prepared!

Since the mails are rather slow, it is August before friends are able to bring her a long letter from Jérôme, a letter that is as affectionate as it is vague. But Betsy, filled with renewed hope since the birth of the baby, feels that this news is reason for optimism.

"You know how distressed I was to leave you in Lisbon, and God, who knows my heart, also knows that I breathe only for my dear wife. Not doubt I am a father by now; I hope it is a boy. As soon as I arrived at Madrid I wrote to you. Then I rushed off to Alexandria [Italy], where I met my brother. No one but I, Elisa, when I have the happiness of holding you in my arms, can tell you what happened then. . . . Trust your husband, and believe in your heart that he breathes, dreams, and works only for you. . . . The Emperor is such a kind father that we have everything to hope from his heart and his generosity."

For some time now, William has been pressing his sister to return to the United States, but she refuses. He can go back by himself if he so desires, she tells him, or he can take along Eliza Anderson, who desperately wants to leave. She will join them later with Robert, who has just come to London.

She is simply in no hurry to go back to her cramped middle-class life in Baltimore. Here in England she is fawned upon, fêted, surrounded by admirers, and watched with flattering curiosity by all and sundry. The Monroes have presented her to the duchess of York, who reigns over a veritable court at her castle of Oatlands Park. There she has met politicians like Lord Alvanley, the Irish dramatist Richard Sheridan, and the famous dandy George "Beau" Brummel, arbiter of elegance, whose famous cravats are copied by everyone, including the Regent, and whose sharp tongue can make or unmake a person's reputation based on a single glance.

After Eliza has left, Betsy is invited to a performance at the Drury Lane Theater, and then to a ball at the Marquess of Hertford's. She is fascinated by this brilliant society, but still too worried about her future to let herself be fully absorbed by it. The Prince of Wales, the future George IV, has sent word that he would like to receive her at his court, but she feels that it would not be proper for her to accept. After all, she is the wife of a Bonaparte and the mother of a little Jérôme-Napoleon of the same name.

"Mlle Patterson has been in London, causing a great stir among the English; this has compounded her reprehensible behavior." Hearing of this statement by the Emperor greatly dampens Betsy's spirits. Why does Napoleon not understand that she did not know where to turn six months earlier, when she was drifting on the waters of the Zuiderzee?

She also learns from a letter of Lecamus that Napoleon offers her a yearly pension of sixty thousand francs if she returns to Baltimore and gives up the name Bonaparte. "Return to Baltimore, perhaps, but give up the name to which my marriage has given me the right — never!" she has exclaimed. Yet a letter from Dr. Garnier, and then one that arrives in September from Jérôme, urge her to return to her family until matters are settled. Jérôme continues to exhibit great epistolary tenderness toward her. "My dear and beloved wife," he writes,

> my life is nothing without you and my son. We will, my Eliza, be separated for a while longer, but eventually our misfortunes will come to end. . . . If you are not recalled [to France] within two months, go back to America. . . . Do not worry, your husband will never abandon you. . . . Be persuaded, my dear wife, that I only work, only suffer, for you and my son. . . . Tell him, "your father will always prefer you to grandeur, wealth, and any position of exalted rank."

Jérôme has also asked his wife to adopt a lifestyle commensurate with her rank as soon as she returns to Baltimore: she will have to "keep open house, a carriage drawn by four horses, and numerous servants," as if his return were imminent. These calming words have been a balm to the young mother's afflicted heart. By the end of October she decides to wend her way home with Robert and the baby, for it will be best not to wait until the nor'easters that blow along the American coast in late autumn become too troublesome.

As our three travelers make their way on the brig *Mars,* and as Betsy hopes to avoid further imperial edicts, she does not know that great events are unfolding in the Mediterranean: on 21 October 1805 Napoleon suffers his first defeat at Trafalgar. Nor is this a minor setback: his fleet and that of Spain have been decimated by the English Royal Navy under the command of Admiral Nelson, who has lost his life in that engagement. What is being heard are the first sounds of the death knell for Napoleon's power.

Part 11

AN AMERICAN HIGHNESS

9

*M*ARY-ANN! . . . JÉRÔME! WERE IT NOT FOR the accent of the black nursemaid who is watching the children, one might feel carried back twenty years to the old *casa* in Ajaccio's rue Malerba.

But no, we are in Baltimore, and it is the autumn of 1806.

Elizabeth has returned to her family, her head held high. To those who would offer her sympathy, she has shown a smooth and smiling face. All it will take, she has told them in confident tones, will be a little patience. Jérôme has been ordered to take a new command and has had to go to sea again, as is only normal for a naval officer, but as soon as he returns and has done well, he will bring the Emperor around to his views and extract his permission to send for his wife. This is also what Alexandre Lecamus has asserted in a letter to Mr. Patterson: "If Jérôme successfully carries out his mission, he will ask for his wife as a reward."

Following her husband's advice, Betsy's first step has been to take up residence, with her son, in a house provided by her father. Before going to sleep at night she often imagines the joyful life she will lead as soon as Jérôme returns: once again she will go to fêtes and balls. She will leave this town she detests, where she feels cramped, and she does not care about the breeze of liberty that fills the dreams of so many Europeans. The breeze that fills her ears comes from the old continent, from its history-laden streets, from its frills and furbelows, and even from its wars, where lace is no longer in evidence.

Yet the wind from Europe sometimes brings bad news. Thus word

71

comes during the winter that Napoleon has had the Senate annul his young brother's marriage. So as to leave nothing to chance, he has also sent a long and detailed letter to Pope Pius VII, asking him to have this union declared null and void by the Papal court of Rome.

> I have several times already spoken to Your Holiness about the young brother whom I sent to America on a frigate and who after a month's stay, although a minor, was married in Baltimore to a Protestant, the daughter of a merchant who is a citizen of the United States. He has just returned to France. He is well aware that he has done wrong. I have sent Miss Patterson, his alleged wife, back to America. According to our laws the marriage is null and void. A priest has strayed from his duty to the point of giving his blessing. I should wish to obtain from Your Holiness a bull annulling this marriage. . . . It would be easy for me to have this done in Paris . . . but it would seem more befitting to me that the immediate intervention of Your Holiness should give prominence to this matter, if only because it involves a member of a sovereign nation. . . . It is important in many respects and in the interest of our religion in France that I should not have a Protestant girl near me.

But this has not worked out for him. Yes, Napoleon is powerful, but not enough to force a pope's hand. Moreover, his letter is filled with deliberate inaccuracies, and the pope knows it. He replies that he is extremely sorry but that he cannot accede to this request.

Learning of the pope's refusal, Betsy has felt her hopes revive: in the Church's eyes, at least, she is still Jérôme's wife. . . . She continues to receive enthusiastic letters from that husband who, having assumed command of the *Vétéran*, crisscrosses the Atlantic under the orders of Admiral Willaumetz. He has become second-in-command to the admiral, he is gaining fame and glory, and he harangues his sailors in Napoleonic tones: "Sailors, and you, soldiers, today we are entering the year 1806, which must become the year of our naval successes. . . . As for me, whose only concern is your happiness and your glory, I expect from you that some day it can be said: 'He was a gallant fighter, he sailed on the *Vétéran*.'"

Off the Cape of Good Hope, he captures two enemy vessels.

Betsy is proud of her husband's achievements; after all, as long as he is at sea, she has nothing to worry about, particularly since he assures her that he is doing all this only for her. Forsaken as she is, she avidly drinks in his comforting words; they help her ignore the malicious rumors that are beginning to fly in Baltimore. The most rancorous of these are spread, of course, by the Federalists, who are delighted: they have known all along that the French are sly and fickle, always ready to turn their coats, and totally untrustworthy! Betsy hears a great deal of such talk. Even in her own family, hitherto Republican and staunchly supportive of Jefferson's policies, the wind is beginning to shift. "After all," says Mr. Patterson, "three-fourths of our trade is with the English, even if they make us pay heavy customs taxes. From France we hardly import anything but silks, brandies, and a few manufactured goods."

Betsy shrugs as she hears her father and her brother discuss ballast, freight rates, and prices. Some of their friends, the Bayers and the Cunninghams, have had their cargoes confiscated by French raiders as they were making their way to Saint-Domingue with supplies of food, arms, and printed materials for the black insurgents. Complaints are constantly lodged with Arcambal, the French consul-general in Baltimore, or with his superior, General Turreau, who is still the acting minister plenipotentiary.

President Jefferson is disturbed by the French arguments. Yet how can he prevent American merchants from pursuing their business? More than in any other country, politics is secondary to business in the United States. "It pains me to see," the President confesses, "that our people have an inclination for commerce that no other area of interest will be able to counter-balance." Braving his fellow-citizens' incomprehension, he decides to submit to Congress a bill to regulate commercial relations with the Antilles.

When this "Bill Prohibiting Intercourse" was published in the press, Betsy was jubilant. This would shake up the complacency of the American merchants. Her family, however, was dismayed.

In Baltimore, as in other American cities, everyone peruses a newspaper first thing in the morning and last thing at night. And there is no lack of papers in Maryland. One can read the *Maryland Observer,* the

Federal Republican, the *Baltimore News,* and others as well. In 1806 and 1807 all of them are overflowing with sometimes disturbing news: Aaron Burr, the former vice president of the United States, is trying to bring about a split between the northern and the southern states, and to create an independent confederation. French Canada, for its part, is rebelling against English domination, and a majority of its population demands to be reunited with France. Turreau has been appraised of these sentiments by a delegation from Québec but lacks the funds to take action. However, this rumor has caused concern in American public opinion. To be sure, France has given up Louisiana, but its presence in Canada would be even less reassuring, it is whispered. At a time when France is feared as an expansionist nation on the Old Continent, what are the prospects for the young United States of America, a nation that is still struggling to consolidate its institutions and does not even have a real army? True, every state has its own militia, but no one knows if that of the New England states would be willing to fight in Georgia, for instance, or vice-versa.

Certain opposition papers (financed no doubt by the English), attribute even darker motives to the Gallic rooster. France, they assert, would be ready to force the United States to return to the bosom of England, which would place it under the jurisdiction of the Duke of York. But the English, kind souls that they are, do not want to hear of it!

"The amount of foolishness that one can read from the pens of the Federalists is not to be believed!" Turreau writes in a fury. "And there are people naive enough to swallow it all, hook, line, and sinker! This can only harm us! Why don't we too finance French papers that would allow us to set matters straight?"

At the time of General Moreau's arrival in New York, for instance, it had been believed for several weeks that the Napoleonic Empire was about to collapse, for false rumors to this effect had circulated.

One evening John Patterson, returning from New York, had told his family what he had seen: Several armed ships had surreptitiously left the East River, one of them, the *Leander* carrying six guns. This was an enormous frigate, outfitted by a certain Miranda, a handsome Venezuelan with a glowering face who was suspected of subversive activities in the Spanish colonies. Was he in cahoots with the English . . . or with the Americans? The Pattersons are inclined to go along with the latter hypothesis. Or rather, they think that their government deliberately closes its eyes to Miranda's machinations. For there is every reason to wish for a rebellion in the Spanish possessions. They are really quite poorly run, and their independence would allow the United States to open new routes to the East and to establish branch offices there.

But was it not possible also that the ships were simply off on an expedition to Saint-Domingue? This has happened before. . . . It has almost become a routine undertaking.

One morning, when Elizabeth and Jessie had gone to Lexington Market, they witnessed a most unusual pageant. A group of Indians dressed in trousers and blue blazers, with long straight hair, and wearing rows of something like dog collars on their arms, were parading through the streets behind a bugler, escorted by armed soldiers. They were, it seemed, the first Indian delegates admitted to the Congress of the United States; they were presented everywhere to the population as "adoptive brothers brought into the great American family." Everyone was invited to step up and embrace them or shake their hands. They had also been made to parade in these outfits in Washington and Philadelphia. Although fed and housed by the government, they were dying rapidly, unable to adapt to a way of life for which they were not suited.

Elizabeth had shrugged her shoulders about all of this. She is more anxious to hear from Jérôme than to learn about the fate of the Indians or indeed the Americans in general. Whenever a ship arrives in the harbor, a wave of hope washes over her, but alas, news is rare. But then one day, Commodore Lewis, a friend of her father who has just returned from Cayenne, reports that he has met Jérôme there, where he had stopped over with his three-master. Lewis had been besieged with questions: "How is little Jérôme Napoleon? Who does he look like? And Elisa, is she as pretty as ever?" "As you can imagine," Lewis says with a laugh, "I gave him as faithful a picture of reality as I could. And he was very moved by it. I saw his eyes fill with tears, and as he took both my hands into his, he murmured, 'My little wife . . . my dear little wife . . .' Before I departed, he entrusted me with a letter for you, and here it is."

Do you believe, my good wife, that if I had given you up I would still be commanding His Majesty's ships? For an ordinary officer the position I occupy is quite good, especially at my age, but for me, who with one word could rise to the very top, it does not amount to much. . . . Do not believe, my beloved, that your good husband will ever regret all he has done and suffered for you; I have preferred you to a crown and I will always prefer you to everyone else. . . . You must have unlimited confidence in your husband; let the little girls and the bad tongues of Baltimore say what they will and enjoy your happiness, for it is a happy thing to be loved as you are loved. . . . Do not make yourself unhappy; take care to bring up my son properly; and especially do not make him into an American, he must be French. See to it that the first words he speaks are those of his father and of his sovereign. He must learn right away that the great Napoleon is his uncle and that he is destined to become a prince and a statesman.

Tears blur Betsy's vision, she is flooded with happiness. Jérôme still loves her after this long year of separation! And since he is near, having stopped in the Antilles, perhaps he will repeat his escapade of the last time, when he landed on the Virginia coast? For weeks on end, Betsy lives on that hope.

She has gone back to live at her parents' house, and Jessie has followed her as a matter of course. The two often take the child for a walk along the Patapsco or at Fells Point, where a whole slew of shipyards have sprung up. Baltimore has become famous for a special kind of schooner with fore-and-aft sails and for the ultra-rapid brig that has been developed there. Better than all of these, better even than the Bermuda schooner, is the Baltimore clipper. Slender and well-proportioned, this schooner is very responsive to the tiller and clips through the water (hence its name). Its two masts and its stern post are bent slightly backward in order to offer as little resistance to the wind as possible, and its hull has the shape of a V. The deck is as close to the water as possible, the poop deck and forecastle are only slightly higher, and the stem post is very slender.

Elizabeth and Jessie fill their nostrils with the smells of cut wood, which must be allowed to age for several months before it can be used, and watch the precise gestures of the master carpenters who wield their adzes, augers, and saws as they cut, assemble, and peg the wood.

Returning from these outings, Betsy desperately scrutinizes the horizon: will she see, far off on the Chesapeake, the arrival of the superb flagship *Vétéran* followed by its squadron? But the days go by and no French sail appears on the horizon. The English, for their part, are running more and more patrols, boarding American ships under the pretext of looking for deserters from the British navy, and using this opportunity for pressing Yankee sailors into their own service, where treatment is harsh.

Betsy receives one more letter from Jérôme, written in Martinique: "I am well, and it pains me to be 150 leagues away from you, yet unable to enjoy the happiness of seeing you," he writes. But he also has some belated reproaches for her. Why on earth has she sought refuge in Eng-land, last year? If she had gone ashore in Holland and given birth there, might not Napoleon have accepted her as his sister-in-law after all? "What is this?" Betsy asks herself. "Did I read this correctly? And what about the orders of the Grand Elector of Batavia, did I dream that?"

Jérôme is not coming to the United States. On the contrary, before long he is chasing an English squadron in the waters off the Azores and captures eleven vessels. Flushed with pride after this exploit, he makes straight for France, where he is henceforth bound to be showered with honors.

Months go by, slowly, slowly. American relations with the English are becoming increasingly strained. It is learned that in New York one of their sloops, the *Leopard*, has fired point blank at an American frigate, the *Chesapeake*, which had refused to submit to a "check." Three men have been killed and eighteen wounded. "How can we tolerate such treatment from the English in peace time!" is the general cry. The situation on the high seas is becoming intolerable for the neutral powers. When the Orders in Council of the British government forbid all American trade with Europe, Napoleon replies with his decrees of Berlin and Milan, which prohibit all trade with the British Isles. The French navy is ordered to seize all ships coming from England or her colonies. "This will be our ruin!" the Yankee shipowners and captains wail.

But then they deploy such ingenious techniques that their businesses do very well indeed. Their clippers brave the Atlantic; they are so fast that they can outrun both the heavy English brigs and the French frigates. Some of these American merchants carry their audacity so far as to trade in the Mediterranean, despite the threat of privateers from the Barbary Coast.

THEN, ONE EVENING, DISASTER STRIKES. MR. PATTERSON HAS COME TO Betsy's room, carrying a letter. It was sent by his son John, who is in London. The papers there, he says, are announcing the marriage of Jérôme to Princess Catherine of Württemberg. In the autumn he is to be crowned king of Westphalia. "A fine reward," Mr. Patterson concludes, "for a man who has abandoned his legitimate wife!"

"Father, please, be quiet. He did this for reasons of state. But I can't believe . . ." Betsy lifts her hand to her face, holds on to a nearby console; she is about to faint. As William Patterson contemplates her deathly pale face he is seized by a wave of pity, which he quickly suppresses. After all, he thinks, a clean surgical strike is preferable to letting this romantic little head continue to nourish false hopes. "Peggy," he says to his younger daughter who is sewing in her mother's sitting room, "it would be good if you went to comfort your sister; I think she needs you."

As is learned subsequently, Jérôme has had a princely wedding. In the face of the pope's refusal to have the American marriage annulled by the ecclesiastical court in Rome, Napoleon has had it declared invalid by the ecclesiastical tribunal in Paris. Having been married by proxy in Stuttgart, Jérôme married Catherine of Württemberg in a grand ceremony that took place in late August at the Tuileries.

In her mind's eye, Betsy sees a parade of colorful uniforms. Jérôme in a suit of white silk with a lace jabot, Catherine in a Leroy robe of white silk that is fitted rather too tightly, the brilliance of pearls and diamonds, the banquet in the hall of Diana — all the luxuries she has not enjoyed at her own wedding, elegant though her lace dress had been. Fortunately, she hears, there has been torrential rain that very evening, so that the fireworks and the illuminations in the Tuileries Gardens have had to be canceled. . . . Betsy, seized by sobbing, rushes from the room.

Oh, how her heart weeps as the rain pours down the window panes and the autumn winds bend the tree tops, blowing down the first red leaves. The tall oak tree with its black trunk shakes its heavy mane. Overhead, a huge, dark V passes. It is formed by the wild geese that are coming down from Canada to hibernate in the marshes of Maryland and Virginia.

How far away it is, that autumn of 1803, when everything around her seemed to glow with happiness, when life was a perpetual party! Jérôme, Jérôme, have you forgotten everything?

What to do, what to say when people watch you and pity you — Dorcas, for instance, whose heart is deeply pained by the wall of silence behind which Betsy has withdrawn, or William Patterson, whose glances are tinged with reproof when the family sits down to supper around the heavy oaken table?

If the young brothers, George and Octavius, blurt out jokes about the situation, their mother bids them stop. But the worst is meeting neighbors or friends in the street. Hearing the seemingly harmless words they exchange with her as she goes to the market with her mother or with Jessie, Betsy feels touched by a thousand furtive thoughts that twist and coil around her and swarm up her spine as soon as she has turned her back. A thousand tiny arrows, flying from the bows of lilliputian archers, strike her heart every hour of the day.

Fortunately, she has little Jérôme, called "Bo" by everyone here. Mainly because he is a Bonaparte — the first American Bonaparte, as Betsy tenderly whispers into his ear. But also because he already has a certain proud delicacy in his features, beautiful black eyes, and willful jaw that recall those of his all-too-famous kinsman. He is good-humored and boisterous, and his grandfather is crazy about him. Mr. Patterson sometimes climbs up Federal Hill with the child. There, from the very top of the tower, Bo looks out for arriving ships through a field glass, just as his mother has done fifteen years earlier.

Meanwhile Betsy tries to stave off boredom by learning a few recipes from her mother and writing them down in a little notebook. Maryland is famous for its refined cuisine, which is a far cry from the rough communal meals of the Western pioneers or the heavy German cooking of Pennsylvania farmers. Betsy learns all about deep-fried oysters, sautéed crab, and shad croquettes, and knows how to serve some of the old madeira from her father's well-stocked cellars with her lemon custard. Betsy increasingly takes over from her mother in the running of the household, for Dorcas's delicate health has been further compromised by thirteen pregnancies.

In the last two years there have been many marriages in the Patterson family. John, who had planned to go into medicine, has given up on this career and has joined his father's business in order to make a living sooner and be able to marry. Edward, Elizabeth's favorite brother, has also gone into the shipping business, having abandoned his original vocation. The most artistic of all the Patterson siblings, this accomplished pianist would have much preferred a life of concert halls and music lessons to juggling the figures in his father's account books. To Betsy, who sometimes wonders about his docility, he replies that he must be able to make a living as soon as possible, for he is in love with his cousin Sidney Smith and wants to marry her. "Really now, Ed," she tells him in a tone of reproach, "is there anyone in the world worth ruining one's life for?"

Bo has just been baptized (according to the Catholic rite, much to Mr. Patterson's dismay). His godmother is Mary Caton. This beautiful young woman, who has a great deal of style and distinction, has recently been married to Robert Patterson. The young man is madly in love with his wife, but Betsy, deep down, does not like her sister-in-law. She finds her snobbish, disdainful, and consumed by craving for fine clothes and luxury. No wonder, for she and her sisters have been coddled since childhood by their grandfather, old Mr. Carroll, who was the richest man in Maryland. "I am sure she will not make Robert happy," Betsy thinks disconsolately. "And yet he is such a good fellow!"

No doubt she envies Mary for the tenderness and the attentions with which her husband surrounds her. Whenever she comes upon them as they kiss, hold hands, or exchange tender glances, her heart is pierced by thorns. For her, all that is left are a few kind words, like those that were brought to her by Anna Kuhn, an American who has met Jérôme at the imperial court shortly after his marriage.

"I had a few minutes' private conversation with your ex-husband," she has told Betsy. "He seemed very moved when he heard that I was going to see you soon. He repeatedly assured me that you were the only woman he has really loved, and will always love more than anyone in the world; he will never get over having lost you!" "And . . . what does Princess Catherine look like?" — "Oh, she is far from being as beautiful as you are! She is heavy, timid, and poorly put together. But she has an open face that radiates kindness. Jérôme does not seem much taken with her for the moment. You know that this was a marriage of convenience, to which he agreed to please his brother." "I know," Betsy had sighed, feeling somewhat comforted despite herself.

In February 1808 an unusual-looking visitor rings the doorbell of the house on South Street. When she first sees him, Betsy feels transported four years into the past. He is a Creole with matte complexion, a pock-marked face, and a soft and melodious voice. "Allow me to introduce myself. I am August Lecamus, and I have come from Martinique. My brother Alexandre, Comte de Furstenstein . . ." — "Comte de what?" Elizabeth asks, nonplussed. "De Furstenstein," the young man continues without missing a beat, pronouncing the word "Furchetintin," much to his interlocutor's amusement. "Yes, His Majesty King Jérôme has been gracious enough to name my brother grand chamberlain of the court and to ennoble him."

As she considers this, Betsy wavers between irritation and a fit of laughter. Alexandre Lecamus grand chamberlain of the king. . . . More trifling games for Jérôme! Jean-Jacques Rewbell, she also learns, has been promoted to general, and Meyronnet grand marshal of the palace. This is the Meyronnet who liked to go around looking like a pirate, with a gold ring in his left ear peeking out under his curly hair. All of Jérôme's boon companions of the past have been showered with honors and bombastic titles, while she . . .

"My brother has instructed me to ask you for a portrait of little Jérôme Napoleon for the king. I believe His Majesty to be deeply chagrined at being separated from his child."

A few days later Alexandre Lecamus has left Baltimore, carrying in his luggage a carefully wrapped miniature showing the charming face of a pink-cheeked, thoughtful-looking little boy. Surely, this will be a good letter of credit when he arrives in Westphalia!

10

$\mathcal{N}$ANCY SPEAR IS CONCERNED ABOUT HER NIECE'S health; having caught her one day swallowing a large dose of barbiturates, she has immediately alerted the family doctor, who has succeeded in reversing the incipient poisoning. "I can't even do away with myself!" Betsy had sobbed between two bouts of vomiting, "I am good for nothing!" Pale, thin, and depressed, she is a pitiful sight.

"Dorcas," Nancy has said to her sister, "we absolutely have to do something to help your daughter get over her grief. What if I take her to Washington with me? That will distract her." This is an offer Betsy has eagerly accepted.

Aunt Nancy has not given up her favorite habits. Every winter she jumps into the diligence and goes to Georgetown, where she lodges in the boarding house of an Irishman by the name of O'Neale. While she is there, she immerses herself in Republican politics while Congress is in session. Everyone recognizes her puce overcoat and her mauve hood.

Under the prodding of the wife of the secretary of state, James Madison, the presidential palace has been considerably spruced up. New furniture has been purchased and the old fence has disappeared. A certain refinement is becoming evident: next to Chippendale or French-inspired Directory chairs one now finds genuinely American-style furniture from the workshops of Boston, Baltimore, and Philadelphia: inlaid desks and bureaux, sometimes decorated with mother-of-pearl or tinted glass, armchairs in beechwood, birch, or mahogany with delicately sculpted backs or ornamented with charming landscapes.

Dolly Madison, who is as pretty and spirited as her husband is puny and retiring, enjoys taking snuff, playing cards, and giving balls. It is she who now presides over the receptions at the "palace" and receives all of Washington's society there — young and more-or-less unmannerly congressmen, foreign ambassadors and chargés d'affaires, and wealthy citizens of the new Republic. At these gatherings the oriental style favored by the wife of the secretary of state is all the rage: turbans trimmed with jewels, aigrettes, and cashmere shawls. The men have still not made up their minds between knee-breeches and white silk stockings and the trousers inherited from the French Revolution. Cravats and excessively high collars are due to the influence of Beau Brummel.

In the evenings gigs and cabriolets drive along the dark and muddy streets of Washington and Georgetown that are still separated by immense deserted spaces. They are taking all these elegant people to the "palace" or to one of the foreign legations, which try to outdo all the others with their parties. In that society one meets all kinds of different faces; there is the inscrutable one, for instance, of the new British minister, Mr. Erskine, whose courteous manners have charmed the president and the Madisons to the point that for a few months the balance has seemed to shift toward the pro-English Federalist Party; then there is the enigmatic Miranda with his swarthy complexion and the scowl on his face, a man who is always ready to scatter the seeds of revolt in South America although no one understands the exact nature of his political dealings. One can also meet the American engineer Robert Fulton, who has recently invented a propeller-driven submarine, the *Nautilus,* and has also proposed to build motors that can propel the frigates and catamarans of the American government — without, however, being taken up on this offer. To be seen also is General Turreau, once known as the Ogre of the Vendée, whose heavy-set figure and grim face, complete with long whiskers, sideburns, and bushy eyebrows, greatly impress the secretary of state when he comes to see him and, in his poor English, presents the grievances of the French government.

"I hope, Betsy, that you are not going to wear one of your transparent dresses to Dolly Madison's next ball?"

"How about my muslin dress with the embroidered silver tears? It would be quite appropriate to my mood and is also quite modest because I wear it over an undergarment of white satin."

"Whatever you decide, my dear. All I want is to see once again a smile on that face of yours, which lately has too often been bathed in tears."

If Aunt Nancy seems to have had trouble snagging a husband in Washington where people are getting engaged right and left, Betsy soon becomes its darling. People call her *Madame Bonaparte*, they crowd around her to pay homage, she dances and plays cards — especially the game Loo, which is all the rage — and she once again has the smile and the pink cheeks of her girlhood.

A young English naval attaché cannot take his eyes off her. He is Samuel Graves, the son of the admiral of the same name who long ago, during the American Revolution, was defeated by Admiral de Grasse in the Chesapeake and has been harboring a fierce hatred of the French ever since.

General Turreau, who is watching these goings-on from afar, bites his lip and does not say anything, for he has received orders from his minister to keep his distance from "Mademoiselle Patterson." Still, he feels compelled to express his worries to his superior, the Duc de Cadore. In his opinion, this is nothing less than an attempt on the part of the English to get hold of both the mother and the child. He feels that behind the amorous glances of Samuel Graves, behind the poems and the ardent notes he sends to Betsy ("In bed, dejected and depressed/ Wearied I turn from side to side/ Impatient to obtain that rest/ Which to my troubles is denied") there lurk the black intentions of perfidious Albion.

"Suppose that, later on, the English were to pursue subversive ends by means of this young American Bonaparte, whom they could convert to their own views and then manipulate like a chess piece against the other heirs to the name? One never knows!"

However, the French plenipotentiary has other worries. America is a moving terrain, where wildly ambitious schemes are being pursued. While the American presidents are encouraging the pioneers to push their incursions further West and to drive out the Indians they find there or, alternatively, initiate them into the dominant culture, and while the English nourish their dreams of taking over the Spanish possessions in Latin America or at least carving out lucrative markets for themselves in these regions, Napoleon is beginning to think of regaining Canada or founding French establishments between Louisiana and Mexico. Why not a New World France to counterbalance a New World England?

The American government, for its part, has also recognized the importance of dominating the Gulf of Mexico. And so it haggles and quibbles over the western borders of Louisiana: given the artistic vagueness of the borders between that territory and western Florida, surely there must be a way to lay hands on a little piece of that land? And indeed, why not on all of the two Floridas? Now that Jefferson, without firing a shot, has obtained from France the cession of Louisiana, Madison would be pleased to see the prestige of his administration enhanced by the addition of the two Floridas to the young nation's patrimony.

But certain parties are deaf to such arguments. First and foremost are the Spanish, who are outraged. Yrujo, who is no longer minister plenipotentiary of His Most Catholic Majesty but has stayed on in the United States for personal reasons, fills the newspapers with his verbal outbursts.

Turreau, who tries his best to run with the hare and hunt with the hounds, has promised Madison to act as moderator if it should come to negotiations. For France does not want to fall from favor with the American government. But is it really in France's interest to see the United States extend all along the East and the West Coasts of the continent, develop its power, and protect its commerce? At the very least, the American government should ally with France against England. "If, for instance, the English were to attack Florida, the Emperor would find it appropriate if the Americans were to bring in troops to defend these territories." By means of such euphemisms the young nation is steadily strengthening its position. When all is said and done, it is doing rather well for itself in this fierce struggle between France and England, the two European superpowers of that era.

However, other forces are beginning to stir in the background. The former vice president, Aaron Burr, continues his plotting, and it is said that he plans to overthrow the government and to bring together Louisiana and Mexico in the empire he intends to carve out for himself.

All of this goes to show that amidst all the balls and fancy receptions, Washington is the scene of an intense struggle in the year 1808. But for Betsy, to whose beauty everyone pays tribute, all that counts is little Bo, his chestnut-brown curls, his black eyes, and the glorious future that is in store for him.

And oh, how monotonous her life has become, now that she has returned to Baltimore! Once again she faces her father's remonstrances, the neighbors' whispers, and the long evenings of mortal boredom. She crosses the paths of the Caton sisters riding in superb carriages and dressed in clothes of the latest fashion, while she herself is still wearing the gowns and jewelry that Jérôme has given her three years earlier. These are things she keeps as if they were fetishes.

But then she is hit by a bombshell. Auguste Lecamus has returned from Westphalia. This time King Jérôme has asked him to bring back his son, so that he can be brought up by his side and "receive all the honors to which he is entitled." August carries two letters, one for "Elisa" and one for "the worthy Mr. Patterson."

> I know in advance, my beloved Elisa [he writes], that it will be very hard for you to separate from him, but you will not be blind enough to your true interests and mine not to agree to his departure. A brilliant destiny is in store for him; our son must enjoy all the advantages to which he can lay claim by dint of his birth and his name . . .

As for Mr. Patterson, this is what his former son-in-law writes to him:

> This request has been authorized by the Emperor, and you will easily understand that this is a matter of preparing my son for an existence befitting his birth and his rank. Brought up under my eyes, in the rank that is rightfully his, he will at least soften somewhat the unhappiness I feel at being far away from his mother, and no doubt the time will come when he will be able to overcome the pain that has been inflicted on him by the great political forces to which I have had to bow. In view of my position, as well as Elisa's, it is most important that my son

be living with me. You are too wise not to understand the reasons for this. . . . I fully appreciate how painful this separation will be for Elisa, but I am counting on you, Sir, to point out to her all the advantages that will result from it.

William Patterson is indignant. How now? Jérôme wants to snatch from his wife the only treasure left to her after he has abandoned her? And in what way would the upbringing he would receive in Westphalia amidst the gilded bric-a-brac of a princely palace be better than that of a solid American citizen?

Discomfited by this outburst of anger, Auguste Lecamus hastily blurts out some apologies and hands Betsy a golden medallion that the king has sent for his son. When Betsy opens it, she finds in it a miniature portrait of Jérôme, an almost unrecognizable Jérôme, whose face is barred by a close-cropped mustache that gives him a martial air. She places it on the table.

"Thank you, Sir," she says, "I will keep it for my son. As for the answer I am to give to you, please grant me a few days to think about it."

In due course, mother and son, writing in an approximate French, let the King of Westphalia know that Bo does not want to "break his Mommy's heart" by going to live in Europe. Did I do wrong? Betsy asks herself after Lecamus has left. Should I not have thought first of all of my son's future? But could I even trust Jérôme? Surely, I know all about the worth of his oaths! I would actually prefer to appeal to Napoleon. . . . After all, did he not promise me a pension, three years ago, for leaving England . . .

ONE DAY PEGGY, A PUPIL AT THE CATHOLIC SCHOOL OF SAINT MARY, TELLS her sister that she has met her friend Eliza Anderson. She seems to be on the best of terms with her professor of drawing and architecture, Mr. Godefroy. Eliza, to whom Betsy has given the cold shoulder ever since her precipitous departure from England shortly after the birth of Bo, has just divorced her first husband and gone to live in Trenton. She deplores the silence of her old friend and is very eager to renew contact with her.

If only you knew [she writes] how people crowd around me here in Trenton, where I am living now, when they find out that I was friends with you. . . . They have no end of questions about you. . . . Such as: why don't you go to France? Everyone here thinks that a brilliant future is ahead for you, as well as for Bo. . . . Peggy told me that you allowed yourself to fall into depression. For heaven's sake, stop brooding, and don't let the black monster of despair get hold of a mind like yours. . . . Immerse yourself in your beloved philosophes. Yes, re-read Helvetius and Paley. And above all, write to me!

Betsy will soon find out that her friend is in love with Maximilien Godefroy, who just then is building a chapel for the Sulpician Fathers at the convent of Saint Mary's, where Peggy is studying. This will be the first neo-Gothic church in America, and its style is destined to become highly popular throughout that country, especially during the Victorian era. Godefroy will design many other buildings. He and Benjamin Latrobe, an English-born architect who has designed the Capitol in Washington, will create the physiognomy of nineteenth-century Baltimore.

During the summer, Betsy has seen Samuel Graves again, or, rather, the young Englishman has called on her in Baltimore. Despite her parents' encouragement and the burning love poems Samuel sends to her, she simply cannot see anything seductive in the round face, the receding hairline, and the awkward manner of the Englishman. Her memory is still filled with Jérôme's lively expression, his fiery glances, his sensuous mouth. "It's too soon," she says to Dorcas, who is delighted to see the blossoming of this romance. "No, Mother, I could not."

Even Mrs. Graves has involved herself: "My husband and I will be in London next fall," she writes to Betsy, "and as soon as you have left your son with the Bonapartes, we are ready to celebrate your marriage to Samuel with great pomp." And she adds: "Why would you want to make him unhappy, a young man who loves you so much and who belongs to a most honorable family?"

But Betsy remains deaf to the chiding of her family, who urge her to accept this flattering alliance. Most insistent of all is William Patterson, whose business is in serious trouble now that the president has decided to place an embargo on all maritime trade with France or Great Britain.

This decision may seem suicidal, yet if the American government is willing to give the French government such a break — for it is English trade that will be most seriously affected — it must be because it expects to reap some benefit in return.

Yes, Jefferson does hope to persuade Napoleon to intervene on his behalf to facilitate the American acquisition of the Floridas. However, the Emperor hesitates, wondering whether it would not be preferable to keep eastern Florida for France. No doubt he already regrets having ceded Louisiana, five years earlier, for an absurdly low price. But he is also thinking about other arrangements. If, for instance, he helps the Americans in these negotiations, perhaps he can ask that Cuba be given to France.

Turreau, the French minister, continues to show his cranky airs and his impressive appearance in the halls of Congress without broaching this matter at all. Unlike his predecessor Pichon, he is of a prickly temper and has a poor command of the English language. He flies off the handle at the slightest provocation. But since he is not without a certain sense of humor, his whiskered face can break into a big smile when, in the midst of a heated discussion with Mr. Madison, the office door opens and someone sticks in his head: Dixon, the barber, who announces that he has come to shave the Secretary of State.

". . . Monsieur Turreau," Betsy thinks. "What if I went to ask him for advice? Yes, that's a good idea, I will ask him for an appointment." It takes some courage to face the formidable Frenchman, who in addition has acquired the reputation of a Bluebeard. All Washington had resounded with the noise of his quarrels with his wife, the daughter of his former jailer (for he had had to serve a prison term after the fall of Robespierre), and it was whispered that he beat her. In 1807 he had finally sent her back to France.

At first blush, Louis Turreau is quite annoyed to be receiving a note from "Mademoiselle Patterson" — for while everyone in America calls Betsy "Madame Bonaparte," this is the name by which she is officially known to the French diplomatic service. Turreau had sensed for some time that the young woman had tried to approach him and to speak to him when she met him on social occasions. Whenever their eyes had met, Turreau, obedient to the orders he had received, had quickly averted his glance. However, different people had warned him: "Watch out," they told him, "don't let Mlle Patterson go to England. . . . Can't you see that she is very close to Samuel Graves? They are about to get engaged."

Yet Betsy's letter expresses sentiments that do not match that perspective. She submits entirely, she tells him, to the wishes of the Emperor; she wishes to be removed from the United States and has no intention of going to England, fearing that such a step might displease the French government, "without whose consent she will never settle anywhere."

This perplexes Turreau, and he agrees to receive the young woman. He cannot help being touched by her beauty. As she explains her distress to him, she seems so small and so fragile that she becomes even more engaging. In a trembling voice she answers his questions, twisting a lace handkerchief between her hands. That day she is wearing her Mathilda-style batiste dress embroidered with spikes of grain and blueberries and a Lyonnais bonnet that makes her face look particularly thin.

When their conversation is over, the minister remains silent for a moment and then declares that he will refer the matter to the Emperor. If she so desires, he will let her add to his note a letter of her own, where she can express her wishes better than he would be able to do. Two months later Napoleon therefore receives, at Burgos, a long missive in which Elizabeth lays out for him her situation and that of her child: "the situation of a mother who deserves all testimonies of esteem and attachment with which a woman can be honored, [a mother] who owes her misfortune to circumstances over which she had no control, and who, disappointed in her high hopes without reason to blame herself, is reduced to weeping over the birth of a son whose status and whose very means of subsistence remain uncertain even though he seemed born to enjoy esteem and happiness."

As young Graves, his heart in tatters, sails for England, Betsy is seized by an immense renewal of hope. Autumn once again brings a splendid glow of red and gold to beeches, maples, and black oaks, and red berries to dogwoods and pyracanthas. Cardinals, blue jays and mockingbirds are still singing with all their might in the shiny foliage of the magnolias. It is a magnificent Indian summer, just like that other one.

In November a message comes from Washington. Betsy is summoned to the French legation.

"I have news for you," Turreau tells her, the smile on his face as wan as the winter sun. "The Emperor has received your letter at Burgos and has sent me his instructions through M. de Champagny, Duc de Cadore. He says that he will be pleased to receive your child and that he will take charge of him if you wish to send him to France. As for yourself, you will be granted whatever you desire; you can count on His Majesty's esteem and his wish to please you. The Emperor wants to make it clear that when he refused to recognize you, he was prompted exclusively by considerations of high politics; in every other respect he is determined to provide for your son the kind of destiny that you would wish for him."

"Will I be allowed to accompany my son?"

"That, Madame, I do not know yet. I shall have to ask M. de Champagny."

So the Emperor finally takes an interest in her? Betsy can't believe her ears. Feeling much more at ease she goes about her domestic chores and only half listens to the men of the family as they discuss the day's politics around her. The embargo law decreed by Jefferson is becoming increasingly unpopular. The sight of their ships tied up in the harbor makes the Baltimore merchants very angry. The Federalist press goes wild.

And indeed, Jefferson does play into the hands of France, but better that than a British hegemony. On the high seas, England is more to be feared than her rival. By preventing American merchants from engaging in any trade with Saint-Domingue, the president also calms the apprehensions of the big planters in the South, who fear that the contagion of a black revolution will spread to their own slaves.

However, public discontent with the embargo becomes so strident that a month before the end of his term, in early January of 1809, Jefferson has to rescind his embargo law. By the end of his term, the president is disheartened, for between the Federalists and the secessionists, he seems to be surrounded by enemies. By February he is therefore greatly relieved to yield his office to his successor, James Madison, who had been his secretary of state and a Virginia-born Republican like himself.

In this troubled atmosphere, Betsy keeps watching for news from Europe. Before long, a letter from Jérôme reaches her. He has been disappointed to see Auguste Lecamus return without his little boy and irritated to learn that his ex-wife, over whom he believes he has some rights, has gone to solicit the Emperor's help.

> Am I not a sufficiently good father and friend, and powerful enough to give to my son and to his mother all the titles and the fortune they can desire? Oh, my dear Elisa, you do not properly appreciate me, or perhaps you are not aware of my present position, which is independent in all matters pertaining to my country, and which is only dependent in its relations with France, from which my son, our beloved child, has nothing to expect. . . . I was expecting my son, and yes, Elisa, I was expecting you as well, and an existence worthy of the objects of my most tender affection has been, and remains, prepared for you. If this came to pass, I would at least see my son from time to time, and I promise his mother, Elisa, my most tender friend, that I will leave her son with her until he reaches the age of twelve, in the principality I have chosen for him. . . .

This would be the principality of Smalkalden, situated seventy-five miles from Kassel, and it would come with an income of 200,000 francs per month. Jérôme also assures Elizabeth that he will "always be happy to sacrifice everything so that her days will flow by peacefully and without any other pain than that of their star-crossed connection."

AT THAT POINT THE KING OF WESTPHALIA DOES NOT YET HAVE AN HEIR, and Queen Catherine regularly goes to take the waters to cure herself of her barrenness. Napoleon too does not have any children. Lucien is still on bad terms with his brother, and Louis has had constant tiffs with his imperious elder ever since he has become king of Holland. Betsy therefore nourishes great hopes at the thought that one of these days her little Jérôme will be in great demand. Many of her friends help her maintain this illusion. He is destined for great things, they tell her. No

one talks of anything but you and Bo at the court of France right now
. . .

After lengthy reflection, Betsy decides to write to the Emperor:

Sire, after four years of pain and sorrow, I finally have the consolation of seeing that Your Majesty does not believe me to be
unworthy of your attention. The greatest of mortals is kind
enough to take an interest in the fate of the humblest of women.
The blood and the talents that are the inheritance of my son
and the name that distinguishes him are incompatible with a
humble upbringing or an obscure existence. I owe it to him, to
the world, and above all to Your Majesty not to miss the opportunity to place him into a situation where, taught by the most
enlightened men of the greatest nation in the world and protected by the most august sovereign, his mind, his genius, and
his virtues will acquire all the power of which they are capable.
. . . Proud that Your Majesty has deigned attend to my concerns, I would consider it amiss to place my destiny into other
hands. . . . Whatever will be Your Majesty's orders concerning
the establishment, the residence, and the conduct of my son
and myself, we shall do our utmost to comply with them . . .

Turreau endorses this request. Recognizing that, yes, this young
woman is ambitious, and obviously pursuing a rank in society rather
than a fortune, he feels that she seems to be worthy of His Majesty's
protection.

In Betsy's mind, the image of Jérôme is gradually beginning to
fade, to dissipate like a ghost, replaced by a grander and more awesome
one, whose brilliance is almost blinding: it is the image of the Emperor
of the French, the man who just now makes the universe tremble. A
man? No, he is a god! In a firm hand, Betsy casually informs her ex-
husband that the kingdom of Westphalia is not big enough to hold
two queens . . .

11

*T*HE REWBELLS HAVE RETURNED TO BALTIMORE. They have been expelled from Westphalia, where Jean-Jacques had been appointed general and his wife Henriette lady-in-waiting. Both are very upset and find it hard to come to terms with their disgrace. But Betsy has still not forgiven her former friend for having followed Jérôme and his new wife to Westphalia, where she has been showered with honors for four years.

Yet, a few days later, Henriette rings the doorbell of the South Street house. Betsy immediately notices that she has lost weight; her cheeks are hollow and there are rings under her eyes. After some chilly moments of greetings exchanged with pursed lips, Henriette gradually begins to open up. She tells about her life in Kassel, the capital of Westphalia, about Jérôme's lavish lifestyle, the continuous round of balls and receptions, the sumptuous furnishings of two palaces, one at Kassel and the other at Napoleonshöhe, and the pomp and circumstances at a court attended by a crowd of marshals, prefects, head chamberlains, masters of ceremony, paymasters, and so forth.

"It was great fun," she says, "and there was never an evening without a ball, concert, or theater performance. Sometimes the king set up a lottery, where everyone was a winner and received a piece of jewelry, or else there was bowling, or a game of high-cockalorum. Sometimes one was also called upon to pick a gold ring out of a big bowl of flour with one's mouth or to participate in sleigh races. The king and queen were full of high spirits and a good-natured atmosphere prevailed. The pages took full advantage of this to play a thousand tricks, such as placing pins or toot-horns on the chairs of ladies before they sat down or sewing their dresses together while they were sitting. They were given a good scolding . . . and went right on. Jérôme had many mistresses but always managed to keep up appearances; the queen had no idea of what was happening. She was so much in love with him, it was positively touching! He called her his Trinette . . . and cheated on her at every turn!"

But eventually things turned sour. Queen Catherine's uncle, the duke of Brunswick-Oels, some of whose land had been taken from him in order to be added to Westpalia, had raised a free corps, the Black Legion. At the head of these terrible fighters, whose uniform featured a white embroidered emblem of skull and crossbones, he had invaded Saxony and given the signal for an uprising. General Rewbell had failed in his mission of stopping his advance. Accused of treason, he was to be court-martialed on orders of Napoleon. King Jérôme helped him escape and secretly got his family out of Kassel. "Henriette," he had told the distraught wife when giving her the news, "it would be better for you if your husband were already dead. . . ."

Betsy has no trouble imagining what it was like, this headlong flight through the night in a post chaise, ending only when the mother and the children have found a ship to take them back to America. She too has experienced this, the Tarpeian Rock after the Capitol, flight after grandeur, and then Baltimore, this haven of peace she detests.

During the winter, Betsy has sometimes made her bumpy way to Washington to see her aunt Nancy. Dolly Madison now reigns as First Lady at the "palace," where she gives lots of dinners and receptions to enhance the prestige of her timid husband. She is very popular, and everybody likes her.

"Mrs. Madison too likes everybody," she cheerfully replies when complimented on this point.

However, tensions in Washington are mounting, especially with the British government, and despite the evident good will of its representative at that time, Mr. Erskine, who is doing his best to keep the machinery functioning smoothly.

Young Madame Bonaparte is paid the most assiduous attention by the members of the English legations, among them a certain Sir Richard Oakley, who, after Samuel Graves, has been set aflame by her beauty.

Meanwhile, Louis Turreau sulks in his own corner. As long as he has not received precise orders from his government, his hands are tied. Moreover, his still unsettled family situation prevents him from giving receptions at the French legation. Not that he could afford them anyway, for the Emperor, however lavish at his own court, is much less so when it comes to his agents abroad. And finally, Turreau cannot attend any social event, except at the White House, where he does not risk running into English diplomats.

But then summer arrives with its heat and humidity and the unhealthy effluvia that rise up from the port. Having spent a few weeks at Coldstream, the country place that has been assigned to her brother Edward, Betsy decides to spend the month of August at Three Oaks, in Virginia — to which her father had exiled her when she had first fallen in love with Jérôme.

In this peaceful countryside with its gentle valleys, between the cotton and tobacco fields and pastures surrounded by white picket fences where white and brown cows are grazing, Betsy enjoys a quiet life in the company of Bo, Jessie, and the many slaves of the plantation. She is not much more than fifty miles from Charlottesville and Monticello, the beautiful neoclassical house to which ex-president Jefferson has retired. It occurs to her that she should visit him. After all, he is a philosopher, a very open-minded man. He may be worth consulting . . .

High up on a wooded hill, the "Sage" of Monticello has had a superb house of stone and brick built from his own design, which called for a cupola and a portico in front of the entrance. Architect, engineer, botanist, and astronomer, Jefferson is friends with the greatest scholars of his time, among them Alexander von Humboldt, who has recently paid him a visit in connection with his plans to continue the research of the explorers Lewis and Clarke on the Pacific coast.

From France, where he has served as his country's minister plenipotentiary between 1784 and 1789, the former president has brought back an immoderate liking for a classic and sober architecture. The construction of the town house of the princes of Salm[1] in particular has

---

[1] The present-day museum of the Legion d'Honneur, rue de Bellechasse in Paris.

delighted him to the point of inspiring the conception of his future dwelling. Similarly, some echoes of the old covered grain market of Paris can be found in the dome of the University of Virginia, whose creation at Charlottesville has been overseen by Jefferson.

Monticello is filled with clever inventions, such as the weighted clock, conceived by the ex-president, that shows both the day and the hour, the automatic doors, the small elevator concealed in a side panel of the mantelpiece in the dining room, by which wines can be brought up from the wine cellar at the proper temperature, or the butler's trays placed at the guests' side at small dinner parties, so that they could serve themselves without having to call on the servants.

As Betsy follows her host up the staircase leading to the room where Jefferson's grandchildren are playing, she is amused to see a mocking bird hopping from step to step behind him.

"It's my favorite bird," Jefferson says with a smile; "I prefer his song to any other, even that of the nightingale I have brought back from France and tried to acclimatize in Virginia. But a propos of acclimatization, I must show you my plantings. I may be an old man, you see, but I am a young gardener."

Long after his return from France Jefferson has kept up the correspondence with his French friends, among them Madame de Tesse who has a green thumb and with whom he has exchanged cuttings. But there are more than just French plants in the large gardens, which are both useful and agreeable: one can also find there Chilean strawberries, Columbian lillies, franklinias (a Georgian bush with white blossoms), sugar maples, and Maltese crosses.

That evening, as Betsy takes leave of Jefferson and his daughter Martha and contemplates the sunset over the rolling terraces that stretch into the far distance toward the Blue Ridge Mountains, her host remarks: "Does not nature deploy for our eyes a rich coat of mountains, forests rocks and rivers. Could we dream of a more enchanting sight?"

Betsy feels at peace as she leaves the president-philosopher. True, he has not sought to influence her in favor of a possible remarriage. After all, he has told her, she is surrounded by many friends who can give her useful advice. But, out of his usual anglophobia, he has warned her. He definitely does not like Napoleon and his expansionist policies. However, as far as he is concerned, the English are even more cruel and more to be feared. She would do well to keep that in mind.[2]

In September Betsy has returned to Baltimore. She sometimes visits the Rewbells, who are living at the home of Henriette's father, the old Marquis Pascaut de Poléon. Jean-Jacques Rewbell has become stout and acrimonious. He cannot tolerate to have the detested name of Bonaparte mentioned in his presence. Crimson-faced, he breaks into invective as soon as the conversation at his father-in-law's house turns to politics. And yet Louis Pascaut, who in fact has a great deal of respect for his son in-law, takes a malicious pleasure in goading him. Any time there are guests and the men move on to the smoking room, the father-in-law cannot resist teasing the younger man.

Also in September — surprise, surprise — Richard Oakley, whose ardor has been fanned by this two months' separation, appears in Baltimore and calls on the Patterson parents to ask their permission to frequent their daughter. The Pattersons are delighted . . . but Betsy is cautious. What will happen if she agrees to marry the young Englishman? She definitely likes him better than Samuel Graves. He has a certain vivacity, a tall and slender figure . . . and a great fortune. Moreover, Mr. Patterson, who is all in favor of this project, promises his daughter a royal dowry: fifty thousand dollars, and an equal sum after his death. On the other hand, if she persists in refusing any kind of "establishment," she will be disinherited.

The English minister, John Erskine, and one of his attachés, a certain Jackson, put their shoulders to the wheel to push this marriage and often accompany Richard Oakley when he calls on the Patterson family. They soon become regular visitors at South Street, a fact that quite upsets General Turreau when he learns of it. He has tried in vain to send messages to the young woman, but has never received a reply. Have his letters been opened by Betsy's parents? Or does she herself refuse to speak to him? "I cannot really go out to see her myself," he writes to M. de Champigny, "for I am liable not to find her at home and to run into one of these impertinent Englishmen whose gigs are often waiting by her door."

[2] "Reflections on Jefferson's Old Age," from Lawrence Kaplan, *Jefferson in France* (New Haven: Yale University Press, 1967)

But one day Jessie does bring him a message. It is not encouraging, and consists of only a few lines. There is no use talking, Betsy tells him directly, for she has received the latest news from Europe from her brother John, who is there now. She has been duped, he asserts. There never was any question of providing an establishment for her or for her son.

Turreau panics. As the rumors of an engagement between Betsy and Oakley become more detailed, he sends another message to the young woman: "Do not listen to such rumors, they are being put out by the English: they simply make this up in order to discredit us!"

Turreau has rented a house at the outskirts of Baltimore in order to be closer to mother and son. And finally, one day, he receives word: Betsy is willing to meet with him. She looks awkward and embarrassed and lowers her head as he questions her. Yes, she admits, she is almost engaged to Oakley. Her parents are pushing her hard, and so do her brothers. They are pointing out to her that she and her son are a heavy burden for the family. There are lots of children, times are hard, and the embargo has not been helpful. . . . Her father has threatened to throw her out in the street.

"But I thought Mr. Patterson is very wealthy?" Turreau asks in surprise.

"He is, but he is very tightfisted," she replies. And besides, he is afraid of reprisals from the English. Surely, you are aware of the extent to which they exercise the right of impressment on our ships?"

"Well now," Turreau continues after a few moments of reflection, "would you be willing to defy your parents if I took it upon myself to offer you financial help that would allow you to set up your own household? In this manner you could await the right moment to send your son to France."

"You have not told me whether I would be able to accompany him."

"I have not yet received a reply on this subject."

Betsy has another concern. If she is to travel with her child, she cannot and will not do it under the name "Mlle Patterson." Yet the Emperor will never allow her to use the Bonaparte name. Might he perhaps be willing to bestow a title on her? At this point Turreau becomes evasive, almost sarcastic.

"In my country," he says, "we do not give titles to women without husbands. And you cannot make your own law. I shall submit the matter to my minister, M. de Champigny."

Meanwhile he takes it upon himself to pay her the sum of 25,000 piasters, which will allow her to establish herself with her son and to free herself from the hold of her family.

Turreau is moved by the young woman's expressions of gratitude. How quickly the young English lord has been forgotten! Very proud of himself, he writes to the minister to tell him the whole story: "I have pulled Madame from the clutches of her family and of England," he writes in all modesty; "and I have given her the independence I felt she deserved, given the memory of the ties she had formed, the great qualities and the generous spirit that distinguish her, and also her honorable conduct, which does not need to be proven by four years of privation and misfortune . . ."

Are we seeing the terrible Turreau, the "Ogre of the Vendée" falling for Betsy? He often goes to see her at her new home on the pretext of making sure that he has what she needs. He also assigns her a bodyguard, Colonel Toussard, vice consul at Philadelphia, who is made to leave his family in order to be close to the young woman.

> Your age, your moral qualities, your experience and your zeal have determined my choice [Turreau writes to him]. You will have to watch very carefully over Madame and her son and guarantee their safety, for the English are still planning to kidnap them and to take them to London. . . . Having exhausted all the resources for seducing Madame, the agents of Great Britain are now working on the means of taking at least her son from her, if they cannot kidnap both of them. . . . You will have to live under the same roof, Monsieur, eat at the same table and, in a word, never leave Madame and her son except insofar as the proprieties require it. . . . And on this point there is no need for me to specify what is proper and thoughtful in dealing with a young lady distinguished by her honorable and pure conduct as well as by the qualities of her heart and mind, a lady, in short, who is worthy of the brilliant fate that is in store for her . . .

So now Betsy and Bo have a bodyguard whose zeal is so great that before long his presence in the house becomes indispensable. He takes care of the minor problems of day-to-day life, props up Betsy's morale when she feels blue, and serves as private tutor to the little boy.

In December Louis Turreau finally receives a response from the Duc de Cadore, which he eagerly communicates to Betsy: the Emperor still takes a great interest in her fate, but marrying an Englishman is out of the question!

That danger seems to have been averted for good. Elizabeth is so busy furnishing her new home that during this winter season she has no regrets about giving up her escapades to Washington. Actually, it is just as well that she keep her distance from the English legation. Lord Oakley has been rather surprised and hurt to receive his walking papers. Once again, Betsy has put her son's interest first, for it takes precedence over everything.

As for Turreau, who derives considerable satisfaction from the contemplation of his handiwork, he is increasingly spellbound by the beauty of the young American. One evening when he finds her alone he declares his love to her. Since she wanted a name, he is ready to offer her his. He has an impressive number of years of service to his credit, he is a grand officer of the Légion d'honneur, and he will receive the title of baron of the Empire as soon as he returns to France. . . . A beauty and a mind like Betsy's are not made to vegetate in a place like Baltimore. In Paris her position would allow her to move in the most brilliant circles, whereas her son would be brought up at court. Furthermore, this would be a marriage of convenience, if that is what she desired.

Speechless at first, Betsy replies with a firm and clear refusal, alleging once again that her son needs his mother's care. Deep down, however, she is boiling with anger. How can this terrible man, who has just repudiated his wife after months of stormy marriage at the French legation that has set tongues wagging in Washington, this man who is her senior by thirty years, and whose past glory is stained with blood — how can he think of uniting his fate with hers?

In January 1801 there is another letter from the Duc de Cadore, which voices some criticism about Turreau's prodigalities for the "Belle of Baltimore." "What magnificence!" he exclaims. "Some limits will have to be set for it."

Then nothing more is heard. Betsy would be very bored if Colonel Toussard, who has become a veritable guardian angel, were not doing his best to distract her. This is the beginning of a solid friendship. Louis Toussard sometimes takes her in his calash to Philadelphia, where his brother lives.

Philadelphia has returned to its austere bearing, now that it is no longer the seat of the Congress, and the influence of the Quakers once again makes itself felt. But it is an agreeable place, which boasts two theaters. Rumors that "Madame Bonaparte" is in town have spread rapidly, and one evening when she appears at the Old Chestnut Tree Theatre in her friends' box, the public wildly applauds her. When she receives visitors at the Toussards' home, they are made to wait in the front hall before being ushered ceremoniously into the room where the mother is seated with her child, who is granted the title of prince.

Does this mean that Napoleon has designs on little Jérôme-Napoleon? The English, in any case, are growing suspicious. The Emperor, who is beginning to tell his entourage, "this old Europe is beginning to bore me . . . ," might well at a later stage think of carving out for himself an empire in the New World, where his American nephew could play a prominent role.

In this year 1810, Betsy can indulge in a good bit of hope. For the sake of peace, her family has ceased to put pressure on her. Being a smart woman, she therefore decides to save some of the money she receives from the French minister by moving back to her father's house, since everyone at the Pattersons has promised to leave her alone. She is also concerned about the health of her sister Peggy, who is suffering from tuberculosis, and about that of her mother, who is declining from month to month. Little Mary-Ann has already died three months earlier.

Turreau points out to the young woman that since she is once again living at her father's house and has thereby cut her expenses, it is no longer necessary to pay her as comfortable an allowance. Having consulted M. de Champigny, he proposes to allocate to her sixty thousand livres per year, payable in installments every trimester. Out of this pension Betsy sometimes pays for jewelry and clothes — gloves, shoes, and bonnets — she asks friends to bring from Paris.

One day she learns that the French consul in Philadelphia, Félix de

Beaujour, is about to depart for France. He offers to serve as her spokesman with the Emperor, if she has a message she wishes to transmit. She
eagerly accepts. It seems to her that at the imperial court not enough
attention is being paid to her in her Baltimore retreat!

It so happens, however, that Napoleon, having repudiated Joséphine
and concluded a second marriage with Marie-Louise, the daughter of
the Emperor of Austria, is thinking about other things than an encounter with the charming American. Months go by, and Betsy is becoming
discouraged. According to the rumors that reach her, Napoleon is very
much in love with his young wife, who is expecting his child. "He'll
forget the very existence of his American nephew," she thinks in bitter
disappointment. How fondly she had dreamt of playing a brilliant part
at that court of France. And perhaps even of conquering the heart of
the man who to her is still the "Steward of the Universe." Her relations
with Turreau have grown increasingly tense. The general must have
been offended by the cool reception of his proposal.

Meanwhile, Samuel Graves makes another attempt, writing to Betsy
from England that he cannot forget her!

As for Jérôme, to whom Queen Catherine has still not given an
heir, and who is beginning to worry, he has decided that he must post
haste dispatch Auguste Lecamus to America. This time he is indignant,
takes offense: How could Elisa implore the support of the Emperor and
refuse help from him, Jérôme? Nonetheless he continues to assure his
ex-wife of his deeply felt affection. But she remains unmoved. "I would
rather," she says bluntly, "take shelter under the wings of an eagle than
hang from the beak of a gosling." This remark reached the ears of the
Emperor, who was delighted by it.

Then, one day, Turreau informs her he has asked to be recalled and
that he will be replaced by Sérurier. Sérurier? The man who as consul in
Lisbon in 1805 had refused to issue her a landing permit? Dreadful
memories crowd into Betsy's mind. She may not be terribly fond of
Turreau, but at least she has become accustomed to his gruff manner,
his big mustache, and his airs of an elderly beau.

As soon as Sérurier arrives in Washington, he contacts Colonel
Toussard to find out how things stand with respect to "Mlle Patterson."

"Monsieur," he is heatedly told by Louis Toussard, whose service with the young mother has largely won him over to her cause, "you cannot call her by her maiden name without offending her, a respectable person, whom everyone here knows by the name of 'Madame Bonaparte.' Because of her marriage, she is entitled to it under the laws of this country."

"I beg your pardon," replies Sérurier, "but in France she was always mentioned to me under this name. Perhaps we can agree between us on a name that would be something in between, for it runs counter to my duty as an envoy to qualify her as "Madame Bonaparte."

"Since princesses are called by their Christian names," Toussard suggests hesitatingly, "how about calling her Mme Elisa?"

"Agreed!" exclaims Sérurier, much relieved. "There will be no difficulty whatsoever about this."

"What are the Emperor's orders in this matter?"

"His Majesty is still quite interested in her case, but right now he is greatly preoccupied by the Spanish situation, as you surely know. With respect to her, I was advised to continue the line of conduct pursued by General Turreau, but not to promise anything more. We must take our time."

"Will she receive the title she has requested?"

"I have received no orders to this effect."

That winter, Betsy decides to move to Washington for good. Her son will receive a better education there, she claims. She just wants to get away from Baltimore, where Peggy has died three months earlier, and where her mother rarely leaves her room: she simply cannot face the prospect of spending icy evenings alone with her father. On Capitol Hill, the atmosphere is stormy. The English harassment of American ships has been such that there is now open talk of war with Great Britain, especially among the so-called War Hawks.

— We have put up with this abuse until patience ceases to be a virtue, they exclaim.

— Do you want to play the game of France by declaring war on her worst enemy? retort their adversaries.

It is true that the French government continues to keep a tight check on all American ships arriving in its ports, and those who do not have a proper license are held up for months on end, at the risk of having their merchandise spoil, while their crews are kept under surveillance until their identities are established. Meanwhile the English, not satisfied with impeding the Americans' commercial activities, continue, by fair means or foul, to take sailors off American ships.

Mr. Erskine, the English envoy to Washington, who had promised the Madison government a softening of the Orders in Council from London, has been recalled and disavowed by his government. He has been replaced by John Foster, a former embassy attaché under the orders of Mr. Merry. It has taken a bit of arm-twisting to make young Foster take this new assignment in America in a difficult period, particularly since he is in love with Lady Annabella Milbank (who is also courted by Lord Byron, and whose husband he will be a year later).

Like his predecessor, Foster tries his best to smooth the hard edges, but without success, for his government is as intransigent and the English raiders are as enterprising as ever. His instructions are few: do everything to prevent the Americans from occupying Florida, counterbalance the influence of the French and prevent their raiders from taking shelter in American ports. Act in a conciliatory manner, though without promising anything tangible.

In Washington one encounters all kinds of people at this time, some of whom offer their services alternatively to the French and the English, while others, such as Simón Bolivar, have come to solicit help for uprisings in their countries from the Madison government.

The residential hotel O'Neale, where Betsy and her aunt Nancy are living, is sometimes the scene of violent incidents, when swearing and pistol shots are heard at night. Also, rather improper poems are sometimes slipped under the young woman's door, verses like the following:

To this bed, where I stretch my weary frame
You have revealed your most secret charms.
To possess them, Madame, I would gladly give,
Without hesitating for a single moment
Twenty Westphalias and fifty Germanies . . .

The English and the French envoy vie for the distinction of giving the best dinners and parties, but of course neither ever attends the other's receptions.

Sérurier, who does not want to pressure the Americans openly to go to war against England, invites small groups of War Hawks, flatters them and makes promises, although he is alarmed at the designs on Canada harbored by some of them. Young Foster, for his part, gives lavish balls, to which he invites all of the area's good society, and above all Betsy, whom he considers "the most beautiful woman in America."

When Sérurier hears about this, he is worried.

"Really now," he writes to the young woman, "you cannot accept such invitations from our enemies. If you do, you close your door to me forever . . . and you know what that would mean!" "Nonetheless," Betsy responds, "I intend to be governed by my own rules, not by yours."

Oh these French, they seem to be interested in her only when they sense that the English might become dangerous. . . . And could that be? After all, John Foster is quite attractive, with his sandy hair of an Irishman, his tall stature, and his affable manner. He has become the stepson of the Duke of Devonshire, through his mother's second marriage. His diplomatic service in Washington and then in Stockholm has broadened his view of the world. Yes, it would be tempting. . . . But on the other side there is the French imperial family, and above all Napoleon, by whose image she is obsessed. Just then rumors of war are arriving from Europe. The Emperor, it is said, is ready to launch another campaign, this time in Russia.

In the United States as well, war is smoldering. The conflagration is sparked by the Indians who, armed by the English, are descending from the Canadian Great Lakes and attacking the farms of the young newly created states of Ohio and Kentucky, devastating the harvests and massacring the population. The United States will have to invade Canada and take it from the English. This will be a way to break the lock that has held back American expansionism!

"Let's go to war against the English!" cry the War Hawks. "They impress our sailors, they take our ships and arm the Indians who scalp our women and children!"

"You are just playing Napoleon's game," others retort. "He will surely ask for something in exchange for his help!"

As it happens, Napoleon has finally understood that he has nothing to gain from impeding American commerce. He orders large numbers of confiscated ships to be returned and revokes the decrees of Berlin and Milan. Meanwhile, London sticks to its Orders in Council.

Hesitation is no longer possible: in June 1812, at the very moment when Napoleon is poised to march on Russia with his Grande Armée, Madison asks the two Houses of Congress for a declaration of war against England.

Despite the strenuous opposition of the Federalists and the threat of secession on the part of New England, the declaration of war passes by 79 to 49 in the House, and 19 to 13 in the Senate.

Betsy, Aunt Nancy, and Bo have beaten a hasty retreat to Baltimore. There they encounter rioting. The director of a Federalist newspaper, the *Federal Republican,* has taken it upon himself to publish an article in which he protests against the declaration of war that has just been passed. The vast majority of the city, however, is pro-Republican, and during the night a crowd armed with axes and iron bars has gone to destroy the paper's print shop and everything in it. But never mind! The paper's director, Alexander Hanson, barricades himself in a neighboring house and resumes his activities and the publication of his anti-government pamphlets. All of the city's Federalists are on his side. Soon the population has mounted a veritable siege, people are killed and wounded, and the militia has to intervene. The besieged are ordered to leave their stronghold and taken to prison, where some of them are massacred a few hours later. All of this characterizes the stormy atmosphere that pervades Baltimore in these early summer days.

Betsy has not seen John Foster again, for the English legation has had to leave Washington precipitously and take a route around Baltimore, which is considered unsafe because of the riots. The young English envoy subsequently explains to his superiors that he has failed to see the impending catastrophe. He had not believed his ears when Madison — a livid Madison, his face distorted — informed him of the declaration of war after the vote by the two Houses. He has not seen Betsy again, but her lithe and nymph-like shape floats in his memory as he flees on horseback on dark and deeply rutted paths toward Halifax, the English base of operations. Nor does he know that two days earlier his government has revoked the famous Orders in Council that were among the major reasons for the war. But news travels slowly . . .

From her window, Betsy contemptuously watches the street demonstrations of the populace. "Ah, yes!" she mutters, "a fine thing, this democracy." In Baltimore, and everywhere else, the people are seething. Every state is raising its own militia. Large numbers of ships, outfitted for long voyages, are carrying cannon. Along the shores of the Chesapeake a profusion of these new privateers can be observed; from the port of Baltimore alone some fifty of them will fan out into the bay over the next few months. Even Commodore Barney has gone back to sea, not in the regular navy but as a privateer. He is commander of an entire flotilla. Henceforth the clipper ships, dozens of which are being built in the shipyards on the bay, will play a decisive role. They can outrun the English patrols and, despite their instability, which is the counterpart of their large sail surface and their high speed, cross the Atlantic and stop English ships as far away as the Irish Sea or even the English Channel.

When Admiral Cockburn, the commander of the English fleet, is apprised of these exploits, he swears that he will take his revenge on this "pirates' nest" that Baltimore has become.

News from Europe is now very scarce indeed. The Imperial Court and the new foreign minister, Duc de Bassano, have become mute. Betsy has no way of knowing that Napoleon is stuck in the ice of the Beresina with his soldiers and that he has called on his brother Jérôme to command the right wing of the Grande Armée in Poland. So it's war everywhere. Betsy is again getting terribly bored. The popular war songs she hears leave her cold. She misses the society of Washington. Perhaps if John Foster had stayed . . .

Before long, Mr. Patterson confronts her. She must make up her mind. She wants to have control over her dowry, so that she can live independently. Very well! But then she will have to clarify her situation. Under Maryland law, a married woman is considered to be under her husband's control and cannot administer her own property. Only her spouse has this right, and under American law she is still married to Jérôme. And Jérôme seems to be a regular sieve. Betsy has the impression that the finances of Westphalia are not exactly flourishing. . . . Through Henriette Rewbell, who has kept some written contact with her former friends (ladies-in-waiting to Queen Catherine), she has learned that Pichon, whom Napoleon had sent to Kassel to handle the kingdom's finances, has finally become discouraged with this overwhelming task and resigned his post after three years.

Betsy certainly does not trust her ex-husband. If he were to find out that the laws of Maryland can be used in his favor, who knows whether he would not try something? . . . No, she does not dare face such fears; this would be the last straw! She does not believe Jérôme capable of such base behavior, but in the present circumstances, and with the haze of war obscuring everything, would it not be better to make sure of the ownership of the handsome properties in Virginia her father has transferred to her name, along with the house in Charles Street, to which she wishes to return?

Eliza Anderson has left Trenton and has come to live in Baltimore with Maximilien Godefroy, the young French architect who has become her second husband.

"Oh Betsy," she says to her friend, "when will you stop running to catch the moon and thinking about glory and highfalutin' titles? When will you realize that a more ordinary man who shares your tastes could make you happy?"

"I don't want to hear of these Baltimore merchants, who have a cash-register where their heart should be, and I don't want to marry any one of them. A dull existence, with a slew of kids — thanks, but no thanks!"

This is not exactly the kind of life led by Elisa Godefroy, who just then is deeply involved in the affairs of her husband, Maximilien. After a brilliant rise to prominence, Godefroy has failed to receive the commission for a monument to George Washington that is to be erected in the heart of the city. The commission has gone instead to Robert Mills, a young American of the school of Latrobe. As for the chapel of Saint Mary's School, Godefroy has never been able to finish it, due to lack of funds. Elisa, who knows all about money troubles, does not understand how Betsy can refuse to sign a document that would allow her to clarify her legal situation and give her control over the property she has received as a dowry.

But things are not as simple as that. For Betsy it is not a small thing to give up bearing the name of Bonaparte, which is famous throughout the world, even if Napoleon is entering his decline and if everyone predicts that the Empire is about to crumble. In her heart she still hopes to go to France and to be received there with all the honors to which she rightfully aspires. Yet for the French legation, the Minister of Foreign Affairs, and the Emperor himself, has she not been "Mlle Patterson" all along? Will this ever change? But then, what really counts is that she is the mother of a little Bonaparte!

And so it is that Sérurier is amazed to learn that "Madame Bonaparte is suing for divorce." For a few days the newspapers of Washington and Maryland make fun of this news, which even eclipses the war. "This can only harm us and strengthen the pro-English party," Sérurier says to himself. He therefore chides Betsy, asking her to put off her suit. She confesses that she is tired of waiting. And now that the procedure is launched, things will just have to take their course. Sérurier insists that all she would have needed was a bit of patience. The kindness of His Majesty the Emperor is boundless. Why not trust in it? Can't she see that for the time being traveling is out of the question? In any case, she must avoid besmirching the name of the king of Westphalia; at the very least she must not mention His Majesty . . .

"Tell me another way to do it," Betsy says ironically.

The French envoy wonders whether by any chance John Foster has anything to do with this decision. He does not, as all of Betsy's acquaintances confirm.

In January 1813 the divorce is ratified by the two houses of the Maryland legislature, along with the creation of the University of Maryland and the decision to build a bridge over the Choptank River. "Well," Sérurier petulantly says to himself, "after all, I am not the envoy of Westphalia. My orders I take from the Emperor."

But Napoleon has just returned from Russia and sees the clouds of the sixth coalition forming on the horizon. He certainly has other things to worry about.

At the same time, bloody battles are also fought in Canada, which has been invaded by troops from the frontier states, except those of New England, which do not want to fight. The American army suffers defeats, and for a moment it looks as if Canada in turn would invade the United States. Happily a young American commander, Oliver Perry, wins a decisive victory on Lake Erie and reconquers Detroit, which had fallen into the hands of the English.

In this fall of 1813, unusual commotion fills the Fountain Inn. It has been run by the brother of Commodore Joshua Barney for the last two years. The innkeeper has spared no effort to prepare a sumptuous celebration for the hero of Lake Erie: an enormous eagle hangs from the ceiling and a platform represents the poop deck of the *Niagara*, the ship on which Perry has won his victory. President Madison is seated there, side by side with the glorious commodore. A sumptuous banquet, replete with crabs, lobsters, and oysters from the bay, is served to the notables of Baltimore. Betsy has been invited with her father but has sent her regrets.

Out at sea, clippers and frigates perform valorous deeds and sailors board enemy ships. Joshua Barney alone collects nine victories. But then the collapse of the Napoleonic Empire in Europe allows the English to free some of their troops and their ships and to send them to fight in America. They receive orders to block the entrance to the Chesapeake Bay and the Delaware River. From now on, the bold American captains are cut off from all trade and in May, when Commodore Barney sails down the Chesapeake as far as the mouth of the Patuxent, he faces a much superior English force and has to burn his ships in order to prevent them from falling into enemy hands.

Before long the English sail up the Potomac and come within sight of Washington. The militia, hastily summoned the night before, is at no more than a tenth of its strength. When the enemy enters the city, there is a general rout.

James Madison, his wife Dolly, and the inhabitants of the presidential residence have to flee into the night in all haste, taking with them their most precious possessions, papers, jewelry, silver dishes, and George Washington's portrait by Gilbert Stuart. In the city, the English are having a riotous time. Reveling in vengeance — for the Americans' requisitions in Canada have exasperated them — they go in for shameless looting, burning, and wrecking. The presidential residence and the very recently completed Capitol flame like torches. Charred walls will be all that is left of the residence. Once the war is over, it will be rebuilt and its blackened outside will be replastered. It will become so white that henceforth it will never be called anything but "The White House."

Baltimore is not about to give up. When the news of the fall of Washington arrives, an observation corps has been formed, and Betsy's uncle, General Smith has been put in charge of defending the city with his troops.

From his grandfather's windows Bo has seen the militias file by; arriving in large numbers from all parts of the state, they are composed of men of all ages, including adolescents. Betsy's brothers are among them, even the youngest, Octavius, who is only fifteen. But Edward is aide-de-camp to General Smith.

"Father! You are not going to let Octavius go, I hope?" Betsy implores, for she still thinks of the family's Benjamin as that little boy whom she took for walks along the Patapsco with Bo and Mary Ann.

"He must do his duty like everyone else," Mr. Patterson replies bluntly.

Huddled deeply into her sickbed, Dorcas keeps silent. Her gentle face has become even more emaciated, her eyes seem huge, sunk into their orbits.

Betsy approaches the bed and embraces her. "If you would like us to, Mother, Bo and I will stay with you tonight."

"I want to go and fight," Bo shouts.

"Don't talk nonsense," Betsy replies with some irritation.

The black servants too are in a state of excitement: all the freedmen have been armed.

One segment of General Smith's army corps is marching along the Philadelphia road in order to surprise the English army from the back; Joshua Barney's sailors, who no longer have any ships, have joined them. But during the night the English sail up the Patapsco and noiselessly land at North Point at dawn. They are firmly resolved to teach a thorough lesson to this rebellious city that has given them a great deal of trouble on the high seas and represents the epitome of America's hostility toward Great Britain. Having taken Washington with almost disconcerting ease, they expect to swallow Baltimore in a single bite.

In the morning, the city's inhabitants awaken to the sound of cannon fire. Everyone hurries to his post. Fort McHenry, which defends the entrance to the harbor, has been equipped with cannons and a solid garrison. Over the past few days all the bridges over the rivers near the city have been destroyed and trenches have been dug. For two days the battle rages. From the terrace at South Street, Bo and Betsy try to follow it, but all they see in the distance are thick clouds of smoke, sometimes rent by flames. Armed with his field glass, Mr. Patterson desperately scrutinizes the horizon.

"As long as our flag waves over the fort," he mutters, "we will be saved. For if the fort falls into the enemy's hands, all is lost. Baltimore will be bombarded until not one stone is left."

The flag that waves over the fort at this moment has quite a history. The preceding one was worn out and its colors had faded, and a few days before the attack this had concerned the commanding officer of the garrison, Colonel Armistead. He needed a flag that could be seen from very far away, and he needed to have it made in record time. Joshua Barney had proposed his sister-in-law, Mary Pickersgill, who was an expert in this kind of work and had often supplied flags for his own boats. But since her house was not large enough for work on a project of this size — thirty feet wide by forty-eight feet long — she and her mother, Rebecca Young, had gone to work in the premises of an abandoned brewery and finished the job in a few days. The brand-new and magnificent "Stars and Stripes" showed fifteen stars, one for each state of the young United States, two of which had been recently admitted.[3]

On the evening of 13 September the flag over Fort McHenry can still be seen between two clouds of smoke. In the afternoon, Edward, sent by his uncle, has arrived in town, riding full tilt, out of breath, his hair dishevelled. He brings the news that they had to fight the English on the Philadelphia road and were badly outnumbered. But the enemy's commanding general, Ross, has been killed, a development that further enraged the British.

The situation, in short, is anything but reassuring: Colonel Brooke, who has replaced Ross, is planning to attack Baltimore by land, whereas Admiral Cockburn continues to fight on the water.

In the city all those who are not fighting in the ranks of the militia or in the regular army observe the development of the hostilities from

[3] The "Flag House" still exists in Baltimore and is open to the public.

their windows or their rooftops. The noise is tremendous, and it is pitch dark. The only guiding mark is Mary Pickersgill's flag, which waves way down there over the fort. When night comes, hardly anyone can get any sleep. All hearts are anguished. But when dawn comes, the noise seems to have abated. A few cannon shots are still heard here and there, but they seem to be going away, regretfully, as it were.

Early in the morning, Betsy, who had gone to lie down without being able to sleep, slips on a déshabillé and climbs up to the terrace from which one has a view of the harbor. Her father has not budged from there all night. She sees his tall, dark silhouette against the silver-white horizon. Holding his field glass in his hand he does not turn around when he hears his daughter approaching.

"Our flag still waves over Fort McHenry," he tells her. "The English frigates have turned around, it looks as if they were sailing out of the Chesapeake. . . . We are saved."

All Baltimore is wild with joy. The next morning it is learned that a young Maryland lawyer, Francis Scott Key, has composed a hymn in honor of Mary Pickersgill's "Stars and Stripes," deeply moved to see this flame of hope continue to wave over the ramparts of the fort by the dawn's early light. He had jotted down the first verses on a scrap of paper while he was watching and then finished them at the Fountain Inn while taking a hearty breakfast.

A few weeks later this poem would be set to music by the cast of the Holliday Street Theater and sung in Baltimore for the first time. It was to become so popular that one day the entire United States would make it the national anthem.[4]

Alas! At the Pattersons the joy is short-lived. For when all the combatants return home, they learn that Octavius was missing at the roll call. One of his comrades brings the news that he has been killed on the Philadelphia Road as he was bringing supplies to the troops. This last blow saps the last of Dorcas's strength: she will gently pass away during the winter.

Of the thirteen Patterson children, only eight are still alive.

In February 1815, Great Britain and the United States sign a treaty

---

[4] The original text of this hymn is on exhibit at the Maryland Historical Society.

of peace at Ghent. Each of the two nations makes concessions to the other, but the Americans are pleased at the thought that they will finally be able to exercise their trade freely on all of the world's oceans. No more blockades of any kind, no more "right of impressment" against their sailors. Ship owners and captains heave a sigh of relief; American commerce is headed for a fabulous boom. Europe, meanwhile, is far from calm; Napoleon, having abdicated a first time, has left his exile on the island of Elba and marched to Paris, from which the Bourbons have fled. Everywhere he has been greeted by enthusiastic crowds. But a new coalition against him is formed and he must once again go to war.

With a delay of several weeks, Betsy has received an avalanche of news. Jérôme, who has had to flee Westphalia when it was invaded by Russian troops, has taken refuge at Trieste, where his wife has given birth to a son — another little Jérôme.

Upon learning of his brother's return from Elba, he hastens to leave his exile. Wearing a disguise, he has fled to Italy, where he has met up with his mother and his uncle, Cardinal Fesch, who will travel to France with him. But first of all, they have made a stopover in Corsica, disembarking in Bastia, where they were given a triumphal reception. "Jérôme must have been so happy to be in his native island and to breathe in the scent of its mountains, of which he has so often spoken to me. Oh, how sad it makes that I could never see that famous "Kallisté" from close by!"

At last, Jérôme has joined Napoleon in the capital, along with Joseph and Lucien, who has recently become reconciled with his brother. Together with them he has participated in the ceremony on the May Field, where the new constitution is celebrated and each regiment receives its eagle. But after these days of euphoria the war has reclaimed everyone's attention. For in Belgium the armies of Blücher and Wellington have gathered, ready to pounce on France.

Jérôme, who has been given charge of a division under the orders of General Reille, has fought valiantly at Quatre-Bras, where he was wounded, and then at Waterloo. It fell to him to lead the tattered remnant of the Grande Armée as far as Laon, where he was relieved by Marshal Soult. Napoleon commended him. . . . Yes, he is brave, but if he has shown courage on the battlefield, this is not the case in his private life.

The empire has collapsed. The Bonapartes are sent into exile. A welter of confused feelings fills Betsy's heart. So now her idol has fallen. At this very moment Napoleon is sailing toward the exile he has been assigned by the English, his implacable enemies. Should this make her happy? Should she, like everyone around her, heave a sigh of relief in the face of this renewed peace in the world and applaud the demands of the Congress of Vienna? Or, on the other hand, should she shed tears about the cruel fate that now awaits the man she admires most in the world, and whom she had hoped to meet for so long? Ah, how she would have liked to present her son to him, live in his orbit at the Tuileries or at Saint-Cloud, and meet the glance of his eagle eye . . . and see his face break into that smile which people called utterly charming.

One day Elisa Godefroy tells her friend that her husband Maximilien has decided to return to France. They will move there as soon has he has finished his current project, which is the construction in Baltimore of a monument honoring the war dead of 1812. Why could Betsy not follow their example and also make a dash for the seas, now that they are open? Elisa Godefroy's suggestion makes Betsy think, even though the France of the Bourbons has little attraction for her. But then, why should she not go to Europe? Bo is older now, she can leave him for a few months. In fact, during the winter he is going to board at the Sulpician School of Saint Mary anyway. And during the summer her brother Edward offers to have him stay at Coldstream.

Even Aunt Nancy has offered to help. She has many connections in Washington and will be delighted to let her niece make use of them. She can, for instance, obtain a letter recommending her to M. de Talleyrand through her friend David Parish, who knows him well. Her uncle Samuel Smith will surely give her a letter of introduction for General La Fayette, his one-time comrade-in-arms. In Paris, she will see the newly appointed minister plenipotentiary, Albert Gallatin, an old friend of her father's who has just participated in the signing of the Treaty of Ghent.

But Betsy does not yet quite dare tell her father about her European plans. Still not recovered from his wife's death, William Patterson is becoming more and more taciturn and spends days on end closeted in his office on Gay Street. In the evening he comes home just at dinner time, and his somber looks and his cold demeanor do not inspire Betsy to pour out her heart.

But one day she can no longer hold back; she has decided, she tells him, to go to Europe, if possible on one of his ships. William Patterson is shattered by this news. How can she think of leaving him? Forsake her father's home when he has just suffered the most cruel losses: her mother, Octavius, and Peggy, three years earlier.

"Father, my life is in Europe, not here. You cannot force me to stay against my will in a city I detest. I have waited long enough for my hour. The war is over, and I want to make use of the freedom of the seas."

It is a dialogue of the deaf. Her father feels that she is pursuing a chimera and chasing after a discredited family that is scorned by all of Europe instead of giving Bo a father by marrying an upstanding American. But Betsy is single-minded: she desperately needs a change of air, in every sense of the word, for the climate of Baltimore does not suit her at all and she is suffering from continuous stomach aches. Whenever she spends a few months in the city, she loses her appetite and is seized by uncontrollable nausea, as if she were being poisoned. The family doctor whom she has consulted is not sure whether to blame this on the unhealthy air of the port or on emotional problems. On the off-chance that it will help, he prescribes "the waters."

"And there is no better spa for stomach troubles than the one at Cheltenham in England."

Not long thereafter, Betsy learns that one of her Washington friends, a Mrs. Ashley, is planning to sail soon for Southampton. She thinks that this would give her a traveling companion and that after two or three months in England she might go on to France.

Once Mr. Patterson finds out that his grandson will be left in his care — at least on school-free days and during vacations — he feels better about his daughter's leaving. What he does not know is that she intends, once she is over there, to look for a good boarding school for Bo. After all, he needs a European education.

Part III

The European Dream

12

*L*ONDON! IT IS THE SUMMER OF 1815, AND ONE cannot dream of a happier city, a city more intoxicated with its own glory, and more relieved to be at peace once again.

After Waterloo the defeated Emperor has placed his fate in England's hands. Everyone knows what the result has been. "Boney" as the man in the street calls him, has been exiled to a deserted island. Here in London, just about everyone has the impression of breathing easier. Only a few are protesting, among them George Gordon Lord Byron, who will write an ode in honor of the fallen eagle. Others think that Lord Liverpool and his government have dishonored England by sending a former enemy who had surrendered to them to the bare rock of Saint Helena.

"I solemnly protest here, in the face of the heavens and of men, against the violation of my most sacred rights committed when my person and my liberty were forcefully seized." But the wind blows away the complaints Napoleon voices aboard the *Bellerophon*. London, and especially the Regent, could not care less. Celebration follows celebration, and there are balls and fireworks every night.

Betsy experiences a mixture of feelings as the small steamboat she has boarded at Dover makes its way up the Thames. A rapid craft, it threads its way among the fine sailboats. From afar one sees the London Tower, Westminster, Saint Paul's Cathedral, the Stock Exchange, Billingsgate, and the docks, the famous docks of the port of London that have just been created. The busiest among them is the West Indies dock.

Leaning over the rails with Mrs. Ashley, Betsy contemplates her situation. She has carefully thought out her journey, and she is no longer the hapless young woman chased out of all the ports of Europe who had landed here ten years earlier barely in time to give birth. Now she is just a tourist among many others who has come to take a close and admiring look at the English people, whose tenacity has made the final victory of the coalition forces possible.

London has developed considerably in the course of these ten years, it population has grown, and the city now has almost a million inhabitants. New houses have been built, and the entire borough of Westminster is lit by gas. Marylebone Park has become Regent's Park in honor of the future George IV, and the elegant Regent Street district is under construction.

Having gone through the lengthy formalities of the Foreign Office, Betsy is finally seated in a cabriolet with Mr. and Mrs. Ashley. She is greatly entertained by the spectacle of the streets: newspaper vendors who shout the latest news and sell or rent for a penny an hour the *Times,* the *Globe,* or the *Courier.* The gas lanterns of Westminster fascinate her. But everywhere else, where it is dark, the night-watchmen or "charlies" are making their rounds. Shaking their rattles, they call out: "Ten o'clock! And all is well!"

Later, when she has settled down in her little room, all covered in cretonne, at the boarding house where she and her traveling companions have taken lodgings, she feels a great sense of security. She briefly thinks of Bo, whom she has left in the good care of his grandfather and of the Sulpician Fathers of Saint Mary's. How far away Maryland seems to be! She goes to sleep, a smile on her lips.

My friends have advised me to move, for society people do not live in boarding houses. I have therefore rented a house right next to that of my new friends, Sir Arthur and Lady Brooke Falkener, who have sort of taken me under their wing.

Betsy has established residence at Cheltenham, where she is taking the water cure that has served as the pretext for her European trip. It is a very fancy resort frequented by the British aristocracy and the upper crust of the bourgeoisie. When it comes to the rules of society, she has become as punctilious as an elderly British lady.

> In this country [she writes to her father], one is so particular about social position that relations with persons of obscure background, however honorable and respectable they may be, are not tolerated. This evening, I am invited to a ball at Lady Condague's, tomorrow at General Trivine's.

These great names do not impress Mr. Patterson, who writes back distressed letters. "I am convinced," he writes to her, "that the happiness you are seeking is not true happiness; I pray to God that you will see your error. As for your letters, I am so ashamed of them that I do not dare show them to anybody."

Oh well, thinks Betsy, who has made up her mind to kick over the traces, just let him stew in his own juice. No more evenings of deadly boredom, when she worked on her embroidery while her father played faro with his friends. No more looking over her younger brothers' and sisters' homework. No more being in charge of a large household as she had been because of her mother's illness and death. And no more also of the humiliation of seeing people turn around when they passed her in the street. "Did you see? . . . That's the Patterson girl. The one whose husband left her. . . . A lot of good it did her to act so stuck-up!" Or those who, on the contrary, averted their eyes and pretended not to recognize her.

Here she is anonymous in the street. But when she enters a ballroom — embroidered high-waisted muslin dress, ermine-lined cloak, diamond-studded tiara in her "Ninon"-styled hair, emerald necklace once given to her by Jérôme in Lisbon — a ripple of flattering comments runs through the company. Lords and generals bow deeply to her, offer her their arm, and ask for a quadrille or a schottische. And of course, there is whispering behind the fans. But what do they say, these English voices with their delightful singing accent: "Look! Isn't she lovely!" they say.

The name Bonaparte is on all lips, but, by an irony of fate, it is spoken without animosity or pejorative connotation. Bonaparte, yesterday a fierce enemy, today fallen from greatness, has become the object of general admiration. Betsy has noticed this right away.

> People recognize his incredible genius and his enemies almost respect his misfortune. I listen to all discussions about him in silence. And I realize that he is treated more fairly here than in our country.

> Yes indeed, the English are serious about *fair play*.

As for Betsy herself, victimized but haloed by the ephemeral glory of a name that has never really been hers, she still and always wavers between contradictory feelings: even on his rock of Saint Helena, Napoleon, this brother-in-law whom she has never met, continues to weigh on her destiny. Eternally absent from her life, he still haunts her dreams. She has hitched her fate to that faraway star that sparkles in the South Atlantic and treasures that "bonapartian" identity, proudly displaying it here like an escutcheon.

London is empty in this month of August. The heat is stifling. The court has taken refuge at Brighton, in a kind of oriental palace built by the Regent and called "The Pavilion." One day Lady Falkener tells her friend that she would like to have her invited by the Prince Regent to one of his parties. The two young women see each other every day. There is even a door to communicate between their adjoining houses. Lady Falkener is amused by the unsophisticated ways of the young American and initiates her into the secrets of the English court — not that they are all that well kept.

Ever since he was Prince of Wales, the Regent has continued the habit of having numerous mistresses. His marriage in 1795 to Caroline of Brunswick has not changed this, quite the contrary is true, for the two spouses have never gotten along. Caroline, who has given George a daughter, Charlotte, is traveling all over Europe, where she leads a giddy life. "They even say," Lady Falkener adds, "that she fell madly in love with Murat when he was king of Naples. George has asked for a divorce a hundred times. But the people, who do not like him, and from whom he has not hidden his life of luxury and debauchery, are on Caroline's side. Whenever she returns to England, she is greeted with ovations. The Whigs too have rallied to her."

"As for King George III," she continues, "he is going more and more out of his mind. One day, when a huge blackbird pie with a thick crust was brought to the royal table, he exclaimed as it was cut open: "Ah! How very odd: how could these little birds get inside this dish?" He did not allow the pie to be eaten and called in a philosopher to study this question in detail. He is also losing his sight and can be seen groping his way through his palace like another King Lear. Sometimes he sits down at his piano and plays a sonata by Händel or Scarlatti. He has locked himself up in another world . . ."

One day a messenger brings Betsy an envelope sealed with the Regent's coat-of-arms. It is an invitation to a garden party on the grounds of the Pavilion. How wonderful! She will go with Lord and Lady Falkener.

This involves going back to London on a road along the Thames, which wends its way among cottages surrounded by green lawns and weeping willows. Along the way the travelers visit Oxford with its twenty-five colleges.

The next few days are filled with a bustle of activity. Lady Falkener has a French dressmaker and a French milliner, both of them refugees from the French Revolution. They have many clients in high English society, that "Silver Fork Society" as the satirists call it, which is steeped in luxury and mad about fancy frills and furbelows. These French refugees have placed their own stamp on English fashion and toned down the extravagant style of some of the ladies.

The great day has finally arrived. Sumptuous carriages drive into the Pavilion's park, crossing gardens of exotic flowers where a few couples are already enjoying the scenery. Betsy is a bit shocked when she sees the cupolas and the little bell towers of the Moorish-style palace. "Funny," she murmurs, as a lackey comes rushing to open the carriage door and Lord Falkener courteously holds out his hand to help her step down. At the door of the Pavilion an usher calls out the name of the new arrivals.

Here she is, at the very center of that lavish Regency society, that "sparkling sea of jewels, plumes, pearls and silk," she thinks, citing Byron. How she would love to see the author of *Childe Harold,* whose poems she has read in their entirety, make his way through this glittering crowd in his limping gait, buttoned up tightly in his strict black coat, with his disdainful mouth, his determined chin, and his blue gaze filled with *ennui*. . . . But no, she has no chance of catching a glimpse of him, for he has been embroiled in marital troubles for a few months already and has taken refuge in his lair at Newstead Abbey. Moreover, the Regent has never forgiven him for his opposition to the government.

As Lady Falkener wanders through the suite of rooms with Betsy in tow, she points out to her a tall, severe-looking man: it is Lord Castlereagh, the minister of foreign affairs. Further on, they see Lady Melbourne and Lady Hertford, two former conquests of the Prince Regent. And the young woman over there, with the high-pitched voice, around whom a whole crowd has gathered, is Lady Caroline Lamb, who was once madly in love with the handsome Byron.

But now the Regent is announced. He makes his entry, accompanied by a few dandies. Betsy finds him tall, dignified, and well-proportioned, if a bit corpulent. He is superbly attired in a crimson velvet coat encrusted in gold, a powdered wig of the Ancien Régime, and a high white cravat.

The Regent smiles benevolently at all and sundry, and affably shakes hands. He is an aesthete, a friend to artists and writers. Unfortunately, he has alienated many of them politically, among them Byron and Shelley, who support the Whig opposition.

"He likes for people to call him 'the first gentleman of Europe,'" Lady Falkener whispers. "And maybe that's what he is — until he has had too much to drink!"

Betsy marvels at the decor of the salons and makes one discovery after the other: here she sees superb wall coverings of Chinese wallpaper which on three walls depict a landscape or the story of a battle, there, enormous chandeliers in the form of dragons. There are several music and game rooms.

From the distant gardens one hears the first sounds of quadrilles and Scottish dances. But over the last two years the favorite dance of the English has become the German waltz. And since the victory of the coalition forces, it positively reigns supreme.

"You think this is a beautiful party," observes Lady Falkener, "but this is nothing in comparison with the fairytale spectacles that were put on in July in London to honor Wellington. If you had seen the capital at that time, it was delirious! The day the victory of Waterloo was announced, people embraced in the street, some were weeping. . . . Imagine also what it was like a few months earlier, when it was believed that the defeat of the "ogre" Bonaparte was assured, and all those foreign princes came to town, the czar and his sister, the king of Prussia and his escort, the royal family of France. There was a ceremony in which the Regent exchanged decorations with the future Louis XVIII: while the Regent received the Ordre du Saint Esprit, the French sovereign was given that of the Garter. This actually did not work out too well, for George insisted on attaching the decoration to his guest's huge thigh in person. This was not an easy thing, and the poor man worked up quite a sweat. He felt as if he were putting a belt around a fat baby!"

In this second half of September, the people of London — the London of Mayfair, Saint James Street, and Pall Mall — have returned, except for a few lords who are hunting foxes or pheasants on their estates. Distractions abound once again. "The little Bonaparte woman" is the center of attraction for the very people who not so long ago had enthusiastically received the French royal family.

The great nobility has opened its doors to Betsy. "I am so happy to find myself in the best society that I only regret the absence of American friends who could testify to the esteem in which I am held," she writes. She adores masked balls and particularly that of the Duchess of Rutland, where the members of Parliament wear the masks of the opposition, and vice versa. She has actually succeeded in gaining admission to Almack's, the most exclusive club in London, where the tone is set by Brummel, Alvanley, Pierrepoint, and Byron (although the poet, alas, has quit the scene and is preparing to leave for Switzerland, Italy, and Greece).

Brummel still has the same cold stare, disdainful mouth, caustic humor, and supreme elegance. "How little he has changed in ten years," Betsy says to herself. Yet she is witnessing the last of the flashes with which the Beau has dazzled this "Silver Fork Society." Ever since his falling-out with the Regent, which caused quite a stir in 1811, he has become more and more haughty, defying his former friend (whom he calls Big Ben in private), and making him look bad by comparison with the elegance of his own carriages and his impeccable attire — for the future George IV has an immoderate taste for luxury that at times brings him close to bad taste. In the political arena, the Regent is also furious to see that Brummel has gathered around him members of the Whig opposition as well as lords who disapprove of their future sovereign's scandalous way of life.

In any case, a few months later George Brummel will follow Byron's example and leave England in the deepest secrecy. Crushed by gambling debts, he will one day sail from Dover and take up residence at Caen, where he will die in poverty twenty years later.

Fortunately, Betsy does not like to gamble. But some of her friends do sometimes invite her for an afternoon of whist or faro. This fashion was started by Lady Archer and Lady Buckingham, who have opened gaming tables in their homes, complete with banks and croupiers, by way of getting even with London clubs like Brooke's, White's, or Watiers, to which only men are admitted.

Included in Betsy's program of pleasure are also, of course, outings in Hyde Park, where gigs, cabriolets, and tilburys cross paths and where every kind of fashionable dandy — from the *Corinthian* to the *exquisite* and the *offensive* — struts his stuff. And then there are the theaters, Drury Lane, the King's Theatre, and above all Covent Garden, which boasts of being the largest hall in Europe.

So there is no lack of distractions in London, but Betsy often thinks of her son. What might he be doing at this moment? Is he working hard enough? It has been some time since her father's last letter. Each time she has to wait for the arrival of the "packet boat," and the next one is due only by the end of the week. She sits down and writes to Baltimore:

Everyone here feels that my son should be educated in England and people are kind enough to flatter him by saying that the talents of a Bonaparte should receive an English education. There is no question that he would enjoy much more consideration in Europe than in America, where he has no social rank, and if I could combine with the interest he arouses here the advantages of a vast fortune, I would be very happy indeed! As a last resort, he must have a career and the talents with which nature has so profusely endowed him may well lead him some day to play an eminent role in Europe. When it comes to its institutions, America is still in its infancy and, given the commercial character of the aims it pursues, does not offer as good a terrain for exercising the kind of mental superiority your grandson possesses, for better or worse.

Betsy has no illusions; she is not likely to convince her father, who is intent on one thing only: making little Jérôme into a good American, endowed with a common sense that will enable him to stand up to everything — especially his mother. But Betsy's mind is made up, for she has not come to this still war-torn Europe as a simple visitor. No, what she intends to do is to lay the groundwork for her future and that of her son. While others pursue the American dream, hers is the European dream. But does she have an inkling that the alluring perspectives held out to her may not be altogether innocent? Just the name Bonaparte continues to arouse fear. Now that the different members of this detested family have scattered to different places — some to Italy, some to Württemberg, some to the shores of Lake Constance — does it make sense to allow an American branch to grow freely? Would it not be more astute to neutralize her, Anglicize her, and spirit her away? And in fact, these unspoken fears are not limited to England. Unbeknownst to the beautiful American who dances the waltz or the schottische at Almack's or at the duchess of Rutland's, coded letters of Louis XVIII's secret agents are traveling back and forth. Will Mme Patterson, ex-Bonaparte, be permitted to set foot on French soil? For different reasons than ten years earlier, Betsy is no more welcome today than she was then. Yet in the end Fouché, still the minister of police, shrugs his shoulders. "What of it," he says, "let's allow this pretty woman to enjoy a taste of Parisian life, seeing that she wants it so much!"

And so it is that one day Comte de la Châtre hands her her passport for France.

Paris awaits her, Paris is open to her!

13

*M*UCH TO HER AMAZEMENT, BETSY FINDS OUT that General Wellington is fêted almost as much on the banks of the Seine as in his own country. Even a liberal like Mme de Staël has sharpened her best pen to write to the victor of Waterloo: "Milord, there has been glory in the world before, but I do not know if there is another example of glory as unimpeachable, as unalloyed, and as universally recognized and appreciated. . . . You must be feeling a foretaste of the other world . . ."

She is not the only Frenchwoman to receive the English general with open arms: all Paris, it seems, has eyes only for him. On the evening when Betsy attends an opera entitled *La Bataille de Waterloo,* whose hero is an English officer, there is thundering applause. "How fickle these Parisians are," she writes to her father, fascinated in spite of herself by this sparkling city, which as yet she only half understands. For she does not suspect that side by side with the exultant joy of the legitimist and the satisfaction of the emigrés who are gradually regaining their landed estates and their town houses, side by side with the colorful uniforms of all those Russian, English, and Prussian officers who have poured into the French capital with their troops, there is distress among large segments of the population: soldiers and officers of the Grande Armée put on half-pay by the new government, a modest middle class whose businesses are flagging, peasants who are terrified of a return of the privileges of the Ancien Régime.

If she had gone walking under the arcades of the Palais-Royal and stopped by the doors of such places as the Café Lemblin, she would have seen them entering there, these whiskered, somber-looking men in long riding-coats buttoned up to their necks, wearing the rosette of the Légion d'Honneur in their buttonholes and carrying rattan walking sticks with lead knobs. They are the living antithesis of the old dukes and marquis who, going around in the powdered "pigeon wing" wigs of the Old Regime, are once again living in their town houses of the faubourg Saint-Germain.

At night, under the floods of light shed by the crystal chandeliers of the cafés around the Palais-Royal, one can often hear male and slightly drunken voices intone, "Let us look out for the safety of the Empire." Sometimes members of the Bourbon king's elite troops and musketeers come from the nearby Tuileries and sit down to have a drink; brushing back their long mustaches they look with contempt on the crowd around them.

The old officers of the Old Regime, called "Louis XIV's light infantry," have chosen the Café Valois, next door to the Lemblin, as their base. Here they solemnly sit in their antiquated uniforms or their court attire in front of a table of baccarat or whist. And woe to anyone who would mimic or mock them. Six young men who had dressed up in "light infantry" outfits — chiné stockings, silver-buckled shoes, tailcoat, variegated epaulets, white kerseymere knee breeches, tri-cornered hat with an enormous white cockade — and had sat down at a café table along the boulevards were sent to prison for three months. Despite their lip service to strict legality, the monarchy and the nobility have no tolerance for political allusions and unruly behavior. Paris should have a good time, of course, but always within the bounds of propriety.

Betsy, who has been introduced into certain salons of the faubourg Saint-Germain by her English friends Lady Redd and Lady Drummond, watches with a curious eye as it swirls around her, this society that has joyfully returned to its town houses, its servants, it Sèvres dishes, and its salons where there is dancing and where there is talk, a great deal of talk. Here the business of the kingdom is conducted, malicious gossip circulates about nearly everyone, and particularly about the Napoleonic nobility, whose bombastic titles do not sit well at all. Anglomania is raging among these aristocrats, who are likely to have a British jockey or riding master to teach their children riding and who, in addition to the gavotte, dance such fashionable dances as the cossack, the Russian dance, and of course the waltz.

In these circles, which are luxurious and aristocratic to the very core, Betsy would be supremely happy if she did not frequently have to hear people speak in contemptuous tones of the Corsican *Buonaparte* or of the *Usurper*. These words grate on her ears and make her shake. Why does she always have to feel so deeply torn in her heart? But then, the present is here to enjoy, and so for a time she lets herself be absorbed by this idle and distinguished life.

The outings in the Bois de Boulogne have taken the place of those in Hyde Park, except that it is a very long way to the Bois. Fashionable people go there only three times a week. On Sundays it is left to middle-class families, who come there with their children and their housemaids. Betsy likes the Monday outing, which is known in the faubourg as the "petit Longchamp."

Not that the Bois is all that attractive, what with its clipped hedges and trees that have been decimated by the Allied armies, with the walls that enclose it, and the muddy marsh of the lake at Auteuil, where a few ducks are listlessly paddling about. But it is an opportunity to meet elegant people and to be seen.

Betsy would not dream of going there by herself, for one must take the Champs-Elysées once one has crossed the muddy and garbage-strewn Place Louis XV. And the Champs-Elysées, though lined with wine shops and a few rural houses, marks a truly cutthroat neighborhood. A year later, Wellington will almost be murdered there. For the moment the troops of the Holy Alliance are encamped in the neighborhood: the English on the banks of the Seine, the cossacks in the lower section of the Champs-Elysées. They are exotic, these cossacks, with their rough manners and their way of rolling their Rs. Since they are prone to getting drunk, their officers do not allow them to consume alcoholic beverages in the cafés of the capital. Consequently, as soon as they feel unsupervised, they rush to the first tavern they come to and hastily order a glass of wine or brandy. "Bistro! Bistro!" they shout, which means "Quick! Quick!" This word sounded so amusing to French ears that certain tavern keepers are using it to designate their businesses.

Very different from the faubourg Saint-Germain is the area around the Chaussée d'Antin, whose inhabitants are for the most part businessmen, foreigners, and wealthy bourgeois. Fewer noble titles here, and more great fortunes. It is here that the Gallatin family has decided to live. Provided with a letter of introduction from her Aunt Nancy, Betsy has gone to call on them.

Albert Gallatin, a white-haired gentleman of austere appearance, but blessed with a good sense of humor, has retained a great simplicity, despite the important position he occupies. His very sober black attire contrasts with the luxury of the Bourbon court. He and his wife receive Betsy in a most affable manner. She tells them that her mother has died a year earlier and talks about her own life over the last few years, as well as about her decision to leave Baltimore against her father's wishes. The Gallatins listen in silence.

"Poor young woman," Albert thinks with a heavy heart. "So young, and so pretty. . . . She does not deserve to be treated in this way. Ah! If I had been in her husband's place!" Mrs. Gallatin is not quite as indulgent and soon remarks that while Betsy is clever, she does have a sharp tongue. Nonetheless she kindly asks her young compatriot to stay for dinner.

"This evening, "she tells her, "we will have, aside from our son James, who is his father's secretary, some intimate friends, Baron von Humboldt and the chemist Laplace. So it will be a serious, even scientific dinner."

In the course of that evening — where eighteen-year-old James cannot take his eyes off her — Betsy learns from the mouth of Albert Gallatin, who as a diplomat is kept well informed of all developments, about the fate of her ex-husband. After Napoleon's second abdication, he had first returned to Paris, where he had lived for some time with his uncle, Fesch, and then fled with the help of Fouché. After a stopover in the Sologne region, he found refuge at Niort. No doubt he had hoped to follow the example of his brother Joseph and head for America, to be followed by his wife later. But this did not work out. At the instigation of Fouché, he went instead to place himself under the protection of his father-in-law, the king of Württemberg. Skirting great danger and repeatedly changing his identity and his clothes, he finally arrived at the court in Stuttgart. But a golden retreat was not what Frederick of Württemberg had in mind for him; Jérôme and his faithful wife — who despite her father's remonstrances had insisted on following him into adversity — found themselves in supervised residence at the fortress of Ellwangen.

"So you see, my dear," Albert tells Betsy in a tone of irony, "when all is said and done you are probably better off than he is."

There is some truth to this, for while the ex-king of Westphalia is reduced to a prisoner, his American spouse cuts a striking figure in Parisian salons, where everyone raves about her beauty. "Too bad that she never reigned," Talleyrand is heard to mutter one day as he walks by her, obviously forgetting his panicked exchange of correspondence with Pichon at the time of the Baltimore marriage, or his threatening letter to the Grand Elector of Batavia when the *Erin* was about to land in Amsterdam.

One evening when she is invited to a reception at the British embassy, Betsy is surprised to see the crowd part and fall silent as she passes; a few ladies curtsey to her, while others blush and hide their faces behind their fans. All eyes follow her in utter stupefaction. Fortunately the ambassador puts an end to this embarrassing situation when he approaches her and offers his arm to take her in to dinner.

"They mistook you, my dear, for the Princess Borghese," he whispers into her ear. "And I must say, the resemblance is astonishing, especially with the coiffure and the tiara you are wearing this evening. And since it was assumed that she is in exile, there was reason to be surprised."

At Lady Drummond's, Betsy has met a slightly older Irishwoman, who, having earlier written several best-selling books, among them *The Irish Girl* under the name of Sidney Owensen, has subsequently married an English lord by the name of Sir Charles Morgan. Betsy was immediately attracted to this small woman who looked at her with bright, shining eyes set in a face which, without being pretty, was full of animation. Betsy's usually caustic wit pays no attention to her new friend's physical defects, even though she is slightly deformed and somewhat cross-eyed — but this "coquetry" seems to be part of her charm, for she is very sought-after in society.

"How lively and clever she is," Betsy thinks. Here, finally, is someone who can keep up with her, and in her own language, too. Lady Morgan is working on a book about the France of 1815. She is taking notes and with a kindly eye observes the different segments of society that swirl around her. She even tries to fish some scattered political ideas from the muddy waters in which the second Restoration is floundering.

She loves France and is crazy about Paris, where she enjoys the lively street life and happily walks for hours, much to the amazement of the ladies of the faubourg, who only venture out in a sedan chair or a calash.

"If only you knew how much fun this is," she says to the young American. "Come on, you should go with me sometime, if you feel like it." That day marks the beginning of a solid friendship between the two women, a friendship that would end only with the death of Sidney, many years later.

Through her, Betsy will make the acquaintance of an Irish poet by the name of Thomas Moore, a childhood friend of Lady Morgan, who has once written a volume of *Irish Melodies* in her honor. One day he rings the bell of the small apartment Betsy has rented in the rue du Rocher, close to the town houses where the Bonaparte family lived not long ago. Moore tells her that he too is a great friend of Byron, and that the poet, who has recently left England to get away from his wife and his creditors, wrote a few verses just before he took ship and dedicated them to Moore:

> My boat is on the shore
> And my bark is on the sea;
> But, before I go, Tom Moore
> Here's a double health to thee!

He soon falls for Betsy. They have many memories to share, for Moore was attaché at the Washington embassy in 1805; however, he says that he did not appreciate the desert Washington still was at that time, any more than the cavalier ways of the young congressmen whose backslapping was a bit too familiar for his taste.

In Moore's company the young woman discovers the boulevard cafés, the Café Tortoni, the Café Riche, the Café de Paris. What a pleasure to sit down there for a moment on a sunny day, have a hot chocolate or a dish of ice cream, and watch idle strollers, fancy cavaliers, and *grisettes* go by. One hears the cries of water and lemonade-sellers, of knife grinders and newspaper hawkers, of women selling wafers, mixed with the shouts of barkers who, from the height of a stage, try to lure the public to an open-air show. It is a perpetual party! A little farther on are the theaters: Le Gymnase, Les Funambules, Le Théâtre Historique.

Among the cafés of the Palais-Royal, Betsy's favorite is the Café de Foy. In the back of the room she has spied a group of young men in smocks who affect an artistic demeanor. One of them scrawls something into a sketch pad he holds on his knees. From time to time he steals a hidden glance at the young American, who blushes with pleasure when she notices it. "I wonder if he is sketching me," she thinks. She learns that he is Horace Vernet. He and his father are regulars at this café. His father, Carle Vernet, has painted the bird with outspread wings one sees on the ceiling.

One evening, Thomas Moore takes Elizabeth to the Théâtre Français, where the great Talma is playing *Britannicus* opposite Mlle Georges.

Not long thereafter, Betsy receives a note from Mrs. Gallatin: "If you are interested in meeting our cousin, Mme de Staël, before she leaves for Italy, come and have dinner with us Tuesday night." The fact is that, despite her admiration for General Wellington, Germaine de Staël has grown tired of the sight of the Allied occupation troops in Paris clearing the Bois de Boulogne as fast as they can. She has decided to take a trip to Italy and then return to her château at Coppet on the shores of Lake Geneva.

She is a cousin to Albert Gallatin, whose family had come from Geneva. Like the Neckers, they were descendants of Jacques Coeur. The two are on most familiar terms, and Albert jokingly says that if Joan of Arc in her time had not had these absurd visions, he, Gallatin, might have inherited the wealth of the famous silversmith!

Betsy, who has never seen Germaine but has read several of her works, among them *Delphine* and *Corinne en Italie,* is delighted to meet her. She is spellbound by her conversation, by the sparkle of her black eyes and the intensity of her conversation. Young Gallatin, who is present at this dinner party, is more caustic.

"Don't you find," he whispers into her ear, "that she gesticulates a bit much, with her olive branch? I think it's funny."

"No, I think it marks the rhythm of what she is saying. It is almost as if she were wielding a musical instrument," observes Betsy. "And anyway, one is so fascinated by her face and her lips that one does not even notice the rest. Is she beautiful? Is she well dressed? One doesn't even know — and anyway, it doesn't matter!"

The effect she has produced on the young American is not lost on Germaine de Staël. She is flattered and intrigued by it. She has always been attracted by the United States, she tells Betsy; her father had bought some land in Kentucky and thought about joining his friend Dupont de Nemours in America. But she herself is content to navigate between France, England, Germany, Italy, and her château at Coppet. But Betsy could easily come to visit her there, since she will soon accompany the Gallatins to Geneva, as Albert has told her.

That same evening Betsy learns that in a few days a great friend of Mme de Staël, Juliette Récamier, will host a distinguished assembly in her salons in the rue Basse-du-Rempart, near the Church of the Madeleine. The writer Benjamin Constant will present a first private reading of his translation of Schiller's work *Wallenstein,* which the public does not know yet.

"I will take you," James Gallatin proposes.

He too has become a fervent admirer of Betsy, despite the great difference in age between them, and sometimes makes her the confidante of his youthful escapades. He tells her how he has sat for the painter David — who unfortunately is in disgrace because the *ultras* consider him a regicide (and it is true that he had voted for the death of the king) who used his talents to promote the Revolution and the Empire. He has been replaced as head of the Institut by Gérard. In painting a vast composition entitled *Amor and Psyche,* David has used James as model for his Cupid, but has never allowed him to meet Psyche, much to the young man's disappointment.[1]

At Mme Récamier's Betsy encounters a brilliant assembly. There is General Bernadotte, who will soon become king of Sweden and who was tapped for the throne of France before the return of the Bourbons. Also present are Matthieu de Montmorency, Comte de Forbin, Ben-

---

[1] The picture now hangs at the Cleveland Museum of Art.

jamin Constant, the painter Gérard, the actor Talma, the sculptor Canova, Prince Metternich, André Pozzo de Borgo (the Corsican who, from sheer hatred of the Bonapartes, has gone into the service of the czar of Russia), the philosophers Humboldt and Sismondi and, last but not least, the Duke of Wellington.

It is a very odd mixture of *ultras,* liberals, foreign princes, marshals of the Empire and former members of the Revolutionary Assemblies, among whom Mme Récamier, dressed in white and unadorned by any jewelry, moves with her habitual gentleness and grace, receiving homages here and there and exhibiting a marvelous ability to maintain harmony among such a variety of guests. Rumor has it that Benjamin Constant is crazy about her, as is August of Prussia, the nephew of Frederick I, with whom Princess Charlotte of England, the Regent's daughter, was so much in love the year before.

The tall, thin, and rigid man leaning against a console over there is Wellington, the victor of Waterloo. He too is in love with Juliette de Récamier. Having learned from Mme de Staël that she was among those exiled by Napoleon, he was sure that after Waterloo she would receive him with open arms. And so he had rushed to the rue Basse-du-Rempart and thrown himself at Juliette's feet, exclaiming: "I defeated him!" At first she had burst out laughing, but then, shocked by her own tactlessness, she had gently rebuked him.

Betsy, for her part, sees no reason to show a surly face to the English general whom James Gallatin would soon thereafter present to her; she is delighted when he proposes to show her around in Paris, which he is beginning to know like the palm of his hand. How can this fail to go to her head: here she is, seated at the side of the victor of Waterloo as his gray phaëton streaks up the Champs Elysées or through the streets of the faubourg Saint-Germain. This will cause a lot of gossip and a certain amount of jealousy in the American colony.

But the brilliant warrior is also quite a ladies' man, who prides himself on "conquering by the heart as well as by the sword." And so Betsy, like Mme Récamier, soon has to fend him off. No harm done, though! Lord Wellington does not hold it against her and one day brings her a little lapdog — with which Betsy is at first enchanted, although it soon gets in her way! — and has her invited to all the balls at the embassy.

A few days earlier, Thomas Moore too had been given his walking papers when he sadly came to take leave of her before returning to England.

Betsy's most relaxing moments are those she spends with her new friend, Lady Morgan. The two ladies go shopping for clothes together, take tea or lime punch at the Belle Madeleine café near the Tuileries, and visit the antiquities collection of the famous egyptologist Baron Denon, who at the time accompanied Bonaparte to Egypt and subsequently founded the Louvre Museum. He is a major attraction for visiting Englishwomen. They simply cannot get enough of hearing him tell stories about his travels, which he likes to embellish with spicy details, for he has a sense of humor and takes a malicious pleasure in scaring his pretty visitors.

One day Lady Morgan proposes to take her friend to the first-night performance of Lemercier's *Charlemagne* at the Théâtre-Français. She and Sir Charles have an extra seat in their box. Betsy eagerly accepts, for she knows that the main role will be played by a certain Lafond, who is very popular just then. But she still does not know that she will witness a momentous event, which will show her to what extent France is still divided in two.

It turns out that two factions confront each other in the auditorium. One is in the pit, the other in the boxes. Even before the curtain goes up, one hears noises resembling the rumble of thunder. As the play begins, the tumult only increases. Behind every utterance the audience thinks it perceives veiled allusions to the present regime or to the fall of the previous one, greeting them with whistles of displeasure or ovations, depending on their opinions. Soon the situation comes close to a riot, a riot that fortunately remains purely verbal. It is an anticipation of the battle over *Hernani*.

With a sparkle in her eyes, Sidney Morgan is enjoying this spectacle. She loves, she says, "this wonderful youth, so full of energy and vivacity." How far these young people are from the mincing little marquis of the court of Louis XIV in their red heels! And also from the dandies of London with their disdainful vanity.

"The other day I watched as one of them arrived at a Parisian gathering; he produced as big a sensation as if a dinosaur had walked in!"

14

*G*ENEVA, WHICH HAS JUST REGAINED ITS independence — for during the Revolution the city had been incorporated into France — has become a kind of crossroads, where one encounters people of all European nationalities, and above all the English. This is not surprising, since they have actively worked for this emancipation and have contributed to the enlargement of the Genevan territory — which, as Voltaire said, was so small that by powdering one's wig one powdered the whole country — at the expense of Savoy and France. Geneva has thus become a canton.

It is love at first sight for Betsy when she sees this tidy town at sunset, nestled inside its ramparts at the foot of the mountains, sitting next to the tranquil lake, its houses covered with round tiles, and its *domes,* which are enormous overhangs that shelter artisan shops, tanneries, and wash houses. If she can find a suitable school for Bo, she has no doubt that she will happily live here with him, far from her father's reprimands and all political passions.

The Gallatins, with whom she has traveled here, are filled with excitement. "Just think," James confides to Elizabeth, "this is the first time that Papa has returned to the country of his birth after years and years of absence."

The Gallatin house, which belongs to another branch of the family — Comte Michel de Gallatin — is a fine building on the rue de la Corratrie. The family coat-of-arms over the main entrance has been torn off during the Revolution; only the two lions holding it remain.

On the first morning after their arrival, a whole group of noble citizens has come to greet the representative of the United States, along with a delegation of municipal officials in dress uniforms complete with ceremonial swords at their side. The Swiss historian and philosopher Jean-Charles-Léonard Simonde Sismondi addresses a long and flattering speech to his "enlightened compatriot," and this is followed by an interminable lunch lasting two hours. Frances and Albert, the two youngest Gallatin children have been excused from this ceremony, but James desperately winks at Betsy who, sitting on Sismondi's right, pretends not to see them. In this austere company, she stands out by the elegance of her attire. And she does remark that the Genevan ladies are dressed very simply and do not wear much jewelry.

Sismondi is a charming man. A liberal who has protected the *carbonari*[1] and formulated the first theories of labor conditions, he is a kind-hearted man capable of great efforts to help his friends. He is not handsome with his big face, his heavy-set body, and the thick spectacles to correct his myopia, but he radiates kindness and good nature. He is instantly seduced by the spirited demeanor of his luncheon companion, by her flawless French and her cheerfulness. Reminding her that he has seen her once before, a few months earlier at Mme Récamier's, when Benjamin Constant read from his translation of *Wallenstein,* he tells her that he would like to invite her to his residence of Chêne, a simple country house near Geneva, where he lives with his wife Jenny, an Englishwoman whom he has recently married.

Mme de Staël too has come to greet her cousin Gallatin. In her green, sable-lined greatcoat and her turban of the same color, she looks rather odd, but her cordiality is so contagious that everyone is delighted to see her.

"Come and visit me at Coppet," she tells the Gallatins, "and of course," she adds, turning to Elizabeth, "I hope you will come along."

The little town of Coppet, where Mme de Staël has her château, is located between Lausanne and Geneva. After Germaine's falling out with Napoleon, the château has become a veritable international court of intellectuals of varying tendencies, the place where they remake the

---

[1] Members of a secret society who oppose the policies of the Holy Alliance.

world, plot to place Philippe d'Orléans on the French throne, and where all the best minds of Europe talk from morning until late at night.

"Geneva is Europe," Napoleon had laughingly told Fouché. And the intellectual crossroads of that Europe is Coppet. When those who come here are not talking, they read aloud from their works, go for walks, act in plays, and dance. There are never-ending verbal jousts. At this miniature court, the dinner table usually holds some thirty guests, while fifteen cooks, waitresses, and kitchen boys officiate in the kitchens.

That spring, Mme de Staël, who has just returned from Italy, has with her her son Auguste, her daughter Albertine, recently married to the Duc de Broglie, and her youngest son Alphonse, whom she calls "Petit Nous." He is the fruit of her secret marriage to John Rocca, a man twenty years her junior.

Soon Betsy becomes part of this little group. She is admired, praised to the skies; Germaine de Staël cannot stop talking about her "virtuous beauty" and listens in wide-eyed astonishment one day as Betsy resolutely puts a rather impertinent Englishman in his place.

That day Betsy had been very late for lunch and found herself seated next to a certain Mr. Dundas, who had stopped by for the day. Having risen early and gotten very hungry during his long ride, he is in a foul mood. Wanting to take a little revenge on his table mate, whose lateness had irritated him, he leans over and asks: "Madame, have you read Captain Basil Hull's book on America?"

"Euh, yes, I have."

"Well then, Madame, have you noticed what he says of the Americans? He finds all of them extremely vulgar."

"I agree with you," Betsy replies without batting an eyelash. "I am not the least bit surprised; if they were the descendants of Indians or Eskimos, this would be astonishing, but since their direct ancestors are the English, it is perfectly natural that they should be boors."

A long silence falls around the table. Flushed and red-faced, Mr. Dundas rises, brusquely pushing back his chair, and leaves the room, stammering some excuses. He will never again be seen at Coppet.

"Well, my dear Albert, she has quite a temper, your young compatriot," Germaine de Staël observes, turning to her cousin. "I really like that!"

Betsy would have liked to stay longer on these delightful shores, but she must return to Paris and from there go to Le Havre to take the boat to America, where her son demands her presence. "Never mind," she thinks, "I'll come back, now that the Gallatins have helped me find a fine school for Bo."

Just as Betsy is leaving Geneva by travel coach, a man, a poet whom she would have liked so much to meet, comes to spend some time on the shores of Lake Geneva. It is Byron who, accompanied by his friend Dr. Polidori, has for a few months rented the Villa Diodati, which is located across the lake from Coppet. Nearby is the house of the poet Percy Bysshe Shelly and his wife Mary. The two men will buy a boat and crisscross the lake in all directions, preferably in rough weather, for Byron considers himself a good sailor and loves to confront danger. Meanwhile, as an evening thunderstorm is raging, Mary Shelley will create the famous figure of Frankenstein. Byron will often visit Coppet and soon become friends with Germaine de Staël.

These images — the limping and sarcastic poet, his hair flying in the wind, the boat under full sail — float before Betsy's eyes as in a fog when her Genevan friends recount their memories of that summer. Alas! Once again, she has missed Byron!

15

*E*IGHTEEN SIXTEEN. GREAT EXCITEMENT IN THE French capital! Preparations are under way for the sumptuous wedding, two weeks hence, of the Duc de Berry, younger son of the Comte d'Artois (the future Charles X). There will be a ball, fireworks, a gala wedding procession, and a high mass at Notre-Dame. Lady Morgan, who loves to see the sights, invites Elizabeth to go with her to admire the trousseau of the future duchess, for she has been able to obtain complimentary tickets.

The Duc de Berry is marrying Princess Caroline of Naples, a pretty, mischievous, and lively blonde who will bring a little cheer to the rather austere and staid court of Louis XVIII, where a rigid court etiquette has been reestablished at the behest of the Duchesse d'Agoulême (formerly Madame Royale, the daughter of Louis XVI). Thus, following tradition, the trousseau will be exhibited. For three days, royal highnesses, nobles, and other people of privilege will be able to look at it at the Palace of the Menus Plaisirs.

But, oh dear! the crowd of the "privileged" is so thick that Sidney and Betsy are just about crushed to death. A veritable human torrent rushes through the hallways, kept in its banks by the palace guards, who try in vain to maintain some kind of order. After two hours of being pushed, jostled, and bruised, the two women finally come to a suite of salons where they see, tacked to the walls, hundreds of dresses of all forms, colors, and kinds of materials: linen, taffeta, embroidered silk, muslin shot through with gold or silver threads, blond lace, and English lace.

Arranged on consoles and warming tables are pieces of head gear, ranging from a diamond-studded crown to a simple night cap, along with many toiletry kits in gold-plated or massive silver.

"Why, it's enough to make the Queen of Sheba die with envy," exclaims Lady Morgan.

After such an immersion in a crowd, Betsy is only too glad on the day of the wedding, celebrated a few days later at Notre-Dame, to watch the arrival of the bridal procession from a balcony in the rue du Vieux Pont. Thirty-six carriages drawn by eight horses, glittering uniforms, sparkling diamonds, the pealing of bells, the Duc de Berry in a cloak of gold-embroidered satin, wearing the Order of the Cordon-Bleu, the duchess looking fragile in her silk costume with the crown jewels in her blond hair, the Hundred Swiss in Renaissance uniforms — what a sight!

It is a far cry from the bourgeois evenings in South Street and a sight that confirms Betsy in her conviction that it takes a monarchy or an imperial regime to bring forth such luxurious displays. All that is left now is for her to be presented at court!

And sure enough, Mrs. Gallatin, who this very morning at eleven o'clock has been presented to the Duchesse d'Angoulême in formal court attire, has come home exhausted from this ordeal and tells Betsy that Louis XVIII has expressed the desire to make her acquaintance.

"That's impossible!" she exclaims. "How could I ever agree to be presented at the Bourbon court after having received a pension from the Emperor all these years! No, ingratitude is not one of my vices! And besides, after all you have told me about the deadly boredom of the receptions at Madame la Duchesse d'Angoulême's and the staid atmosphere that pervades it, I have no desire to stand around there or to try to snatch a tabouret as the French duchesses do!"

Lord Wellington, having returned to Paris after a short trip to England, is glad to see the "Belle of Baltimore." He has some news to tell her: at his home of Twickenham Castle, he has been visited by his brother Robert and his wife the "charming Mary," and his two sisters-in-law, Louisa and Eliza. He, Wellington, has been very pleased to make their acquaintance and has been fascinated by the beauty of Mary . . . (Lucky Robert!) All four of them expressed the desire to visit the battlefield of Waterloo, and he felt duty-bound to take them there himself.

"The Catons!" Betsy thinks with some resentment. Really, here she has fled Baltimore, where she has suffered a lot of bad gossip, especially from the Caton family, and now she has to run into them again? She is sure that Mrs. Caton, who had been the first to criticize her departure, has sent her two younger daughters to Europe with the firm intention of having them wrangle a husband. Nor will that be too hard for them, what with the wealth of their grandfather!

According to Edward, who writes to her from time to time, Bo seems to be interested in religion. To the point where the priests of Saint Mary's have asked him why he prays so much. He did not want to answer, for he does not like it when people pry into his business! He has a strong personality, but he is working well. Right now he is lovingly tending two rabbits that one of his grandfather's friends has sent him.

The thought of returning to America is so repugnant to Betsy that in the end she decides to prolong her stay in France. She spends the summer making excursions here and there, to Bagatelle, to Saint-Cloud, and walking about in Paris. In the evening she dreamily contemplates the shadows of dusk as they descend over the Seine and soon cover the Tuileries Palace, the long façade of the Louvre, the Palais-Bourbon, and the Institut.

Lady Morgan, who knows everyone, has introduced her to a charming old lady with a face as pink and wrinkled as a lady-apple, the Marquise de Villette. She is none other than the Reine-Philiberte de Varicourt, whose godfather, long ago, was Voltaire. He called her "Belle et Bonne," and she later married the Marquis de Villette. It was to her and the marquis' home that Voltaire had come to die, and Reine, who adored her benefactor, considers herself the high priestess of the cult of the great philosophe long after his death.

She now lives in the hôtel d'Elbeuf, a town house in the rue de Vaugirard, which she has transformed into a kind of temple dedicated to the memory of Voltaire. The bookcase holds all his works, and the desk is covered with his hand-written letters. The armchair in which he used to sit stands by the fireplace. In the bedroom and in the drawing room various busts of the patriarch and the model of the famous statue by Pigalle are displayed.

In honor of Sidney Morgan and her young American friend, Mme de Villette has decided to give a little party to celebrate the memory of Voltaire. She has invited all the old friends and contemporaries of the patriarch of Ferney. This makes for a rather high average age of the guests! But Betsy is thrilled. Books, manuscripts, and items of clothing — among them the famous dressing gown — are deployed; incense burns before the bust of the laurel-crowned *philosophe*, and someone recites the ode Marie-Josèphe Chénier composed at his death.

"Here you see one of the finest aspects of the French national character," whispers Sidney Morgan, "which is enlightened, orderly, and passionate about the arts and letters. . . . All this country needs to be one of the greatest nations of the universe is a free government."

During the ceremony, Mme de Villette has surreptitiously watched Betsy and found that she looks rather like her daughter, who would now be about the same age if she had not died before she was sixteen. Upon her death, the marquise has become a recluse in her town house in the rue de Vaugirard. She rarely goes to Plessis-Villette, her husband's family château, which evokes sad memories for her.

Her husband has died twenty years earlier; all she has left is one son, with whom she is not on good terms. A difficult young man, he communicates with her only through letters, transmitted by his solicitor, concerning financial matters.

"Come and see me again, my pretty child," the marquise tells Betsy as she takes her leave.

In the course of this summer and fall of 1816, the two women establish a tender intimacy between them, and before long the presence of the young American has become indispensable to the old lady. Three times a week they go for an outing or to the theater together. Since Betsy does not have a carriage, Mme de Villette often sends her coachman to fetch her in her own.

"I am sending for news of my pretty little one," she writes, "and I want to know if she is alone or if her black moods are tormenting her. Since it is such a nice day, I urge her to come to me; we will dine together, and then we shall see what we will do this evening . . ."

"How far away you live!" she sometimes exclaims. "Why don't you spend the night here? We could just sit by the fire and talk, without, of course, slandering anyone." And so, the next morning Betsy, wearing a cotton dressing gown, goes to find the fresh eggs laid by the gardener's chickens. This is the best moment of the marquise's day. Sitting up in her bed amidst cascades of lace, she sees her young guest come in, her shoulders covered by a scarf, with pink cheeks and laughing eyes, carrying a little basket of eggs. How she reminds her of her daughter Charlotte, years ago, at the château of Plessis-Villette! The two even have something else in common: Charlotte too had a marriage proposal from a Bonaparte, Louis, when he visited his brother Joseph at the château of Mortefontaine, whose park adjoined that of the Villettes. But she was not interested!

"Belle et Bonne" has a great many stories to tell, about her youth in an impoverished gentry family; about the time she spent helping Mme Denis, Voltaire's niece, run the philosophe's household and keeping him company; about the elderly maid servant at Ferney, Barbara, called "Baba," whom the patriarch obeyed without arguing, like a schoolboy; about her meeting M. de Villette, a charming man and sometime poet whom she had loved very much, but who, alas, also loved young boys.

During the Revolution, and after the death of her husband — who had been a member of the Girondin faction at the Convention — she had been imprisoned with her daughter, whereas her son, who had been given the first name Voltaire, was with a wetnurse at the château of Plessis-Villette. After the death of her daughter, this boy had given her no end of trouble.

"So you see that my life has not always been a bed of roses either," she observes with a smile. Framed by her lace nightcap, her delicate face is lined with the marks of sorrow, and yet it radiates benevolence. "I have come," she says, "to that season in life when the flowers of beauty have lost their brilliance."

In a sudden flashback, Betsy sees the sweet and tired smile of her mother Dorcas, long ago.

The salon of the marquise is still the meeting place of poets and artists. Her guests try to outdo each other in song and verse-making. There is little talk of politics. The marquise is an ardent monarchist and positively worships the duchesse d'Angoulême, whom she met at the Conciergerie when she was Madame Royale. But her loyalty to the crown is tempered by generous and liberal ideas that she owes to her famous godfather.

"France is really as I dreamt it would be," Betsy says to herself as she attends all these intimate literary gatherings and sometimes accompanies "Belle et Bonne" to a concert at the Tuileries or a ball at the opera. "And how I will miss it!"

Meanwhile, though, her days are filled with activity. Invited to all the balls given by the embassies or by grand duchesses, she positively shines at those of the Duke of Wellington.

"Truly," Nancy Spears writes to her, "you are the main topic of conversation in London and Paris, and the chorus of praise for you has even reached our ears. . . . But Betsy, when are you going to get married?"

Not that she is lacking suitors. Every morning, the hall of her hotel is crowded with callers. On the other hand, she keeps her distance from her compatriots, finding that they are given to moralizing.

"You cannot imagine how hypocritical they are," she tells Sidney Morgan. "They only want to be admitted to French drawing rooms the better to criticize the mores of this country. And because I myself swim there like a fish in water, they consider me an apostate from the American Republic, whose virtues they praise to the skies. Well, if you want my opinion, I prefer the company of French sinners to that of American saints, for the French, at least, are amusing."

"What I find funny in this country," says Sidney, "is that I might easily lunch at a royalist's, take tea with some ultras, and then have supper with republicans — and nobody minds. What a range of opinions!"

A young habitué of Mme de Villette's salon, the Comte de Saint-Cricq, is madly in love with Betsy. "Why wouldn't you marry him?" "Belle et Bonne" asks. "He is handsome, from an excellent family, and deeply in love with you. This way you would at least stay with us."

"I don't love him. . . ."

"But you could make it a marriage of convenience; it is done all the time in France. Oh, if only I could marry you to my son, it would be my fondest dream to see him marry a gentle, kind, and well-bred woman like yourself."

"He is too young," Betsy objects. "What would he do with a woman of thirty?"

"Age has nothing to do with it, "Belle et Bonne" sighs, "but alas, I can see that you want to leave us."

AT THE URGING OF HER FATHER AND HER AUNT NANCY, BETSY HAS FINALLY decided to wend her way back to America. She will leave the following summer, she says. But she is determined to return to Europe with her son.

She has seen Germaine de Staël again after that lady's return from Coppet, and has found her very thin. She is quite ill and will get worse and worse during this winter and spring of 1817. Betsy sometimes visits her in her home in the rue Royale and finds her stretched out on a chaise longue or on her bed. She no longer has the strength to get up. By her side sits her husband, John Rocca, a ghostly pale, emaciated figure not much better off than Germaine.

Betsy also frequents Mme Récamier, who lives very near her in the rue Basse-du-Rempart, and occasionally sings for her guests, accompanying herself on the harp. She has a delightful voice, which bewitches those who hear it. Aside from the Gallatins, Betsy is one of very few American women to be admitted to the intimate circle of these two famous women. Certain of her compatriots who have just arrived in Paris often ask her to introduce them to the circles in which she moves. "I cannot abuse the kindness of Mme Récamier," she matter-of-factly replies. "Only a few privileged persons are admitted to her salons."

"After all," she confides to Sidney, "I don't see why I should officiate as introducer of Americans in Paris: my government is not paying me to do that job!"

In July, while she is submerged in luggage and busy running a few last-minute errands — she is supposed to bring Parisian gowns to one of her cousins, a set of Sèvres porcelain to another — she learns of the death of Mme de Staël.

Deeply distressed, Betsy rushes over to the rue Basse-du-Rempart to embrace Juliette. The lady of the house is not there. The next morning, just as Betsy is about to set out for Le Havre, she receives a note in the delicate hand she so easily recognizes: "Thank you, dear friend, for having understood how unhappy I was," Juliette Récamier writes.

Betsy will leave Paris with a heavy heart.

Unhappy as well is Mme de Villette, but for a different reason. She will greatly miss her "pretty little girl;" having felt for a few months that Charlotte had returned to her. As a good-luck charm for her long voyage, she gives Betsy the last lines written by M. de Voltaire before his death and three leaves from the wreath that was bestowed on him on his arrival in Paris. And for her father she gives Betsy the volume of her husband's complete works.

As she takes leave of her friend, Betsy cannot hold back her tears. "And do come back soon, my dear little one . . ." the marquise adds.

16

*B*O HAS GROWN. HIS LONG ARMS AND LONG LEGS stick out of his trousers and the smock that has become too short. A true grasshopper! which is why his Aunt Nancy has nicknamed him "Cricket."

He has had a good year at Saint Mary's and claims that he now speaks and writes fluent French. To show his grandfather how well he can do it, he has even sent him a letter in that language from his boarding school the preceding winter.

Mon cher grandpapa. Je ne vous ai jamais écrit une lettre en français parce que vous ne l'entendez pas; mais, pour vous donner une preuve de ma bonne volonté, je prends ma plume pour cela. Comment vous portez-vous? Pour moi, je me porte très bien et je désire beaucoup vous voir et j'espère que vous viendrez bientôt me voir. Adieu, mon très cher grand-papa, c'est tout ce que j'ai à vous écrire à présent. . . ."

[My dear grandpapa. I have never written you a letter in French because you do not understand it; but, to give you proof of my good will, I take up my pen to do it. How are you? I myself am quite well and I very much wish to see you, hoping that you will come to see me soon. Adieu, my very dear grandpapa, this is all I have to write to you for now. . . .]

It is a beautiful day at Coldstream, where Edward and his family spend the summer, and where Mr. Patterson, Aunt Nancy, and Betsy have come to lunch in order to meet Bo. The magnolia blossoms exhale a delightful smell, while ash and tulip trees provide ample refreshing shade.

While they are going for a walk, Edward informs his sister that Bo wanted to stop taking Latin, claiming that it was useless, considering that his grandfather had succeeded in building a huge fortune without knowing a word of it! But he, Edward, has not allowed it.

"Thank you, Edward. . . . And you, how are you? Is your business going well?"

"Oh, that . . . sure. But I would like to travel."

"Why, then, come to Europe with me, when I go back there!"

"I can't, right now; Sidney is pregnant again. I will have to wait."

AFTER HER FIRST IMMERSION IN EUROPEAN LIFE, BETSY FEELS REINVIGORATED and ready to cast a benevolent, almost condescending eye on her American fatherland.

She notices that Baltimore has grown again. One feels that it is a city in full expansion. Two monuments — which will make it known for a time as "the monumental city" — have almost been completed. One is dedicated to George Washington and the other, called Battle Monument, to the war dead of 1812. The first medical school in all of America, a neo-classical building, has gone up on Lombard Street. Merchants and ship owners now have a maritime exchange, located not far from the waterfront.

A few streets have acquired gas lighting, which makes them look much more friendly at night. A highway now links Ohio with Maryland.

Gracious clippers still crisscross the Chesapeake, but some of them are engaged in a shameful commerce: their store rooms have been converted to enable them to bring unfortunate black slaves from the coast of Africa, four or five hundred of them crammed into the hold. This trade has now been outlawed by the European governments, but when the clippers "spread their sea wings" they continue, thanks to their great speed, to thwart the tight controls of the English, who have become the champions of the antislavery movement.

Others leave for mysterious destinations. Are they taking armed support to the Spanish colonies, who are revolting under the leadership of Simón Bolívar? Or will they, on the contrary, help Napoleon escape from Saint Helena, as others suspect.

The first steamships, designed by Robert Fulton, have also made their appearance: gleaming white and outfitted with a paddle wheel and a tall and narrow smokestack, they are used for carrying merchandise or passengers. Some are bound for Norfolk, Virginia, and others follow the coast as far as Brazil, from where they bring back coffee. But they are not yet ready to cross the Atlantic.

One day one of them brings a young Frenchman, who rings the doorbell at Betsy's house on Charles Street. Jessie shows him into the sitting room, a tall, awkward young man who squeezes his hat under his arm and mops his sweat-drenched brow under chestnut curls. It is the Vicomte de Saint-Criq, who has come to pay his respects. Betsy receives him rather coldly, especially when she learns that he lodges at the Fountain Inn, which is still run by the Barney Brothers (although the commodore is quite ill). "This means trouble for me," she thinks. "Pretty soon everyone will know about it, and when it comes to my father's ears, he will not be pleased at all."

A few days later she receives a letter from Mme de Villette. She had had to comfort a tearful Comtesse de Saint-Criq, she tells Betsy. "I pointed out to her that her son is old enough to know what he is doing. After all, travel is educational for young people. I had tried in vain to talk him out of rushing after you, but it was either that or suicide."

For a few days Betsy is on pins and needles. Just so the young man does not make another scene! But no, one day he "takes French leave" as the Americans say, and takes a coach to Washington. There he no doubt finds solace for his sorrow, for Betsy never hears from him again.

Meanwhile "Belle et Bonne" lets Betsy know about her tears. "Your French *maman* really misses you, my dear little girl. . . . I have had two orange trees planted in my garden: one is called 'Elisa,' and the other 'Patterson.' From time to time I go out to water them myself." And in order to show Betsy how much she is missed in France, she sends her a poem written by one of her friends and frequent guest in her salon, a writer by the name of Gérard:

What a blow it is, your departure,
I can see that it's felt by us all.
You have dealt a great blow to La France
When you left it as you have done.

So come back, Baltimorean beauty,
And show us again all your charms.
We don't change on the banks of the Seine,
And love will always be French.

And there is more news. "Belle et Bonne" has become a free mason! She has been asked to become Grand Mistress of a new lodge of the Scottish rite, which has become associated with the Society of the Friends of Arts and Letters that bears her name. Betsy can't help but smile: "Belle and Bonne" as Grand Mistress of a lodge: what next!

Sidney Morgan also sends long missives in her sweeping and energetic handwriting. They are filled with underlined sentences and phrases written between, across, and in the margins of the lines in a torrent of words that intrigues and occupies Betsy, who spends long hours deciphering them.

Sometimes Sir Charles adds his grain of salt in a post-script: "This sounds like a note written to Madame la Marquise by the chevalier, who does not love her with the love of angels, but rather more than that . . . that is, the way sinners love sinful women . . ." and also: "You are both an "*honnête homme*" and an "*honnête femme*," my lovely friend, and in any case *a jolly good fellow.*"

Actually, the publication of Lady Morgan's book on France, every page of which conveys a certain respect for the ideas of the Revolution and for the man who had continued to embody them for a time, has closed the doors of many a Parisian salon to her. And yet it is a carefully written book, cheerful and rather well disposed toward a country that for so long was the enemy of her own. Sir Charles has added some more austere pages at the end of the volume, consisting of medical considerations (since he is a doctor of medicine) and an economic analysis.

DURING THE FALL BO HAS GONE HUNTING WITH HIS UNCLES IN THE MARSHES of the Choptank and the Patuxent, where geese, ducks, and wood pigeons are plentiful. Betsy has sometimes gone with them in the sloop that has taken them into these rivers' inlets, but then has only watched from afar as the big red Chesapeake retrievers joyfully jumped into the water in order to retrieve the birds as they drop. In the late afternoon she has pensively contemplated the sun sinking into the spiked rushes and the cold waters of the bay. Farther on, along the beaches, men with their trousers rolled up to their knees were catching crabs as they scuttled off into the sand. A family of blue herons stalked about among the bushes, and a sea eagle took off, a fish in its talons, amidst a vigorous flapping of wings.

But Betsy is looking forward to different distractions. Aunt Nancy, who has returned from one of her periodic stays in Washington, has come to tea and has invited her niece to go on a little escapade to Philadelphia with her. Her old friend, the banker Stephen Girard, has invited them to the wedding of his niece Henriette. She is marrying General Henri Lallemand.

He is one of the many Napoleonic generals who have taken refuge in America and are living in Philadelphia. A grand celebration has been planned, for Stephen Girard is wealthy. The Toussards will be there, but Betsy's former guardian angel, the colonel, has died the previous year. On the other hand, it is announced that Joseph Bonaparte will attend. He has bought land at Bordentown, not far from Philadelphia, and has built a superb villa there. As a matter of convenience, he has taken the name of Comte de Survilliers. People say that he is a simple and friendly man.

A little change in her routine is bound to please Betsy. After all, even Philadelphia may be a rather austere city — what with its overly symmetrical streets that cross at right angles and the quietist attitudes of its population — but it does have an intense intellectual and artistic life, and lately even an Academy of Beaux-Arts. In the evenings, the society ladies receive in their drawing rooms, where one meets a great many foreigners. And the city's main artery, Chestnut Street, is as lively as New York's Broadway.

The Girard household is hopping. The French chef and his black kitchen boys busily crowd around the stoves to prepare the meal for the great day: oysters braised with bacon and onion, stuffed crab, baked ham, marinated muskrat, ginger cakes, and charlotte russe.

General Henri Lallemand has just turned forty. A fine figure of a man, he has commanded the artillery of the guard at Waterloo, and been sentenced to death in absentia, as has his brother Charles. Also present at the wedding is General Clausel with his handsome, taciturn face, General Vandamme, and Lefebre-Desnouettes, the general who, having rallied to Louis XVIII in 1814, abandoned his post as soon as he learned of Napoleon's landing at Golfe-Juan and hurried to serve his idol.

All these people are friends of the Comte de Survilliers, who keeps in close contact with them and frequently invites them to Point Breeze. But alas, Joseph is not well and will not attend. At dinner Betsy is seated to the right of General Charles Lallemand, Henri's older brother. As she secretly scrutinizes his energetic face, his knotty hands, his bushy eyebrows, and the graying short locks that hang over his neck, she is taken by an involuntary shudder. She suddenly feels an irrepressible need to know more about this man who had been so close to the Emperor and who, to his utter despair, had been unable to follow him to Saint Helena as he had hoped to do. He had been present, his face bathed in tears, when Napoleon sailed on the *Bellerophone.* He would have given his life for him, he tells Betsy. And so, indeed, would all of them, except perhaps Clausel, who claims not to have had any attachment to his person. He simply enthralled his officers!

Lallemand is now thinking about founding a colony in Alabama, where he and some of his friends plan to introduce the vine and the olive tree. While he details to the young woman the itinerary along the Tombigbee River he will follow with his companions, the financial support they expect to receive from Stephen Girard and rich merchants in Boston and Philadelphia, Betsy wonders whether she will dare confess to him that she too loved the Emperor, and that she too is in possession of some Napoleonic trophies. She has, for instance, a sheet of white, completely unmarked paper, a page of the unfinished manuscript of the *Commentary on Macchiavelli* at which Napoleon worked at odd moments during his campaigns, and which was found in the carriage he had abandoned at Waterloo when he fled on horseback. This trophy, which she treasures, was given to her by General Wellington this past winter in Paris . . . but can she admit this?

It has been a jolly party: there has been dancing, people have gotten a little tipsy, the generals have gone in for all kinds of clowning (one of them had the bright idea of imitating the voice of an officer afflicted with a stutter who tried in vain to shout his orders at Waterloo!), and many toasts have been brought: to America, to the republican way of life, to the Emperor, to La Fayette, and to lots of others. . . . They have danced the gigue, the counterdance, and even the French cotillion. Betsy, laughing, her face flushed, and her head spinning, has collapsed on her bed late that night amidst a rush of thoughts that has suddenly obliterated ten years of trying to find her way among anguish, moroseness, resentment, and moments of pride. This evening she has been close to the Emperor as never before. How she would love to follow these men in their epic adventure!

A few months later she learns from Mme Toussard that in the end General Charles Lallemand, with whom she had had such a lively conversation at that wedding, has not gone to Alabama as he had planned. Clausel and Lefebvre, however, have indeed laid the foundations of a colony along the Tombigbee River. Their business is not flourishing, for as convinced revolutionaries, they have refused to use slaves, and they also lack commercial acumen. . . . Lefebvre's farm is doing better than Clausel's, who is going in for market gardening and sells his vegetables on the Mobile market in person. The two have also built small towns settled by French soldiers and officers, places like Arcole, Marengo, and Aigleville (the present Demopolis). As for the Lallemand brothers, they are planning to go to Texas to found a community along the Trinity River, for which they have already found a name: it is to be "Champ d'Asile." This is not quite as straightforward. Why should they settle so close to Mexico? There is a strong suspicion that they are planning to aid that country's uprising. There are those who believe that there is a Napoleonic confederation aimed at freeing the Emperor and creating a vast American kingdom that he would rule. This may be no more than the brainchild of the overwrought imagination of a police obsessed by fears of a return of the imperial regime. But in any case, the French ambassador, Baron Hyde de Neuville, is firmly convinced of its existence. He sees conspiracy everywhere, they fill his dreams. He has received information about a concentration of ships and French soldiers at Pernambuco in Brazil, that is, at America's farthest outcropping in the South Atlantic. These reports say that King Joseph has been approached but refuses to become openly involved in these conspiracies. Speaking of Joseph, Mme Toussard has seen him recently and spoken to him of Betsy, whose son he very much wants to meet. "Send him to me," Mme Toussard concludes, "so that I can arrange a meeting, which will have to be as discreet as possible. Above all, it must not look as if it were planned."

Joseph Bonaparte, who had left France in 1815 after Waterloo, had reached America unimpeded, having sailed from Rochefort, where he had offered to his brother Napoleon to take his place. But the Emperor had refused. Now the ex-king of Spain is in exile, separated from his wife, Queen Julie, and his two daughters, Zenaïde and Charlotte, who had been assigned residence in Italy. Rumor has it that the queen has a few replacements, and that Joseph even has children by them.

After having lived in Philadelphia for a time, he now leads the life of a gentleman-farmer at Point Breeze near Bordentown on the shores of the Delaware. A man of gentle and affable disposition, he has made many friends in the area and frequently receives visitors.

Betsy, of course, would favor a meeting between the uncle and the nephew. She has never forgotten the letter Joseph wrote her shortly after her marriage to Jérôme. This would be a first step toward the Bonaparte family.

During the fall of 1818 Mme Toussard, who sometimes meets the count at the homes of mutual friends, speaks to him of young Bo's good qualities. Once again Joseph expresses his desire to see him. Perhaps his presence will attenuate his unhappiness at the separation from his own daughters. So it is decided that during Christmas vacation "Cricket will visit Mme Toussard in Philadelphia." And sure enough, on 31 December, New Year's Eve, his uncle invites him to lunch.

That morning, Bo is very nervous when he wakes up. His uncle is supposed to send his carriage for him. Meanwhile he must get ready, and the adolescent casts a critical eye on his spencer of beige cotton serge and the striped trousers that form pockets at the knees.

But the boy's worries vanish as soon as he finds himself in his uncle's presence. He is a man of middling size, with kindly brown eyes, dressed in simple, casual clothes. His warmth is so contagious that soon the two talk as if they were old friends.

When he arrived, Bo had admired the superb view one enjoys from that long white villa perched on the top of a hill overlooking the Delaware and the Cross Rivers. As he walked in, he had a glimpse of statues of mythological gods and goddesses in the park; their nudity had intrigued him, for America does not yet share the Europeans' taste for Italian-style antiquities.

His uncle gives him a tour of the long gallery of busts of members of the Bonaparte family that he shows only to intimate friends. The atmosphere of this sanctuary, where Bo is surrounded by white and ghost-like marble faces, makes the young boy shiver.

"This is your father," says Joseph pointing to a curly head with regular features next to the Canova busts of Elisa Bacchiochi and Pauline Borghese. Silently and with pinched lips, the adolescent briefly looks at this father whom he does not know, while his uncle furtively watches him. "He looks intelligent and strong-willed, that boy," he thinks to himself.

Then they have a good lunch and a long horseback ride in the park; it has been a pleasant visit. When Bo takes his leave, Joseph tells him, "Please consider this house your own."

He would like to see him again, he insists, adding that he must go to New York the next week and inviting Bo to accompany him, if he would enjoy that. When Bo hesitates, pointing out that he must have his mother's and his grandfather's permission, Joseph specifies that he will take the Tuesday diligence. If Bo has permission by then, he is to let Joseph know. If not, here is his address in New York: Pension Michel, 7th Avenue. He might join him there, if necessary.

A few days later, Bo receives a favorable answer from Baltimore. Flushed with excitement, his heart beating hard, he climbs into the stagecoach that will take him to New York. This is the first trip he takes by himself! What an experience! Especially since he is going to the liveliest city in the United States, the place of which he has dreamed since his childhood!

The Comte de Survilliers does not disappoint his nephew's expectations. In the three days they spend together, he does his best to entertain him and takes him to a good tailor for a new suit. They go to the theater, to restaurants. Bo, who is accustomed to living with a grandfather who is rather thrifty despite his wealth does not believe his eyes as he watches his uncle's lavish expenditures. Yes indeed, it's not too bad being the nephew of an ex-king!

He would not mind if this fairytale outing continued a little longer, but in Baltimore people are interested in serious things and won't hear of it. One morning a stern letter from Mr. Patterson arrives at the pension Michel: the grandfather is calling his grandson to order. Has he forgotten that his vacation is over and that he is supposed to go back to school? A bit sheepishly, Bo returns to Baltimore, much to the disappointment of his uncle, whom he had greatly amused with the naiveté of his remarks and his ability to marvel at everything.

Betsy had turned pink with pleasure when listening to her son's lively report of his stay in Philadelphia and then New York. "Now this seems to me to be a good omen for his future relations with his father's family," she says to herself. "Of course, Joseph is no doubt the best of them." Mr. Patterson, for his part, has not shown the same satisfaction. His grandson has been overly indulged by his uncle; this is no way to bring him up properly!

Meanwhile, Betsy loses no time writing to the count to thank him for his kindness and to ask him to come to visit them if he ever passes through Baltimore. But the winter passes and this occasion does not arise.

Bo has seen his uncle two or three times, always with the same pleasure. He has had long discussions with him about his plans for the future. Joseph has urged him to go to the military academy at West Point, but Bo is not much of a militarist and would rather go to law school. To hear the boy tell it, Joseph is a sugar-daddy: he loves children and likes to watch those of his neighborhood play, often showering them with sweets and presents.

Spring brings a letter from Geneva: the Collage Saint-Antoine has admitted Bo as a student. Betsy will take lodgings in one of the boardinghouses recommended by the Gallatins. She decides to leave by early summer.

And so it is that when the Comte de Survilliers finally decides to go through Baltimore — on his way to Mount Vernon in Virginia, where he wants to visit the grave of his old friend George Washington — Betsy and her son have already packed their bags and are on their way to New York. There they will board the *Syren,* one of the Patterson firm's brigs, which within a few days will set sail for Holland. From there they will go to Geneva, possibly making a little detour to Paris.

William Patterson. Painting by Thomas Sully.

Betsy Patterson in Paris, 1817. At the time of this painting, she was thirty-two and had been separated from Jérôme for twelve years.

Miniature of Jérôme Bonaparte as a young man of nineteen.

Napoleon Bonaparte, First Consul, about 1800. He signed his name Bonaparte until he was crowned emperor, after which he signed it Napoleon.

The castle of Tuileries, where Napoleon lived as First Consul and as emperor. The central part was called "Pavillon Central." The garden looked like this when Napoleon resided there.

*General Samuel Smith, Dorcas
Patterson's brother-in-law and Betsy
Patterson's uncle.*

*Samuel Chase's son-in-law, Commodore
Joshua Barney, who met Jérôme in
Washington, brought him to Baltimore,
and introduced him to the Pattersons.*

*Letizia Bonaparte, mother of
Jérôme and Napoleon
Bonaparte. Princess Pauline
Borghese introduced her to Betsy
in 1821–22. Letizia treated
Betsy kindly and appreciated her
son, Bo, whom she tried to induce
to marry Charlotte, Joseph
Bonaparte's daughter. She did not
include Bo in her last will.*

Napoleon's Brothers

Joseph, below, about 1806, at his estate near Paris. Painted by K. Girardet, engraved by P. Giradet. (Bibliothèque Marmottan, Boulogne-Billancourt.) Joseph was later exiled in Bordentown, near Philadelphia, and invited Bo there in January 1819. The two enjoyed a close relationship.

Lucien Bonaparte preferred the life of a scientist and writer to political power. Betsy once found him at an archeological site with sleeves rolled up, wearing a straw hat, and carrying a crayon and notebook.

Jérôme Bonaparte as king of Westphalia, about 1810.

Marquis de Lafayette, painted in 1826, at the time he returned to the United States. He was a friend of William Patterson.

Jérôme in 1825 or 1826, at the time he was exiled in Rome. Then in his forties, he probably gave this portrait to his son, Bo, whom he met for the first time.

Mrs. Jérôme Bonaparte, painted by Firmin Massot in Geneva, 1823.

The dining room at Jérôme's palace, Napoleonshoehe, in Kassel, Westphalia.

Throne room of Napoleonshoehe.

Lady Sydney Morgan, a writer and great friend of Betsy's. The two met in Paris in 1815. (Bibliothèque Nationale, Paris.)

Charlotte Bonaparte, daughter of Napoleon's brother Joseph. Bo was almost engaged to Charlotte, but the betrothal fell through. Nevertheless, they remained friends, and she wrote to him often. (Bibliothèque Marmottan, Bologne-Billancourt.)

Letizia Bonaparte in Rome at the age of eighty-five.

Susan May Williams married Bo in 1829. At first Betsy was furious with the wedding and did not meet Susan until seven years later.

"After the fever of a stormy life she has found rest."

— Epitaph on Betsy Patterson's tombstone

Betsy's son, the phlegmatic Jérôme-Napoleon II, or "Bo," looking very much the Bonaparte.

Colonel Jérôme Napoleon Bonaparte, Betsy's elder grandson. He was a close friend of Napoleon III, serving in his army and as the empress's bodyguard in exile. (Bust by H. F. Iselin, 1859.)

Six-year-old Charles Joseph Bonaparte, Betsy's younger grandson, later served President Theodore Roosevelt and created the Federal Bureau of Investigation.

17

$\mathcal{A}$MSTERDAM, WHERE BETSY HAD ARRIVED AFTER a long voyage — seven weeks — had brought back unhappy memories. She had gone to see the consul-general of France to ask for a laissez-passer to cross his country.

She had found herself facing a rather cold-looking gentleman, who had intently stared at her adolescent son before exclaiming: "My word, how he resembles his uncle, the ex-Emperor!" He had hesitated for or a moment, frowning and reading the passports in his hands over and over again, while nervously tapping the table. Then he had looked up: "Well now, Madame, this is impossible. . . . You know perfectly well that all members of the Bonaparte family are proscribed. So I would have to pass this matter on to our minister of the interior, even to the government. . . . All this will take time. Moreover, even assuming that we will obtain this permission, you will be exposed to very serious danger."

So she had had to resign herself to a longer and more costly itinerary through Germany, much to "Cricket's" disappointment.

In Geneva, Betsy and her son take lodgings in the Pension Chougny, which had been recommended by Mrs. Gallatin. They rent an apartment for two years. Even if the cost of living is much less here than in London or Paris, Betsy decides to live as modestly as possible: no butler or footman, just a simple maid. For a very moderate price, the *pension* agrees to send lunch and dinner to her apartment.

To be sure, most of the mistresses of well-to-do households in Geneva also lead very simple lives, doing some of their own housework and going around in sedan-chairs, for almost no one here owns a private carriage. The only luxury of the Genevans is the country house on the hillside of Voirons or Salève, where they go by charabanc or "basket cart." The Genevans are passionate about the countryside. Botany, geology, and natural history occupy all their spare time.

A few days after they have moved in, Betsy and Bo are awakened by the sound of fifes. Bo rushes to the window and sees a battalion of lancers marching by, wearing bicorne hats, their legs covered in white gaiters. Behind them come groups of school children, throwing flowers and carrying long banners inscribed "Glory to Jean-Jacques!" and "Long live Nature!" Mounted on boards, young girls carry a statue of liberty and a bust of Rousseau. This is the nature festival, someone explains to Betsy. Handsome blonde and red-haired peasant women in blue skirts and red blouses laced in front give out carnations in the street; the atmosphere is filled with simple and good-natured gaiety. From afar one hears the chimes of Saint Peter's Cathedral, which play a different tune every day of the week. Today it is Jean-Jacques Rousseau's *Le dévin du village*.

A certain Mr. Astor from New York is also staying at the Pension Chougny. He is with his daughter, a rather awkward adolescent, not very pretty, but pleasant enough. Her father has enrolled her in the same boarding school that Bo will attend, which is not surprising, since the school has been indicated to him by the Gallatins, who are his friends.

John Jacob Astor, a fur trader who has amassed a solid fortune in the United States, is an amiable and thoughtful gentleman. He is elegant, buys his clothes in London, enhances his cravats with a diamond pin, and changes his shoes every day. But Bo finds him vulgar.

"Did you see, Mommy, how he eats his ice cream and his peas with a knife? You would think he has never heard of a spoon." But perhaps Bo is a bit jealous, seeing that the handsome man is interested in his mother. A widower, Jacob Astor would indeed not mind at all to join his life to that of his exquisite compatriot. But Betsy remains ice-cold.

In the fall, Jacob Astor regretfully informs her that his business requires him to leave for Italy. He will go to Rome and Florence, he tells her, in a large coach he has rented with two friends. Would Madame Patterson have a message for the Bonapartes, who for the most part have taken refuge there, except for Jérôme and his sister Elisa, who reside in Trieste? He would no doubt have occasion to meet them.

Six months later, the miracle has happened. Flushed and with a quickened heartbeat, she breaks the seal of a letter from Rome. It is from Mr. Astor, and she slowly reads:

> Last evening we had the honor of being presented to Princess Borghese, who immediately questioned me about you and your son. When I told her that I left you in Geneva, she expressed great regret that you had not come with us. Then she said: "I am very glad to have this opportunity of speaking frankly to you. I very much wish to see Mme Patterson and her son here. . . . I am planning to make a donation to the son of my brother, who is poor and has nothing to give him. But I am rich and childless and feel that I would like to do everything for him." And then she asked me to write to you promptly and to urge you in her name to pay her a visit, bringing along your son.

"What should I do?" Betsy wonders as she puts down the letter. A great many feelings crowd in on her. First of all she is curious to meet this woman who is still famous for her beauty, particularly since some people claim that she resembles her.

But this *Paolina* also has the reputation of being extremely flighty. Can she be trusted? She is rich, that much is certain, for her husband, Prince Camillo Borghese, from whom she is only separated, provides her with a considerable income. She lives alone, served by a large domestic staff, in a superb palazzo overlooking the city of Rome.

"Come to think of it," Betsy concludes, "I myself could spend three months with the princess next fall!"

> I think I shall have to leave Cricket at his present boarding school [she writes to her father], for his education is the only fortune I can provide for his future. I think it is better if for the moment he does not know about the advantages that are being offered to him, for I believe it would make little sense to

count on them as long as he has not acquired a solid education that will allow him to occupy an honorable position in life. Perhaps the princess is sincere right now, but it is risky for a nephew to speculate on the fortune of a pretty woman of thirty-seven. If I took my son to live in a palace, he would naturally prefer pleasure to studying; the Italians have a delightful way of life, but it does not promote anything solid. Once he went down there, I might have a difficult time bringing him back here; and yet the dispositions of the princess, though favorable to us right now, might well change, and the educational facilities to be found down there are much inferior to those I have found here — always provided I would be allowed to exert my authority, which is not likely. I wish to bring him up to think that he must count only on himself to build his fortune, profiting at the same time from his relatives' good intentions but not allowing this to interfere with his career. This point of view has the full approval of the most enlightened persons around me. I see to it that he gets a smattering of Greek, a thorough knowledge of Latin and mathematics, French and English; after that he will take courses in physics and chemistry before beginning the study of jurisprudence. History, geography, and mythology are naturally part of the subjects he is studying now, as are drawing, riding, fencing, and dancing. Not to forget proper manners and the social graces. Every Saturday night he goes to a ball, where he meets some of the most prominent persons in Europe. Sundays are devoted to exercise and visits. I see to it that he works hard at his studies, and I go to see his professors all the time. In short, if he were to remain ignorant and narrow-minded, it would not be my fault. I spare neither money nor effort to give him every possible advantage and to fulfill my maternal duties conscientiously. . . . I hope that he will reward me for my efforts by being a success, and I am glad that he is my only child. . . .

The princess's wish to have me stay with her has advantages as well as disadvantages. Rome is a delightful place, and she occupies a superb palace, where she receives the homage of distinguished foreigners. . . . She lives on a grand footing, but she is spoiled and capricious, which is only natural for a princess and a pretty woman. But people say that she is fundamentally kind. As for me, I would of course prefer Rome to Geneva, a palace to my apartment, pleasure to work, elegance to economy, my liberty to all these lures, and my child's interest to any other consideration. Whether I leave will depend on the reply I receive.

Without waiting for her father's opinion, Betsy decides to write to Princess Borghese:

Madame, your generous intentions that have been relayed to me by Mr. Astor have filled me with gratitude and sharpened my chagrin at not having the advantage of knowing you personally. My objective in coming to Geneva is to provide my son with a distinguished education, which is not available in America, and to give him the simple kind of life that will be appropriate to the destiny I can offer him. I have brought him up to understand that I have a limited fortune to give him and that his rank in the world will depend on his own efforts. Convinced that it is one of the greatest misfortunes to have pretensions without realistic expectations, I have tried to keep him away from false ambition and to direct those he does have toward the cultivation of his intellectual possibilities. He may not have great abilities, but if he works hard enough, they are sufficient to attain an honorable rank in society. So far I have no reason to complain about his application. My first desire, indeed my first duty, is to give him a distinguished education, and I have found all the facilities for doing so in Geneva. This is why I came here, and I shall stay here to make sure he uses them. This will not prevent me from traveling to Italy a few months from now in order to tell you, Madame, how much I am touched by your kind interest in my son and to show you my gratitude. I would even present Jérôme to you if I were less determined never to interrupt his education. Personal merit is the only legacy worthy of his name that I can bequeath to him.
. . .

In April she receives another letter from Jacob Astor, telling her that he has again called on Princess Borghese, who has bombarded him with questions about his young compatriot. Yes, he has told her, her father is very wealthy, but his fortune is mostly in real estate, which for the moment does not produce much income. Also that, in addition to Betsy, he has seven other children. No, Madame Patterson-Bonaparte has never received a penny from the king of Westphalia. On the other hand, the Emperor has for many years paid her a pension, but of course that has ceased after 1814. "If you want my opinion," Mr. Astor continues, "don't budge for the moment and do not entrust your son to anybody."

Betsy does not know what to do.

Traveling is very expensive and the princess is capricious [she writes in a second letter to her father]. Nonetheless, Bo must absolutely meet his grandmother, old Madame Letizia. . . . But what if he were to get caught in the papal states, being included in the list of proscribed Bonapartes? And what if I could not bring him back to Geneva? Moreover, the Bonapartes are not as wealthy as they are said to be, except for Joseph. As for the ex-king of Westphalia, he continues to spend money with reckless abandon, buying houses where he does not live afterwards. . . . I prefer to let some time pass. Actually, Princess Borghese has never written to confirm her offer. It was probably just talk.

Lady Morgan also writes from Rome, where she has met Princess Borghese and formed a close relationship with her. Still, she describes her extravagance and the whims to which she feels entitled as a pretty woman.

Above all [she writes to Betsy] do not entrust your son to her! It would be the end of his education. He would fill his head with hot air and false ideas of imperial splendor. If you could hear them address each other as "Your Highness" and "Your Grandeur" all day long! And make elaborate plans for their approaching return to France and their reconquest of power! As for Pauline, why do you think she is so anxious to invite your son? To upset her brother and his wife, big Catherine,

that's all! She detests them and accuses them of having behaved badly toward the family after they went into exile. She
has broken off all relations with them. . . . As for Madame
Letizia, she is full of good sense and dignity. If such a promise
came from her, one could definitely trust it. Unfortunately, she
has not said a word about it. In any case, what little she has she
will leave to her children, who throw money out of the windows, and there will be nothing left to give to the grandchildren.

Do you know [she adds] that Princess Borghese has asked
me whether it is true that you resemble her as much as it is
said?

In June Jacob Astor returns to Geneva. He is as amiable and eager
as ever, but Betsy calmly and with a smile puts him in his place. He too
advises the young woman against making the journey to Rome. "Listen to me," he says, "and stay here. Soon it will be summer. . . . Who
knows, down there you might not be able to get away when you want
or you might even be made to stay for good. Moreover, even if the
Bonaparte family lavishes fine words on your son, they will probably
not lift a finger to help him, and you will be the one to defray the entire
cost of this journey."

18

*N*OW THAT SUMMER IS HERE, GENEVA IS ONCE
again filled with tourists; foreigners flock in from every side. Here is
Princess Galitzin, who is to become a close friend of Betsy's; also her
cousin, Princess Potemkin; Count and Countess Cavour with their only
son, a boy "with an enormous head and intelligent eyes behind his
spectacles," as James Gallatin puts it in his diary. Here too is Comtesse
de Boigne, and especially Count Demidoff, the most lavish member of
this noble crowd. He is the richest man in Europe, and the foundation
of his family's fortune had been laid by an ancestor, a simple serf, who
made weapons for Peter the Great. The streets of Geneva see a procession
of luxurious carriages, the most extravagant of which, drawn by six or
eight horses, are those of the Russians. At night superb fireworks soar
over the banks of the lake, and fabulous parties for seven to eight hundred guests are given in various châteaux in the surrounding country.

Betsy and her son are invited to all these receptions. There is only
one shadow on this bright picture: the city's gates close at 11:00 PM.
On those long summer evenings, one can therefore not linger in the
countryside or go to see the full moon from the Vevey side. In town all
balls stop at midnight, and one has to play Cinderella and demurely go
home.

Bo obediently goes along with whatever his mother wants to do.
But he prefers the simple pleasures, such as excursions to alpine meadows led by his teachers; these are ideal places to launch the study of
plants and minerals. He asks his grandfather for a little money to buy a

horse, alleging that this will save his mother the expense of renting one every week for his riding lessons. But when Betsy hears of this whim, she puts her foot down, fearing that a horse will give her son too much independence and allow him to ride off into the countryside as he pleases.

Sometimes Bo writes rather sad letters to old Mr. Patterson, who must enormously enjoy what he reads: "Now that I am living here, I dine with princes and princesses and the most important people in Europe, but I have never found any dish I like more than the roast beef and the steaks I had in South Street." He has also adopted a young dark gray dog to which he has given the name Wolf and which follows him everywhere when school is out.

Betsy has a new admirer, Count Demidoff. This elderly gentleman, who loves pretty women, is fabulously wealthy, for he owns mines producing coal, copper, iron, and malachite in the Urals, along with hundreds of villages and thousands of serfs. He divides his time among Florence, where he has a fabulous palace, Paris, where he lodges in his townhouse on the Boulevard des Italiens, and Saint-Petersburg, where his position is not as grand, since everyone knows that his nobility is of quite recent origin.

He is an extremely cultivated man, who maintains his own theatrical troupe known as "The Demidoff Players." It can be called upon to perform comedies, vaudeville shows, and comic operas. Demidoff's parties are unbelievably lavish, and people flock to attend them. For himself, worn out as he is before his time, an insomniac crippled by rheumatism, he is happy above all when he can give pleasure to others; there is little joy in his own life. The only persons capable of making him laugh, he confesses to Betsy, are Princess Galitzin and herself.

How different he is from Sismondi, who sometimes seeks relaxation from his writing by taking his wife for a carriage ride to an alpine meadow or to the terraces of the Saconnex, from where one has a magnificent view of the Alps when the weather is clear. Sometimes their small carriage, drawn by two horses, Brillant and Cadet, stops at the door of the Pension Chougny.

"Betsy, can you come along? Come and admire 'beautiful nature' with us!"

The Sismondis, of course, do not go to Count Demidoff's balls.

They prefer a simple and retiring life in their villa "de Chêne," which serves as a meeting place for liberal philosophers and men of science from all over Europe. They heave a sigh of relief when at summer's end the society of interlopers that has made Geneva such a lively place finally dissipates. "Now all of this belongs to us!" Jenny Sismondi happily exclaims when she sees the promenade cleared of walkers.

Living at the home of the philosopher and his wife is another colorful figure, the charming Charles-Victor de Bonstetten, philosopher and sometime poet, a dilettante interested in everything. The very type of the cosmopolitan man of letters of the Old Régime, he became a friend of Mme de Staël, having much earlier been a disciple of Voltaire. For this Monsieur de Bonstetten is no youngster; he is at the very least seventy-five years old, although he seems ten years younger, and continues to pay court to young women, Betsy in particular, to whom he declares, "You may not have reigned in Westphalia, but then you are the Queen of all hearts, which is much better!"

From time to time he dictates his *Souvenirs* to a young female secretary, and since he has plenty of leisure time, he often calls on Betsy, takes her to a concert or shopping to the city's craft shops — clock makers, goldsmiths, enamelers — where one can admire veritable miniature masterpieces.

He tells her about his travels in Holland, Scandinavia, London, Paris, and Italy, from where he has brought back a *Voyage dans le Latium*.

"Long ago, you know, I almost committed suicide," he reveals to her one evening. "This was at the time when I found myself back in Berne between the four walls of my father's house, after I had known the most brilliant society and the greatest minds of Europe. Yet now the horizon was completely closed to me. . . . One night I wanted to put an end to my suffering. I can still see myself lying on the floor in my shirt, flanked by two loaded pistols, waiting for the decisive moment, when the moon appeared. The moon, denizen of a higher sphere! At that moment the mountain of my suffering was reduced to the size of a mere ant hill."

"I know just what you mean," Betsy says.

Tightly closing her lips and clutching her parasol, she conjures up Baltimore, her father's severe silhouette, and the disapproval in everyone' eyes. How many times she too had thought about this extreme measure, but then there was Bo; happily there was Bo.

In late July 1820, the Gallatins have come for a vacation, bringing news from Paris.

According to Albert, the face of France has changed. People are beginning to reject the king. Even those who acclaimed him five years ago now look at him askance because of heavy taxes, unpopular laws, and the White Terror that has revealed the regime's intolerance. The Pavilion Marsan, still the residence of the Comte d'Artois and his family, has become the rallying point of the ultras, who call for increasingly harsh measures. As bad luck would have it, there have been several bad harvests. Misery is great in the countryside, which is infested by roaming hordes of brigands; there is discontent among the peasants. As time goes on the Emperor, now that he is far away, is acquiring a halo of glory, and a legend springs up around him: he would not have tolerated such social inequality, it is said; had he not liked to sit around the fire with his men at the bivouac? Nor do people appreciate the Duchesse d'Angoulême, daughter of Louis XVI; they can see that she will never forget the tragic hours of long ago. People are wrong, of course, for they forget the heavy costs for the wars of the Empire, the conscription, and the tribute in deaths and injuries the nation was made to pay.

It is also whispered that Napoleon has been able to flee from Saint-Helena and that certain of his officers, who had fled to America, had engineered his escape.

Could this be true? Betsy feels her head swim. Will she finally meet the Emperor? She suddenly remembers what Mme Toussard had told her confidentially three years ago in Philadelphia, namely, that the Champ d'Asile colony in Texas was nothing but a cover for less innocent activities than raising crops on the poor soils of Texas. Ah, that Champ d'Asile! Betsy can still see the grave look of General Lallemand: "I adored the Emperor. . . . If I had been allowed, I would have followed him to Saint-Helena."

But while she is dreaming of what might be, she hears Albert Gallatin say a few sentences that in one fell swoop annihilate this vision of a

Napoleon building a new empire in America, starting out from Mexico. The Champ d'Asile colony has failed. Subscriptions had been solicited from bonapartists and liberals, especially by Benjamin Constant in his review *Minerve*. But these funds never reached their destination, or rather reached it when the colony had disappeared the previous year, decimated by disease, sadness, and flooded fields, whereupon the last survivors had been expelled by the Spanish government. What a sad end to this epic of the "farmer-soldier!"

James Gallatin, for his part, has witnessed a dramatic event, the assassination of the Duc de Berry, the youngest son of the Duc d'Artois, the prince who had been married with such pomp in 1816. Apparently the murderer, a certain Louvel, had acted alone; working as a groom, he was a veteran of the Empire. James, who that evening had escorted Princess Galitzin and her daughter Katja to the opera, talks in a voice shaking with emotion about the horror he experienced: as he left the theater between two ballets to get a breath of fresh air, he saw the duke coming out, held up by the duchess, with a dagger stuck in his chest. The victim was quickly laid on a sofa until help arrived, and he, James, had been asked to help maintain order by standing at one of the doors to ensure that no one entered or left the opera house. What a terrible night! Meanwhile, the performance continued in the hall, where no one knew what had happened. Snatches of music drifted out.

He is not about to forget this, he concludes. No, things are not going well in France. . . . But the Duchesse de Berry expects a child in the fall.

In October, the Gallatins return to Paris, and Betsy stays in Geneva. Still no letter from Princess Borghese! Bo is a good student, "much better in mathematics than in modern languages."

NOW THAT GENEVA IS A LITTLE MORE DESERTED AND GIVEN BACK TO FAMILY life and evenings by the fireside, Betsy sees more of her good Swiss friends. The Sismondis have moved to their winter home and have settled down in their house on the place Bourg-de-Four, where she is a frequent guest. Mr. Astor is traveling again.

But here are a couple of newcomers, whose name and title are painful to hear for Betsy: Prince and Princess of Württemberg. . . . They are the uncle and aunt of Catherine, Jérôme's second wife, the ex-queen of Westphalia.

Having taken the waters at Aix-en-Savoie, they have come to spend the winter in Geneva. Both are dazzled by the charm and the beauty of Elizabeth, cannot praise her enough, and invite her to their house at every turn. The Prince of Württemberg confidentially tells anybody who wants to hear it that Jérôme has made a monumental mistake when he abandoned so delightful a woman.

Has Jérôme gotten wind of these remarks? At any rate, he writes to his ex-spouse from Trieste, asking for her indulgence. His present financial situation, he explains — that is to say the income the receives from his father-in-law and from the czar of Russia — is barely sufficient to feed his family. What he forgets to mention is that his expensive tastes, the luxury and the large retinue with which he continues to surround himself, cause his funds to melt away at a rapid rate. "Elisa," he continues in a playful tone, "you know me too well to suppose that I have ever thought about accumulating a personal fortune!"

These few lines, hastily scribbled by her ex-husband, have awakened some vague yearnings in Betsy. "After all," she confides to her father, "I think that he is not as bad a person as is generally believed, and that many of his flaws and his bad behavior are caused by his extravagance and his follies."

But the oldest of the Bonaparte brothers also writes to her: Joseph, Comte de Survilliers, invites Betsy to live at his superbly furnished château of Prangins near Geneva. No one is using it, he says, since his wife Julie and his two daughters Charlotte and Zénaïde reside in Florence and Rome. Elizabeth only has to say the word and he will send instructions to his agent in Switzerland. The young woman cordially thanks him but tells him that she cannot accept his offer since she does not have her own carriage and would be too far from Geneva. "My son," she adds, "would really like to write to you more often, but his inexperience in writing letters and the timidity that is natural at his age discourage him. He is extremely attached to you. . . . I never cease to regret, Monsieur, the unfortunate circumstances that prevented me from making your personal acquaintance, and to hope that time will repair so grievous a privation by one day taking me to a place close to you. . . .

People who have the honor of knowing you find that my son is fortunate enough to resemble you, and I am extremely pleased to hear it. It is true that he has a fine head, and since he has grown six inches in the last two years, I believe he will be fairly tall. He is doing well in his studies."

Then, in rapid succession, the world learns of two deaths: first that of Elisa, ex-grand duchess of Tuscany, who lived in exile in Trieste and whose children will at least initially be entrusted to Jérôme, and then, in July — with a delay of one month — that of Napoleon, who has died on his rock of Saint Helena.

When Betsy hears the cries of the newspaper vendors: "Death of Napoleon on Saint-Helena, two pennies!" she collapses into a chair, covers her face with her hands, and sobs inconsolably: "Oh, the irony of fate," she thinks. "How quickly everyone has forgotten that for years this man made the whole world tremble!" As always when the Emperor's name is spoken in her presence, contradictory feelings rush through her soul, and a thousand images come to mind. Swept away by grief, she can only repeat over and over: "This is the end, I shall never see him!"

In Paris, Albert Gallatin, who has received floods of letters from Bonapartists imploring him to use his influence with Louis XVIII to persuade him to allow the return to France of their hero's body, is surprised to find Betsy's small handwriting among these letters; she expresses to him the sorrow she feels and the admiration she still has, despite everything, for the great man.

The shock of this death has overthrown Betsy's plans. Considering that the Bonapartes do not seem to enjoy very good health, would it not be better to present Bo to his paternal family, and particularly his grandmother, before it is too late?

Her friends in Geneva now encourage her to do just that. Charles de Bonstetten even offers to draft a letter for her. And so, in the fall of 1821, she decides to take the plunge: She will go to Rome, and not by herself as she had initially planned, but with Bo.

I hope that his education will not materially suffer from this interruption of his studies, which he will in fact be able to continue during the few months we will be spending in Rome.

He can take Latin and Italian lessons while there. I have reserved three seats in a six-person coach at the rate of 15 louis d'or per person from here to Rome; the two daily meals are included in the price, as are overnight stays in hotels and heating if needed. As for the maid, she will be sitting with the coachman; the cost for her will be only seven louis d'or.

And off they go on the route to Simplon!

19

*A*FTER AN EXHAUSTING JOURNEY, BETSY FIRST sees Rome with its seven hills through a haze of tears. Her nose is congested, she has sinusitis, a sore throat, and a terrible headache. Poor auspices indeed for a first meeting with the Bonapartes and the Eternal City! She has caught a cold when crossing the Apennines in the early hours of the morning.

As soon as she arrives at the Hôtel d'Europe on the Piazza di Spagna, where she has reserved a room from Florence, she takes to her bed, determined not to budge from it until she has recovered. Over the next few days herb teas and warm woolens rout this recalcitrant cold. Bo paces in his room like a caged lion, so Betsy sends him to get some exercise by walking with his dog Wolf along the banks of the Tiber and in the ruins of the Forum, where the clearing and the archeological digs begun under the Napoleonic administration continue.

Bo has matured in Geneva. He has grown taller and stronger and no longer deserves the nickname of Cricket by which his Aunt Nancy liked to call him in the past. "I just hope that his family will like him," Betsy says to herself as she fondly looks at her offspring.

Meanwhile, Princess Borghese is beginning to worry, for she has not heard from her prospective visitors. All she has learned is that they have left Florence a few days earlier. What has happened? Have they had an accident? Or were they attacked en route by brigands, which abound in the papal states? Fortunately she is able to track them down through a mutual acquaintance, an American lady, and loses no time in sending word to Betsy.

By return mail, Betsy inquires what day and what time would be convenient for her and her son to call on the princess. But Pauline is so impatient to see them that she gives her response to one of her attending ladies . . . instructing her to bring the two Americans to the palace then and there.

The carriage, whose door is decorated with the Borghese coat-of-arms, drives along the Tiber, climbs up the via delle Ripetta and enters the courtyard of a palace with a rather austere facade. But its luxurious interior — all marble, porphyry and mosaics — enchants the eyes of mother and son. Bo inquisitively looks all around, while Betsy keeps telling herself: "If a chance offers itself, one must seize it. . . ." But her heart beats wildly as she follows the lady-in-waiting down long marble-floored corridors lined with masterworks of Italian sculpture and painting.

She walks through salons whose walls are covered with superb tapestries, looks up at ceilings painted with frescoes, and steps on soft carpets. Then, after a few minutes' wait in an antechamber, she and Bo are ushered into the princess's boudoir. At first she does not see anything, for the shutters are closed and the room is suffused in a gentle half-darkness. Coming out of the bright light of a fresh morning, both Betsy and Bo are unable to see. Soon they distinguish a white figure, stretched out on a sofa. Then the image comes into focus: an admirable shape, a delicate face under curly hair, a languid hand held out to them.

"I am delighted to make your acquaintance, Madame," says a soft and melodious voice.

Betsy stammers a reply and intently looks at this face, which is said to resemble her own. She sees the fine shape of a Greek nose, a gently curved mouth, and a pair of delicately framed eyes, like those of all the Bonapartes. She sees more nobility than she herself possesses, but also more nonchalance.

The princess asks her a great many questions about the life she and Bo have. Insatiably she probes every detail, interrogates the adolescent about his studies in America and his encounters with his uncle Joseph. As the young boy talks about himself, easily and without the slightest awkwardness, Pauline secretly watches him as she listens attentively. Ever since the death of Napoleon — which had plunged her into deep despair, particularly since she had finally received permission to join him on Saint-Helena — Pauline has been searching for a reason for living. Balls, meetings with illustrious foreigners, visits to her mother, and amorous dalliances are not sufficient to fill her life. Over the last few months she has cherished the dream of replacing her son Dermide, deceased at the early age of seven, with her American nephew, the oldest son of her brother Jérôme. She also dreams of forming a solid friendship with his mother, the woman who looks so much like her. Will she be disappointed?

Feigning indifference, she caresses the cat that purrs on her lap, but she has already reached a few conclusions. First of all, Bo is poorly dressed, and it is obvious that elegance is the least of his concerns; in this respect he has nothing of a Bonaparte. Betsy's discreet and calm manner rather pleases her, and she notices that the young woman expresses herself in an almost perfect French, decidedly better French than Pauline's, who has never gotten rid of her Corsican accent and cultivates its melodious, lilting intonations. But she finds Betsy possessed of a cold face and an altogether British self-control, which makes it impossible to guess what she is thinking, what she may be suffering. And yet her eyes sparkle when she speaks. She certainly is very pretty!

After this cursory examination, Pauline rings for her butler and asks for luncheon to be served.

That afternoon the temperature is so pleasant that Pauline and her guests feel inspired to take a long walk in the park. Together they follow the contours of a small pond, pass by fountains surrounded by statues, walk along avenues bordered by live oaks, boxwoods, and cypresses, and stop at clumps of pine trees and terraces that afford a view of Rome bathed in diffused afternoon light. Gradually, Betsy's heart calms down. She is listening to *Paolina* who now tells the story of her life, evoking memories of her youth and of the brother she had admired so much, *Nabulione*. The American is fascinated as her imagination shows her a new image, a slender and wiry young officer full of good-natured teasing, who strikes her as more human than the eagle casting its fearful shadow.

When the two women say goodbye, Pauline tells her former sister-in-law, "Madame Letizia impatiently awaits your visit. But please do not attempt to get in touch with her without consulting me. For your first meeting I had better come along."

Clearly, the princess wishes to remain in control of an encounter she has instigated. As her guests leave, she slips a few coins for incidental expenses into her nephew's hand and promises that from now on and until he marries she will send him $400 per year for his clothes. Betsy for her part is given a ball gown, a bonnet, and a cloak of pink satin, all of which suit her to perfection, for she is of the same size as Pauline.

After this encounter Betsy is reassured, at least as far as her future relations with the princess are concerned. But she has yet to meet the rest of Napoleon's family: Louis, Lucien, and above all Madame Mère. Betsy knows they will soon meet and trembles at the very thought.

Poor Madame Letizia; she still inspires fear, tucked away though she is in her palazzo on Piazza Venezia.

THREE STORIES OF A SOBER BUILDING TOPPED BY AN ENCLOSED TERRACE; the Rinuccini palace does not have the splendor of the Villa Borghese or of the Palazzo Torlonia across the square, the residence of a wealthy banker.

On the tympanon over the main entrance an eagle spreads its wings, and Napoleon's statue stands in a niche at the foot of the stairs.

Madame Mère occupies the main apartment on the second floor. Betsy and Bo walk through Nile-green salons adorned with friezes bearing the initials LB and the imperial crown, whose marble fireplaces have been designed by Antonio Canova. The busts lining the gallery do not show Roman or mythological subjects but all the Bonaparte children. And finally they come to the huge room that has been turned into a kind of museum to the memory of Napoleon. There one can see the iron bedstead on which he died at Saint-Helena and the night light that shone over his agony. Further on stand the busts of Napoleon's father, Carlo Bonaparte, and his son, the king of Rome.

This time even Bo feels overwhelmed by the majesty of the locale. He has seen marble busts at his uncle Joseph's and mythological statues at his aunt Pauline's — but nothing can match this atmosphere. His throat is dry as he approaches the deep armchair where an old lady in a dark gray wool dress, wearing a turban of the same color, is sitting bolt upright. With her still lively black eyes she watches Bo cross the room. By her side stands a tall prelate, somewhat stooped and graying at the temples; it is Cardinal Fesch who has come, as he does almost every day, to play a game of *reversi* with his sister.

"My dear daughter," Madame says to Betsy, drawing her to herself and kissing her on the forehead. "Your visit makes me very happy! But let me take a closer look at this beautiful little Jérôme; he certainly does resemble his father . . ."

It is not long before Bo, who has recovered his natural ease, amuses the old lady with his naive stories about his long trip, about Geneva, and about his impressions of Europe. It is true that hand-kissing, bowing and scraping are not to be expected from him, but Madame Letizia likes his directness.

Meanwhile Betsy talks to the cardinal, telling him that the king of Westphalia has never contributed a penny to his son's education. Fesch, who now feels rather badly about having helped his nephew annul the American marriage at the time, frowns in dismay and grumbles, *"Non è possibile. . . .* We must make Jérôme pay an allowance to his son. . . . After all, he now receives a subsidy from his father-in-law, the king of Württemberg."

He will be very glad, he tells Betsy, to write to his nephew, urging him to do what he needs to do for his eldest son; he himself guarantees that it will be done.

Bo and his grandmother have become fast friends; from now on he will go to see her every day to play cards with her or accompany her on her outings, escorted by his dog Wolf. Madame Letizia has also given him forty guineas with which to buy himself a horse, if that is his desire. But Betsy, looking ahead, has confiscated this sum.

"Your grandmother has not thought about the upkeep of a horse," she points out, "but with this money you can hire one every week, that will be quite enough!"

Very pleased that the grandmother and the grandson are getting along so well, she prefers to leave them alone together. Actually, Madame Mère intimidates her a little with her unflagging dignity and her black eyes, which sometimes follow her intently as she crosses a room swishing her petticoats. What, deep down, is Madame thinking? Does she feel sorry for this young woman whose life has been broken, long ago, through the will of her son? Does she feel remorse when she thinks of the letter disavowing this marriage she herself has written at the behest of the Emperor?

During this time Betsy frequents Pauline's salon, where one engages in *conversazione* and where foreigners flock in large numbers, either because they are attracted by the charm of the hostess or from sheer curiosity. Many of them are English, despite Paolina's vow after her brother's death on Saint-Helena never again to receive a single member of this accursed race. "What can I say," she replies with a disarming smile when called to account for this, "I feel that I am avenged when I see these men, who belong to the proudest nation on earth, lie down in the dust left by my sandals or on the contrary remain standing all day long, waiting to indulge the least of my whims and to hand the pins to my chambermaids when they do my hair. . . . For those who have rheumatism, this is pretty hard."

In Pauline's salon Betsy meets a very distinguished Englishwoman, the Duchess of Devonshire. Tall, slender, and elegant, her face set in a magnificent head of strawberry-blond hair, this charming and spirited lady is interested in archeology. Right now she is financing excavations in the Forum and is very excited to report that "we have discovered the column of Emperor Foca." Around this column great quantities of small and highly valuable antique bronzes have been found. She has brought along a whole basketful of them and precedes to distribute them to her women friends. Betsy is among of them. To her great surprise the young American finds out that Duchess Elizabeth, the second wife of the duke of Devonshire, has been married before to Lord Foster and is the mother of John Augustus, the young British diplomat who courted her years ago in Washington, when the War of 1812 was about to break out! It's a small world indeed!

Lucien Bonaparte — on whom Pope Pius VII, who has great esteem for him, has conferred the title of Prince of Canino — is also engaged in archeological excavations at the site of Cicero's ancient villa. When she goes to see him one afternoon, Betsy finds him with rolled-up sleeves, wearing sturdy shoes and a straw hat, and holding a notebook and a crayon in his hands. Lucien still has the sharp and aristocratic profile of a Roman emperor, but he now wears glasses, which make him look a bit severe. Nonetheless he is full of smiles as he shows his visitors the site of Tusculum, where the famous orator's villa once stood.

A fresh wind, carrying the scent of pines, myrtle, and reseda blows on the hill of Frascati. Lucien leads his guests to his château of La Rufinella not far from there, the retreat where he and his family, along with a few carefully chosen friends, leads a life devoted to arts and letters (he has just finished his great epic poem *Charlemagne*) and the sciences, particularly astronomy. It is a special favor to be admitted to Villa Rufinella and allowed to work in the vast library of the master of this house. Only a few scholars have had this privilege, among them Sir Charles and Lady Sidney Morgan, and above all Lord Byron, who lives in Ravenna and has struck up a friendship with Lucien during his stay in Rome.

Of all the Bonapartes, Lucien, Prince of Canino, who enjoys the protection of the pope and of Cardinal Consalvi, an ecclesiastic well known for his liberalism, is certainly the most fortunate, for after Waterloo he could simply go back to the kind of life he had always led and wanted to lead: he just wants to be a writer and scientist untouched by vain ambitions, a good husband and family man.

Invited to share a family meal at the table of Princess Canino, Betsy feels a pang of sorrow as she scrutinizes the face of this Alexandrine, whose husband has preferred her to worldly honors and has braved Napoleon's wrath, even gone into exile for her sake.

"What does she have that I don't have?" she wonders. "And besides, she was even divorced. . . ."

In Rome one member of Napoleon's family is still missing in Betsy's collection. It is Louis, the ex-king of Holland who, when he is not in Florence, lives like a grouchy bear in his Palazzo Salviati and does not see much of the other members of his family, except for his mother. It is at her home that Betsy meets him for the first time.

She is not exactly dazzled by this ill-tempered hypochondriac who spends his time complaining about various ailments. Yet this is the area where he and Betsy find common ground. He suffers stomach aches when he runs into serious problems (and who doesn't, he says, especially when it comes to marriage). How interesting, says Betsy, she has similar problems, and for the same reasons. When Louis is nervous, his hands shake so much that he can barely write. That happens to her as well. And so, before long, they exchange home remedies: perhaps Louis should try ground stag-horn diluted in orange-flower juice? Oh no, he says, ground quinine on calcinated magnesium is much better.

In the end, Betsy, who has a knack for cleverly mocking herself and others, is able to transform this litany of real and imagined ailments into a repertory of funny stories, and eventually dour Louis brightens. Better still, he takes an interest in Bo, shows him the sights of Rome, lets him see his library, and showers him with gifts — a watch, a snuffbox, knick-knacks made by fine goldsmiths.

Perhaps he misses his two sons, Napoleon-Louis and Louis Napoleon, who are living with their mother, Queen Hortense, in Arenenberg, a Swiss town on the shores of Lake Constance, so that he does not see them often. Hence his need to pour out his frustrated affection on a member of the family who has not yet disappointed him. As it happens it is with him — the crotchety, grouchy bigot steeped in piety — that Bo feels most at ease.

Lucien also receives him warmly and kindly at La Rufinella, but is preoccupied with other things: his household is large, and he is about to marry one of his daughters to an Irishman, Sir Thomas Wyse, and his son Charles-Lucien to Zénaïde, the eldest daughter of his brother Joseph, Comte de Survilliers.

So it is with Louis that Bo and Betsy take walks in the Roman countryside. Together they meditate at the weed-choked tomb of Cecilia Metella or at that of the poet Tasso in the convent of Saint Onulphius. And then they watch as the sunset gradually colors the Alban mountains and the Sabine mountains, finally reaching Rome in the far distance with its palaces, its ancient ruins, the Castel San Angelo, Saint Peter's dome of the Vatican, and the wide staircase of the church of the Trinity that cascades down onto the Piazza di Spagna. Sometimes they hear far-away bells ringing the Angelus. Louis falls silent for a moment. Like Byron, he loves this moment more than any other:

> Ave Maria, blessed be the hour
> The time, the clime, the spot, where I so oft

Have felt the moment in its fullest power
So beautiful and soft
While swung the deep bell in the distant tower.

O this light of Rome, so soon swallowed up by the evening mists! In this almost unreal atmosphere Betsy feels far away from the petty intrigues that are sometimes spun in the drawing room of Madame Mère between two hands of whist or reversi, as the old stewart Cesare Colonna dozes in a dainty couch and the old Corsican nurse, Zia Saveria, bends over her embroidery by the fireside and while the lady companion, Rosa Mellini, softly plays the piano in the next room.

The Bonapartes have decided to find a wife for Bo. Poor fellow, at sixteen and a half years! They have blithely cooked up for him an alliance with a young Bonaparte of his age, planning to look for her, depending on the circumstances, in Lucien's, Joseph's, or Caroline's family. Actually, Caroline is eliminated very soon, for relations with her are cold since Murat's treason. . . . But one day Bo declares to his grandmother, "You know, I will comply with my mother's wishes, but if it were up to me I would rather settle in the United States."

At first everyone had guffawed. But soon an idea has risen to the surface: since Charlotte, Joseph's second daughter, has just sailed for America where she will rejoin her father, it would be nice if Bo were to meet her when he himself goes back.

"That is an excellent idea," says Madame Mère, who is in full agreement with Napoleon's plan to have all young Bonapartes marry among themselves in order to lay the foundations for a solid dynasty.

Betsy had flushed with pleasure when this suggestion was made. She is delighted to watch this intrigue take shape before her eyes. It shows that her son is a bona fide member of Napoleon's family!

Princess Borghese is definitely in favor of this project and promises to provide a capital of 40,000 francs on the wedding day. All that remains to be done now is to notify Joseph, of course — but everyone knows that Bo is already quite popular with that uncle. And, oh yes, to notify Jérôme, the father. Bo must return to America as soon as possible and go to Point Breeze right way. Madame Letizia is very sad to let him go, for he has been most entertaining, but if circumstances demand it, she must go along. As for Pauline, she tells anyone who wants to listen that the more she thinks about it, the more she is delighted with this project.

She often goes to the theater and the opera with her nephew and her sister-in-law. Rossini's music has been all the rage for several years now, and *Tancrède, The Barber of Seville, The Italian Woman at Algiers,* and *Othello* are all on the repertory.

One day when Betsy pays a visit to the Palazzo Borghese, Pauline asks her with a smile: "Have you ever seen my statue?" And when the American professes her ignorance, Pauline hastens to inform her. Face to face with Canova's masterpiece, which has been placed in a remote chamber of the palazzo, Betsy is speechless. Here is a half-naked Paolina, reclining on a sofa, her head delicately resting on a hand holding an apple. The marble sculpture is covered with a thin layer of wax to give an impression of reality. "This is worthy of a Greek sculptor. . . . It has the *morbidezza* of a work of Phidias," Betsy finally mutters, "and how life-like! Did you pose for this yourself?" "Why of course" Pauline, exclaims, "but don't worry, the workshop was heated."

Before long, she offers to take her American sister-in-law to visit Canova's workshop, for he is an old friend. Betsy replies that she will be delighted to do so, especially since she has met the sculptor before at Mme Récamier's, where he offered to make a marble sculpture of her too.

But Canova is not well; suffering from an illness that will carry him off the next year he is unable to receive his visitors. They make up for this by going to see Horace Vernet, who has been living in Rome for several years but has not yet become the director of the Villa Medicis.

He is a skinny little man with a head of dishevelled gray hair, who is never without his ribbon of the Légion d'Honneur. Noticing that he is attentively observing her, Betsy wonders whether he remembers her. They have seen each other at the Café de Foy under the portico of the Palais-Royal six years ago. Has she served him as a model at that time, Vernet asks with a smile; if so, perhaps he will find her likeness in one of his compositions.

EVERYTHING SEEMS TO BE WONDERFUL UNDER THE SKY OF ROME; UNTIL THE day when everything begins to go wrong. The Tarpeian Rock. . . .

Sensational news: the ex-king of Westphalia announces his impending arrival. The Austrian government has agreed to loosen its tight grip temporarily and has authorized him to make a short trip to Rome so that he can embrace his mother — and get some money out of her, the other members of the family mutter under their breath, especially Louis, who has nothing but contempt for his youngest brother. Queen Catherine expects her third child in the fall, and the couple surely needs money. Meanwhile Jérôme has started negotiations with the powers of the Holy Alliance in view of coming to live in Rome near his family, being no longer able to tolerate this separation.

Madame Mère, who has a special fondness for her youngest, is pleased at this prospect, which leaves Louis and Pauline ice cold. "We're headed for trouble," sighs Pauline. A letter from her youngest brother, who has learned from Louis that his ex-wife and his son are in Rome, has arrived at Palazzo Rinuccini. Jérôme acts the injured party: "Pauline must feel that by acting in this manner she has hurt the feelings of my excellent spouse and at the same time criticized the conduct pursued by Emperor and myself in the dissolution of my first marriage," he writes. "What a horrendous position we would have been in if upon our arrival in Rome we had found ourselves in the presence of Madame Patterson, and at my own sister's no less!" The ex-queen of Westphalia herself, the gentle Catherine, has also been offended. "I confess that I would have considered it a special mark of affection on the part of Pauline if she had not called Mme Patterson to Rome and had not received her there, but now that it has been done, I know what to think."

Betsy, who knows nothing of all of this, is astounded to see a complete change in the princess's attitude toward her: no more concerts and *conversazioni*, no more heart-to-heart talks under the live oaks and the magnolias of the Villa Borghese, and no more largesses either. There is no more talk of Pauline paying her nephew's passage to America as she had promised to do two months earlier, when this was a matter of promoting Bo's marriage to his cousin Charlotte. Pauline no longer wants to hear of this alliance. And one fine morning Betsy is flabbergasted to receive the visit of Pauline's lady-in-waiting, who has been sent by her mistress to ask for the return of the cloak and the ball gown Pauline had given her. Betsy will send them back before she leaves Rome.

Fortunately, when this incident occurred, Bo was already on his way to Livorno with his dog Wolf and his uncle Louis, who has driven him part of the way. For the moment, nothing tarnishes the luminous image he carries away from his three months' Roman holiday. "I am happy that I will soon see you, as well as all my uncles and aunts, and also my country," he writes to his grandfather, "but on the other hand I must leave Mommy and my paternal family, who have gone to great lengths for me during my stay in Rome."

Yes, it is a good thing that Bo was not in the gardens of the villa Borghese on the afternoon when his mother and his aunt Pauline walked there together for the last time. Pauline has summoned her American sister-in-law to come and now berates her vehemently.

"You have badly taken care of your son, Madame, ever since he was born. . . . He is uncouth and poorly dressed, and has very bad manners in everything he does."

Betsy does not know what to say, and so Pauline continues: "I am very much afraid that the excessive liberty you grant him will be harmful to the unimpeachable morals that must distinguish a young man."

What an amazing irony to hear these words from the mouth of one who is known as "Our Lady of the Baubles," and whose life has never adhered to the "unimpeachable morals" she now preaches! Betsy has sworn that she will control herself, come what may, but she cannot help protesting: "I at least have the merit of taking care of my son. . . . In any case it is too late to change the manner in which I have brought him up over the last sixteen years; I can only hope that despite the flaws in the system I adopted, my son will have knowledge, virtues, a strong character, a great deal of pride, and the firm will never to forget the obligations his name should impose on all those who have the honor of bearing it!"

Here she falls silent, for she feels choked by her anger.

What is this? Can the princess's words turn all those qualities of spontaneity and frankness that were the joy of Madame Letizia against Bo? Not anxious to be further upbraided, Betsy cuts short her visit. She will never again see Pauline, who shortly thereafter will retire to her country house, the Villa Paolina, which provides a more intimate setting than the Villa Borghese on the heights of Frascati. Rumor has it that she spends happy days there with her new lover, the composer Giovanni Pacini.

But then the young American is utterly astounded to hear certain pieces of gossip that are circulating. It seems, for instance, that her sister-in-law has made it known that she has never invited her to Rome, and that Betsy has come on her own initiative and brought her son, whose presence she has forced on the Bonaparte family. To this Pauline has added a few comments on the temperament of "Mme Patterson," depicting her as cold, selfish, and given to talking about money too much. How unaristocratic of her! Money is made for spending, not for talking about. . . . And when it comes to founding a Bonaparte dynasty, it shows a lack of dignity to think about the large sum Joseph will give his daughter.

When these words are reported to Betsy — for she knows a few hangers-on of the Bonapartes — she feels sorrow plunging into the depth of her heart like a stone, a stone tumbling into a well of ice-cold water, endlessly bouncing off its walls.

No, really, it hurts too much. She goes to see Louis, good, kind Louis, who, having just returned from his trip, sits in his corner ruminating and grumbling, against his family, against Queen Hortense, against everybody, but who is always ready to help those who are even more unhappy.

"How do you think it makes me feel to look like a bothersome intruder, when I only came here to do my duty by my son?" she asks him. "I may have my faults, but no one can accuse me of base motives. I never forget what I owe to myself!"

She is preaching to a convert, the Comte de Saint Leu replies. In any case, she should not fret too much, for as a whole the Bonaparte family has greatly appreciated Bo and his mother. Surely she has seen how much affection Madame Mère had for him? However, if he has one piece of advice to give her — and he will be very sorry about its effect — it is that she should leave Rome before his brother's arrival. This might well spare her some disagreeable situations.

The ex-king of Holland also assures her that she can leave without worrying: the marriage project between Bo and Charlotte will not be dropped. He and his mother are convinced that it is in the family's interest. Perhaps Louis does not know yet that Bo has a serious competitor in the person of his own son Napoleon-Louis, an equally young man; but the fact is that Joseph and Queen Hortense have already exchanged letters regarding this matter.

After having taken leave from Madame Letizia and Cardinal Fesch and asked an American woman friend to deliver a letter to her ex-husband, Betsy has returned to Florence in the company of a couple she has befriended, the Packards. Since they are in no hurry, why not stop in Tuscany instead of rushing through as she had done when she went to Rome?

She knows — and this thought is a great comfort — that in Geneva her old friends are impatiently waiting for her, particularly Baron de Bonstetten, to whom she has written during the winter to tell him about her meeting Comtesse d'Albany, once the faithful companion of the poet Alfieri.

"What a pleasure to see something from Mme Patterson arrive in a sheet of paper," the philosopher had written back. "I found quite a few of her ideas there; in short, I seemed to see and hear you. But you don't tell me anything about your ex-husband, who according to all the papers should be arriving in Rome just now, as if he had a rendez-vous with his legitimate spouse? And then you tell me too much about that princess whom you call the most beautiful woman in the world. Ask her about her secret remedies against ennui, and you will never again suffer it, wherever you go. You will be radiant when you arrive in Geneva, and you will find us charming!"

FLORENCE, LIKE ROME, IS FULL OF ENGLISH PEOPLE. FOR EVERY SCHOLAR, artist, or poet there are many others, young dandies with affected manners, who insolently drag their ennui from place to place and seem to be there as a kind of command performance, obeying the orders of fabulously rich fathers who have sent them on a grand tour of Europe. After all, that's the thing to do!

If there were only Englishmen on the banks of the Arno, it wouldn't be too bad, but there is also . . . Jérôme! What a shock it was when Betsy, looking at a Raphael Madonna in the Venus Room of the Palazzo Pitti in the company of Mrs. Packard, suddenly felt a burning pair of eyes looking at her from behind. She turns around and receives the full impact of velvety brown eyes under a curly head of hair and the astonished half-smile of a full-lipped sinuous mouth. Betsy gasps when she recognizes the face of the man who had left her seventeen years earlier at Lisbon harbor, where she had watched him as he rode off at full gallop through the city's streets.

He has put on a bit of weight, his features have become sharper, and his hair is graying. As elegant as ever, he twirls his Malacca cane. But it almost looks as if his hand were shaking . . .

For his part he sees a woman almost as beautiful as before. The same oval face, the same slender waist, of which Catherine of Württemberg would have every reason to be jealous. . . . But there is cold in these light-brown eyes, in these lips that refuse to smile and are pressed together to contain the bitterness within.

In the space of a second, which lasts a century, the glance between Jérôme and Betsy contains all of the past seventeen years: love, expectation, disappointment, and then forgetting and contempt. Perhaps everything might still have been possible if one of them had spoken a few words, held out a hand. But nothing of the kind happened. Betsy turned her face away, her heart beating hard, as Jérôme walked off, saying to the friend who was with him: "Did you see? That was my American wife. . . ."

"We had better leave," Betsy whispers to Mrs. Packard.

Two days later, she decides to pack her bags. The banks of the Arno are haunted by the specter of Jérôme. She cannot breathe.

20

*E*VEN THOUGH SHE IS WARMLY RECEIVED BY HER friends in Geneva, Betsy does not feel inclined to spend the whole summer there. She no longer has the little apartment she had rented two and a half years earlier and feels rather lonely in the family pension where she has taken lodging. Why not go to Paris, where she will be able to circulate freely, now that Bo is no longer with her? Besides, this will be an opportunity to see the Gallatins, for they are not planning to come to Geneva: "Albert has much too much work to take a vacation," his wife writes.

A few weeks later, she is happy to meet these old friends in the French capital. She will always be welcome at their dinner table, Albert tells her, and a place will always be reserved for her. "You are lucky," remarks James, "for you are the only American Papa tolerates so often at our house. In general, he is rather unsociable when it comes to his compatriots."

Frances has become a very beautiful girl. The previous winter she has been invited to the debutante ball. The proprieties demand that thereafter she must no longer go out unchaperoned. This is most upsetting to her brother, who can no longer drive her about in his cabriolet or, in the winter, skate with her in the Bois de Boulogne. Fortunately Princess de Galitzin has kindly taken her under her wing, along with her own daughter Katia. The two girls are of the same age and equally pretty.

Albert Galatin expects to return to America once his mission in

France has come to an end, and looks forward to leading a very retiring life there. Above all, no more politics; they will settle in Virginia and live in his brick house of New Geneva. There they will savor the pleasures of peace and quiet. This prospect does not hold much charm for Mrs. Gallatin, who hates the countryside. This theme is frequently discussed at the family dinner table. Betsy finds this amusing, but her own preoccupations are elsewhere: she unendingly dreams of Bo's marriage to Joseph's daughter; she speculates about the fortune Joseph, reputed to be the wealthiest member and the most astute manager of the whole Bonaparte family, will give to his daughter; she works out the clauses to be included in the marriage contract (for instance that Bo should be provided for in case his wife should die first . . .); and she tells her friends that in terms of fortune and family connections, the daughters of the ex-king of Spain are the most desirable.

"Madame Mère [she writes to her father] is very eager to see this arrangement made. She has refused to recognize the marriage of one of Lucien's daughters to an Irishman on the grounds that this was a misalliance. She will never forgive my son if he marries a woman of inferior rank."

And indeed, Madame Mère and the Montforts have written to Joseph, Comte de Survillers, expressing their wish to see this project come to fruition. "You made the right decision when you planned to unite Charlotte with Jérôme's son," Madame Letizia had written from Rome in February.

> This young man has been here for two months and I am delighted with him. It is impossible to find such self-assurance and common sense in a person of his age, and he would surely make Charlotte happy. Enclosed please find copies of letters from his father and from Catherine, which will show you that they too are desirous to see this union. I have already informed you that Pauline has promised 300,000 francs at her death if this marriage became a reality . . ."

Lady Morgan is in Paris; like many of her compatriots, she has been dividing her time between England and the continent since 1815. Betsy is anxious to tell her about her stay in Italy and about the bizarre turn in her relations with Princess Borghese. Has that lady not gone as far as taking back her promise after she had told all and sundry that she would pay Bo's voyage to America? Nothing more has been said about this.

"Why should that matter?" Sidney Morgan had asked her. "Have you not brought up your son with the idea that he must count only on himself?"

She has indeed, which is why she has already advised her father to send Bo to Harvard without losing a minute if the prospect of his engagement to Charlotte were to fall through. As for herself, she is ready to jump into the first boat available whenever she learns that things might work out. In point of fact, she is so obsessed by this union that at this moment nothing else interests her. She is also very much afraid that her father will let himself be guided by his family and give only lukewarm support to the promotion of this alliance. Yet in fact William Patterson has dutifully written to Mme Toussard, who acts as intermediary in this delicate matter, and has even gone into some detail:

> When the occasion presents itself, try to find out what the count's intentions are and what the state of his fortune is, particularly with respect to real estate; also give me some indications about the age and the character of the young lady, what people who have met her say about her physical appearance, and so forth. It is true that in America we are not accustomed to setting up marriages in this manner, particularly for young people who are old enough to decide for themselves, but if it should come to pass, I hope that it will work out for the best. . . . Jérôme is considered a very handsome young man, full of promise, and it would make me very happy, as you can well imagine, if he were to get a good start in life before I depart this world . . .

Bo, who has arrived in New York on 12 April, in the company of his dog Wolf, has taken the stagecoach for Philadelphia, and then the steamboat to Bordentown, instead of going directly to Baltimore. "Mommy will have told you about the reason for this trip," he writes to his grandfather by way of excusing himself.

He would of course have preferred to go immediately to Maryland and to enjoy the warmth of the family homestead, but he does not want to thwart his mother's wishes. In addition he is curious to see the new house his uncle Joseph has built at Point Breeze to replace his former home, which was totally destroyed by a fire two years earlier.

Joseph sends his private carriage to pick him up. When he arrives, Bo is once again enchanted to see the dells planted with magnificent tall timber trees as well as magnolias, mountain laurel, and rhododendron; here and there between the trees one has a glimpse of green pastures where Jersey cows are grazing. The road snakes upward among the trees, sometimes following the Creek River and finally reaching a white house flanked by a square tower. Standing on the mountainside a little lower down than the old house, it nonetheless affords a superb view onto the surrounding countryside.

As he enters the vestibule with its white marble flooring, the young boy hardly knows where to look first, for marvelous things abound in this new building, which is even more luxurious than the old one: there are canvasses by the masters of the Italian, French, and Flemish schools, pieces of mahogany furniture, marble consoles. A servant ushers him into a small library furnished with bookshelves and two tables standing on lyre-shaped legs.

And here is his uncle Joseph. He has put on some weight since their last meeting, but he is still dressed in the same simple and informal manner, and he still has that same characteristic kind and affable smile. Immediately putting his nephew at ease, he leads the way to a larger drawing room whose walls are covered in blue merino, furnished with comfortable chairs upholstered in the same material, huge tables topped with black or gray marble, consoles bearing bronze statuary, and pier glass mirrors. The floor is covered by a cheerful Gobelin carpet in a red and white pattern. A wood fire crackles in one of the tall fireplaces covered in white marble that was sent from Italy by Cardinal Fesch.

Inviting his nephew to take a seat, Joseph asks him a great many questions about his mother, whom Bo has seen in Rome, about his uncle the Cardinal, his brothers, and his wife Julie, who still refuses to join him in America. "You lucky mortal, who can travel as you please," he remarks. "Myself, I have asked foreign governments for permission to go to embrace my mother in Italy, but I have been denied."

With a sigh he turns his face, letting his gaze wander through one of the French doors and between the arches of the porch that brings the outside into the house, until it reaches the river that can be seen in the distance. Soon a smile brightens his face, for he is happy in this rural retreat. Here he leads a simple life after having governed a large kingdom, to which he greatly preferred, as he said even then, his "kingdom of Mortefontaine."

Yes, the former king of Spain feels perfectly at ease in this American republic, where he has made many friends and is on the best of terms with his neighbors. Everyone likes and respects him. He continues to receive many visits from distinguished foreigners or compatriots passing through. More than once he has generously opened his purse to help those in need, providing employment or a plot of land for them. There is a long list of soldiers and officers of the Empire who have been saved from destitution in this manner. As for the suspicions of the French secret service that he is involved in Bonapartist plots, Joseph can only laugh at them and point out that he is finally leading a life that suits his taste and fulfills all his dreams, that of a friend of nature and a disciple of Rousseau. How foolish to think that he aspires to another kingdom, even a Mexican one!

Little by little Bo relaxes in the warmth of the flames, as he listens to his uncle talk about his current projects for the clearing of more fields and additional improvements for the house. "If the daughter is as pleasant as the father," he says to himself, "yes, if she resembles him, we might be happy together, especially if she is willing to live in the United States."

As a good host, Joseph himself shows Bo to his room to make sure he has everything he needs. From the window of the little room he is assigned he sees in the distance a young girl dressed in white, her head covered with a large hood tied by a broad red ribbon. She walks with slow and dreamy steps, carrying a notebook under her arm, and stops now and then to pick a flower and to take a deep breath of the fresh air of this April morning before moving on. How small she looks from afar!

In the late afternoon, as the sun begins to cast a red glow on the horizon, he decides to walk his dog Wolf in the park. When he arrived, a servant had taken the animal to the service buildings, and he is anxious to see his old companion. The dog frisks through the paths, delighted to be with his master. Taking the ridge path overlooking the Delaware River, the two of them admire the delicate shades of the countryside under the setting sun. Suddenly the dog dashes forward and barks, stopping by a clump of trees where a white figure moves. Wagging his tail, Wolf waits for his master.

A young woman in a white percale dress has just gotten up from a little bench and begun to pack up the painting implements arrayed around her, an easel holding a canvas that shows the outline of a landscape, a palette, a box of paints, a brush, and a cloth. She is surprised to see the young man.

"Here, Wolf," Bo commands. "I hope the dog has not frightened you, Mademoiselle?"

"He hasn't, cousin," the girl replies with a smile, "for I suppose you are the guest we were expecting today?"

Bo looks at her more closely, a little disappointed to find that she is not as pretty as she had been described to him. Dark-haired and thin, she is very short and has irregular features, but huge eyes in a pointed face. Her eyes bespeak a passionate nature, and she has her father's kindly smile. So this is Charlotte. And apparently she is an artist, too. Painting is her favorite pastime, she says. Her father has had the park cleared of underbrush and ordered openings to be cut among the trees to give her the best views onto the valley. He has also pushed her to exhibit her work, and she has already had two shows at the Academy of Beaux-Arts in Philadelphia. She is never bored. . . . She and her father have traveled a great deal since they have come here. He has taken her to his estate in Black River in New York State, and also to the Niagara Falls. And they have lots of company; Comte de Survilliers often gives dinners and balls.

Little by little Bo is won over by this young girl's charm, by her freshness, her simplicity, and even her silences. Together they walk on the paths that crisscross the property, exchanging a few words from time to time. The next day Charlotte takes him boating on the lake.

At Point Breeze the days pass pleasantly, in an atmosphere of great freedom. In the morning one does not have to rise at any special time.

One is served a cup of coffee or tea in the room, and by ten or eleven o'clock the family assembles for an informal breakfast in the vast dining room with its impressive table. The only time when one must appear in proper attire — dark suit for the men and low-cut dress for the ladies — is dinner, which is served around six or seven.

Jérôme can fill his afternoons as he pleases, with walks or carriage rides on the estate, hunting and fishing parties with neighbors. In the evening he has long conversations by the fireside with his uncle and the uncle's secretary, Louis Maillard. Or else the three of them play billiards.

Sometimes, during the day, he enjoys the company of his cousin Charlotte, sitting next to her as she paints a landscape in watercolor. If she were a better portraitist, she tells him, she would sketch him. He loudly protests that he detests posing for a painter. He has already had to do it for Gilbert Stuart before he went to Europe; the painter was angry because he needed Bo for many more sessions, and so the portrait has remained unfinished.

But aside from a few such intimate moments, Charlotte's presence is evanescent and she seems to crave solitude. She does not dare confess that she has fallen in love with Captain Mickel, who had commanded the *Ruth and Mary* on which she had arrived a few months earlier. But this love is hopeless, for in keeping with the wishes of her uncle Napoleon, she can only marry a Bonaparte.

There is no lack of candidates. There is Napoleon-Louis, the eldest son of Louis, the ex-king of Holland; there is Charles, the son of Lucien; and there are the Murat brothers, both of whom are expected to arrive soon in America, where they will settle. Actually, these young people are interchangeable, depending on what is needed. Thus Joseph has written to his mother: "If Zénaïde (his eldest daughter) marries Charles, we have to marry Lolotte to Louis's son. . . ." And, a little later: "If the marriage with Charles falls through, Zénaïde must marry Louis's son. . . . In that case, Lolotte would marry Lucien's son."

Bo knows all about these little matrimonial calculations, and despite his great liking for his cousin and the considerable attraction he feels for a quiet life at Bordentown in the company of these delightful people, his uncle and his cousin, he balks at the idea of becoming a chess piece that can be moved around on a board at will. No, he will definitely not marry Charlotte. Actually, she does not attract him, for all her charm. And anyway, he is too young!

"WELL, MY BOY," WILLIAM PATTERSON SAYS AS HE WELCOMES HIS GRANDSON to Baltimore a few days later, "all I have to do now is to register you at a prep school in Lancaster to get you ready for Harvard, where your mother wants you to go. For once, I quite agree with her!"

Betsy, who continues to shuttle back and forth between Paris and Geneva periodically reminds her son of her existence by pouring out floods of dreams for his future: a brilliant diplomatic career, a princely marriage, a fortune earned by his work. In this last respect at least, she will be satisfied: having worked hard all summer, Bo is admitted to Harvard during the winter. This also brightens the heart of his grandfather, who has once again suffered a cruel loss. His son Robert has died in an accident. This son, assisted by his brothers, had competently and with a firm hand run the family business and is sorely missed. Robert's wife Mary — one of the "Three Graces" of the Caton family — has gone to Europe to join her sisters, hoping to forget her sorrow.

She forgets it only too quickly, for Betsy soon hears from her English friends that Mary cuts a brilliant figure in all the drawing rooms of London and surroundings, and that she has a faithful admirer, who is none other than the Duke of Wellington.

"What a schemer," she says to herself, "and all this before my brother is even cold in his grave!" Her sorrow at the death of Robert, who has always taken such good care of her, especially at the time of Bo's birth, is aggravated by the jealousy she has always felt for her sister-in-law and indeed the entire Caton family. Once again, her life feels dreary, and her stomach troubles are worse than ever. Betsy is peevish, restless, ill at ease. Her only hope now is that Bo make a really good match. "If the marriage to Charlotte could be brought about after all, I would immediately return. It would almost make me like Baltimore!"

If at least Mme de Villette were still in this world! But she has peacefully passed away at the end of autumn. Betsy has been most distressed to hear this news upon her arrival in Geneva. During the summer in Paris, she had not seen much of "Belle et Bonne," who moved about between the rue de Vaugirard, le Plessis-Villette, and Orleans,

where she had rushed to the bedside of one of her brothers, Bishop
Pierre-Marie de Varicourt. Yet Betsy, wanting to be close to her "adoptive mother" had chosen the Hotel Windsor, located at 32 rue de
Vaugirard, very close to he Hôtel d'Elbeuf. But the marquise was very
busy, serving as president of the Grand Lodge of Scotland; all she could
talk about were initiations, the mysteries of Isis, adoption work, and
Masonic music. "My dear child," she had said to Betsy, "if you stayed
with me a little longer, I could introduce you to all of this. You would
see, it would fill your life."

Clearly, the charming old lady was concerned about the emotional
health of her protégée. "You get much too upset about things that
aren't worth it," she told her. "To be happy as much as one can be in
this world, that is what your mind must strive for. Everything is relative anyway, and real happiness does not exist; so therefore we must
believe that we are happy."

"Belle et Bonne" is gone, but the echo of her voice still reaches
Betsy's ears. She can still see the fire as it crackles in the hearth, Voltaire's
bust on the mantlepiece, the marquise sitting in her midnight-blue
bergère, the kindly smile on her faded face, her hands tightly holding
her own. . . . She has lost a mother for the second time.

THE PROSPECT OF A UNION WITH CHARLOTTE IS NOT GOING WELL, according to a letter from Baltimore. "The young lady has other pretenders,"
Mr. Patterson writes tersely.

"Never mind, then," Betsy replies, "Bo will find other equally good
matches. We must instill ambition in him, keep him from marrying
too low, and give him a sense of economy. Meanwhile, however, he
should continue to see his uncle and his cousin. If they invite him
again, he should go, if they don't, he should not run after them. He
should avoid wandering around in Philadelphia on his trips between
Baltimore and the university, and his conduct should always seem natural, respectful, and as affectionate as it can normally be between an
uncle and a nephew, but without the slightest bit of obsequiousness.
He is their equal in every respect."

Lady Morgan's arrival in Paris prompts Betsy to return to that city
for the summer. Sidney has a plan that greatly appeals to her, namely,

to pay a visit to General Lafayette at his property in the Brie region, to which he has retired many years ago with his large family. On a beautiful August day, Betsy and Sidney have gone by carriage to the château of La Grange. As they approached, the five towers of the imposing castle that had once belonged to King Louis the Fat had come into view amidst woods and orchards. Here Lafayette lives as a patriarch, surrounded by a large household. His smooth face and his firm and upright stance do not betray his age. A warrior and legislator, he is also a competent farmer who is passionately interested in agriculture.

"I am much happier here," he tells the ladies, "than in the corridors of power. Having initially placed my trust in Bonaparte, I disavowed him when he made himself consul for life and then Emperor. . . . And now the Bourbons have returned from exile; they have not forgotten and not learned anything and do not want to hear of a constitution. No indeed, I am the apostle of liberty, and I want nothing to do with them."

In a private moment Betsy asks him if he remembers Baltimore and her father, William Patterson. Of course he remembers! He has always felt very grateful to the ladies of Baltimore for their effective help in difficult circumstances. In fact, he is planning to return there the following year. The American government has invited him to make an official tour. He is so steeped in French political life that it is his fondest dream to revisit his youth on the New Continent!

If Betsy is very proud to show off her family's ties to the famous general, Lady Morgan for her part is impressed to have come so close to the head of the French liberals, the hidden soul of the opposition. She admires him and hopes that he will yet experience his hour of glory.

21

$\mathcal{B}$ETSY IS ON THE VERGE OF DEPRESSION. AND that for two reasons. First of all, she definitely has to give up on a union between Charlotte and Bo. Despite the evident relief of her son who, at the very beginning of his college career, is not anxious to let himself be tied down, Betsy, who deep in her heart had always hoped that this would somehow come to pass, is deeply hurt by this setback. No doubt the family has chosen one of the Murat twins, Lucien or Achille, or else a son of Lucien, rather than Bo.

When she had heard of this failure, Mme Toussard wanted to pour a little balm onto her friend's heart: "There is nothing to regret," she told her. "Charlotte is so short that she looks like a dwarf, and I find her very homely. Jérôme is almost too handsome for her, and he would be making a great sacrifice." Surely this is comforting to the pride of the offended mother! And then too, she hears only good things about the young man's studies; he is only a little behind in Greek, but good in mathematics.

Meanwhile, more bad new reaches Geneva, where Betsy has returned for the winter: Madame Letizia is dead. This truly pains Betsy.

She was an estimable person in every respect [she writes to her father] and she showed great affection for my poor boy. I am very sorry to see her go so soon, for given the perspicacious mind that distinguished her, I am convinced that she would have taken great interest in him if he had stayed with her longer.

She seemed devoid of hypocrisy and the art of double dealing that one so often finds among the Europeans.

Suddenly, disaster! At the same time it is reported that when she fell ill, Madame Letizia drew up a will whose terms are made public: half of her fortune would go to the king of Rome (Napoleon's son, to whom his father, understandably, had left nothing), while the other half would be divided among her children. Among her other grandchildren beyond the king of Rome, only Lucien's sons were reportedly mentioned.

"How could she show so much tenderness to Bo," thinks Betsy, "and exclude him so completely from her inheritance? When I think that just recently she wrote to him: 'Do not forget your *bonne maman,* who loves you with all her heart.'" To obtain some clarification, she writes to an acquaintance in Rome, asking her to make discreet inquiries.

Soon she is reassured on at least one point: the news of Madame Letizia's death was false; the old lady has survived after a long illness and is doing very well indeed. However, the news about the will was true.

Nonetheless, on the advice of her friends, she does not mention the problem of this inheritance when writing to her son, for it might insert ulterior motives into his dealings with his grandmother. But in any case, his mind is far from such preoccupations right now, for he is most unhappy because Harvard does not allow him to bring Wolf, his faithful friend! The dog has had to stay in Baltimore, where he is confined to the kitchen buildings. It has taken him some time to get used to all the black faces around him, for he is a dog who used to call on beautiful ladies dressed in silk and brocade and who slept every night in his master's bed, his head on his own pillow. . . . "If I had known," Betsy writes to a woman friend, "I would have kept him with me, for he was good company. He is a very intelligent animal, and quite superior to half the people I encounter."

THERE IS SOME NEWS FROM PARIS AS WELL: THE GALLATINS WILL SOON return to America, writes James, for his father's mission comes to an end in May 1824. "Will you come to see us before that fateful date?" he asks. He tells her a few bits about his life in Paris: "The day before yesterday we were invited to a party at the Duchesse de Berry's. She had hired a troupe of Neapolitan singers and dancers, who performed in costume. It was good fun. The Duchesse d'Angoulême was present, more rigid and formal than ever. I doubt very much that she appreciated the casual style of this gathering. . . . The Duchesse de Berry has grown fat, but rather prettier than before. She talks very loudly, dresses amazingly badly and has more or less lost her figure. She is said to have quite a few lovers, but I have trouble believing it. . . . We danced until midnight, and then dinner was served. The palace is disgusting, it must not have been cleaned for years. I heard that the royal family will go to live at Saint-Cloud, and that the Tuileries will be scrubbed from top to bottom. It can't be healthy to live in that mess."

"He is so funny, that James!" exclaims Betsy. It appears that he is thinking about getting married. He has had enough of all his adventures. Quite a skirt chaser, he is! I'll advise him to call on my friends, the Pascaut de Poléons in Baltimore. Their youngest daughter is an absolute beauty, perhaps he'll fall in love at first sight? Being so fond of France and of fine manners, he is bound to appreciate this offspring of an Old-Regime family.

WINTER GOES ON AND ON IN GENEVA, AND BETSY IS GETTING THE BLUES. Even her worthy Swiss friends no longer find grace before her eyes. "People here are so reasonable! Everything is regulated like clockwork. Mornings are devoted to the occult sciences, evenings to whist, so that I find myself willy-nilly obliged to read half the day. . . . Also, I am getting pretty tired of all that beautiful nature, the Mont Blanc, Lake Geneva, the lovely sunset, the magnificent moon rise!"

When spring comes, she returns to Paris. What a delight to drink in the smell of the chestnut trees in bloom or the rose bushes at Bagatelle, to listen to the rumors that fly all around her, weigh them and sniff them out. Paris is plotting: There are the ultras of the Pavilion Marsan who, under the aegis of the Comte d'Artois, brother of the king, dream of a reactionary and retrograde France; there are the liberal or Bonapartist newspapers that wish to overthrow the Bourbons; and there are those Parisians who chime in with Béranger's couplets about the

Napoleonic legend: ". . . France, what have you done with your glory?" Under the influence of Sidney Morgan, Sismondi, and other friends, Betsy now sympathizes more with the liberals. Rarely frequenting the legitimist salons of the Faubourg Saint Germain any longer, she will soon climb the narrow staircase of the Abbeye-au-Bois, where Mme Récamier has found a refuge after her husband has ruined himself. Nonetheless she continues to receive French intellectuals of every stripe, ranging from liberals all the way to legitimists, since one can sometimes find Mathieu de Montmorency there alongside Chateaubriand, the star of every gathering.

A great friend of Chateaubriand, who calls her "his sister," also conducts a salon. She is Madame de Duras, a woman of letters who seems to have assumed the mantle of Mme de Staël, even though she lacks Germaine's genius. Authoritarian in temper, she is endowed with a very subtle mind. "I find her ridiculous and almost as ugly as Mme Bernadotte, the queen of Sweden," affirms James Gallatin. "Why does she think that when she speaks she has to wave around long strips of paper which she then tears into little pieces? Is this her way of aping Germaine and her laurel branch?"

The news from America is good: Bo is a freshman at Harvard and already has acquired some friends there; he has made himself popular by generous distributions of cigars he has brought back from Italy. The students wear rather plain black uniforms. They are learning strict discipline: it is out of the question for instance to arrive in the classroom five minutes late or early. As for the food they are given, it is anything but appetizing, according to Bo: boiled vegetables, clear broth, half-baked bread, and meat as tough as shoe leather. . . . Bo and a few others are so disgusted by it that they have decided to board at a professor's house in town. But from time to time Bo also invites some of his less privileged classmates to a restaurant. He is costing his mother a small fortune!

Betsy, with her sense of economy, is very much afraid that her son will develop a taste for luxury and throw money out the window. Given his father's temperament, she has reason to be concerned! She has written to the boy's grandfather, asking him to tighten the purse strings a little. Bo's response has been quick. So he is supposed to tighten his belt? Very well, then, he will begin right away by sharing a room with another student, and during summer vacation he will not make a detour to Point Breeze, where he has been invited by his uncle and his cousin Charlotte, and go directly to Baltimore. . . . And never mind about family relations!

Robert Patterson's widow, Mary Caton, announces her forthcoming visit to Paris. She has made a tour of the European capitals, closely followed by her faithful admirer, the Duke of Wellington. The Gallatins will soon have him at their dinner table.

"Would you like to join us?" Mrs. Gallatin asks Betsy. "I think you should see her. After all, you are childhood friends!"

So they are, but a few years earlier Mrs. Caton had forbidden her daughters to frequent "Madame Patterson" in Paris!

Nonetheless, Betsy, out of sheer curiosity, agrees to meet her former school mate. At a dinner at the Gallatins', where both of them are present along with such guests as the Russian ambassador, Charles-André Pozzo di Borgo, and the learned Alexander von Humbold, both women dazzle the company with their elegance and their spirited demeanor. A sparkling joust takes place between these two Maryland beauties. Which one is the more attractive? It would be difficult to decide.

"Between the one who talks of nothing but the rich alliances in store for her son and the other who brags about her jewelry and her connection with the Duke of Wellington, one can really become fed up," thinks James Gallatin, an amused witness to this memorable evening that closes Betsy's Paris season.

22

*B*O HAS QUITE A SURPRISE FOR HIS MOTHER WHEN he meets her as her boat docks in New York. He has been suspended from Harvard for three months, for unbecoming conduct.

Yet he hasn't done anything serious, he assures her. Here is what happened. He belongs to two clubs at the college and is president of one of them. On Friday of last week he went to a meeting, as he usually does. This time, the election of a librarian was on the agenda. After the election they had some punch that was brought in by the club's president. There was no trouble, no noisy behavior. The next morning, to his great surprise, he learned that he had been suspended, along with some of his classmates. . . . Yet there is nothing wrong with his work. . . . Actually, he does not really mind, for this will give him a chance to study certain matters more thoroughly. What is too bad is that he will not have a vacation. Perhaps his mother would like to come and stay with him in Lancaster? He has taken a room in a boarding house in town.

What an excellent idea! Misfortune has its good side too. Betsy will always remember these three months of peaceful tête-à-tête with her son by the fireside, where she did needlework while he studied or told her in great detail about his life at Harvard, about jokes students play on each other, and about hazing practices.

Thus one day he was made to cross the entire campus on all fours, pushing an apple with his nose! And the story of the fire extinguisher — they certainly had fun with that contraption! The rector was so proud of it — the only one for miles around — that he had ordered the students to go to the scene as soon as a fire was reported anywhere in Lancaster or surroundings. As soon as the alarm bell was rung, they had to don grotesque accouterments and rush to the endangered buildings. It usually took them so long that the fire was out by the time they arrived. In any case, given the capacity of the machine, they would have had just about enough to water a flower-bed. But it was fun anyway! Especially since upon their return they were allowed a *black-strap*, that is, a mixture of rum and molasses. . . . Pretty good stuff it was, too! The college also owned a sloop on which they went in the fall to fetch fire wood for the winter.

Since students are not permitted to go to Boston during the week, Bo uses these three months of suspension to go there with his mother as often as possible. Theater, concerts, dinners with the best people of Boston, one of the most exclusive societies in the United States. In later years, when serious conflicts arose between Betsy and her son, she could never think without secret nostalgia of these three months of calm happiness in the little town of Lancaster.

MEANWHILE, GENERAL LAFAYETTE HAD ARRIVED IN THE UNITED STATES, where he had been received with elaborate ceremony. Bo had gone to greet him in Boston, which was decorated for the occasion with French and American flags, flowers, and triumphal arches. Alas, when the general visited Harvard, where he was greeted with a long speech by the university's president, Mr. Kirkland, Bo was not among the chosen few who had the privilege of approaching the illustrious visitor. "Oh well," he writes to his grandfather, "I saw him in Boston and I think he looks very old. . . . He would do better to take care of himself and avoid all these noisy demonstrations around him. It really doesn't make sense at his age!"

While passing through Philadelphia, the general has made a little detour to call on Joseph Bonaparte. He is a long-standing friend of his and one of the great hopes of the French liberals. Very pleased about this visit, Comte de Survilliers has asked the general, along with his escort, to stay for lunch. What did they talk about during their long walk and their private conversation in the study at Point Breeze? An aura of mystery surrounds this encounter, but it would be learned later that Lafayette asked Joseph to help him restore the Bonaparte family to the throne of France: he would serve as regent for his nephew, little Napoleon II, who would have to be seized from the Austrians. . . . But Joseph refused.

"That doesn't surprise me," Bo was to comment when he heard about this. "My uncle is a dyed-in-the-wool republican. What he admires most in the United states is the form of our government."

— "But couldn't he have accepted a kind of English-style constitutional monarchy, such as it was defined by Benjamin Constant during the Hundred Days in his *"Acte additionnel"*?

— "I think that such an offer to head a coup d'état, which would have made him too conspicuous, did not appeal to my uncle."

"That's too bad," Betsy thinks, "for if Joseph had ascended the throne as regent, there would have been a great deal of hope for my son. . . . For my part, I am sure that the Bonapartes will rule again one day. . . . After all, that's what a clairvoyant told me in 1815. May I live long enough to see it!"

BALTIMORE WANTS TO DO ITS PART IN CELEBRATING THE FAMOUS FRENCH general. Fort McHenry, of illustrious memory, will be the site where the local notables receive Lafayette. Under a tent that had been used by General Washington during the American Revolution, important personalities have assembled, among them the governor of Maryland, old Mr. Carroll of Carrolton, grandfather of the Caton sisters and one of the very few surviving signers of the Declaration of Independence, General Smith, and others.

As for William Patterson, he meets his old friend Lafayette at the Fountain Inn. The Inn has reopened as a venue for festive occasions, but it is no longer managed by Commodore Barney, who has died in 1818.

Triumphal entry, trumpet flourish, sumptuous dinner, ball. Many toasts are brought.

"I would like," says Lafayette, "to drink to the ladies of Baltimore; the gratitude of the young soldier I was is enhanced by the respect of the veteran I have become!"

The noisy joy of the scene is indescribable.

William Patterson is glad to return to the calm of his house on South Street. But he has had the satisfaction of conversing in private with the general. They have discussed crops and livestock, and he has promised his illustrious friend a gift of two of his Virginia cows when he returns to France. They are good milchers and will be useful to him at La Grange if he wants to cross them with other species.

THE HOUR FOR RETURNING TO BALTIMORE WILL SOON SOUND FOR BETSY, who had hoped to spend the winter in Lancaster when Bo went back to school. But the rector had been adamant: "The students' families are not allowed to live in the area." Nothing to be done about it, and so it's off to dreary Baltimore!

Yet Baltimore is not as sad as all that. This city, now the third largest in America, is constantly developing. Many of its streets are lined with brick houses of a uniform type, with marble stoops and steps that are carefully scrubbed every day. Some of them have movable wooden steps: when the owners do not wish to receive visitors, they place the steps upside down by the front door, and then no one will disturb them.

The foundations have been laid for a hotel that will be huge, the biggest in the United States, the Hotel Barnum. Many notables have had luxurious homes built on the heights overlooking the city. General Samuel Smith has been the first to set an example with his "Montebello," to which he has given this name in honor of one of Bonaparte's victories. It is a veritable palace! Albert Gallatin is in Washington, but his wife, who is from Baltimore, lives there with her children. And now Betsy learns a happy piece of news: on her advice, James has called on the Pascaud de Poléons and . . . has fallen madly in love with Josephine, Henriette's younger sister, a very beautiful, delicate, and graceful blonde of twenty-six, who admirably plays the piano and the harpsichord. She does not have a fortune, and neither does her suitor. But then he is an intelligent young man who is headed for a brilliant career, to be sure.

Mr. Patterson has urged his daughter to open her house on Charles Street. "Is that really worth doing?" she has asked him. "I'll be there for only a few months, just long enough to look into some business matters and take care of my son. If Bo were here, it would be different, of course, but he still has more than a year at Harvard. And as long as I can't live close to him . . ."

The young woman has therefore moved in with her father, but within a few short weeks she sinks into the despondent mood that she inevitably associates with the oppressive atmosphere of South Street. Between her father's austere talk and his severe and formal attire — powdered wig, dark suit — and the mannish ways of her Aunt Nancy, who takes snuff all day long and swears like a trooper, life is not very pleasant. Sometimes she escapes to visit her old friend Dolly Madison at her country estate at Montpelier, Virginia, to which her husband has retired. At this point James Monroe, another Virginian, is President of the United States. His daughter Mary, now married, sometimes visits her father in Washington, and this gives Betsy an excuse to take up her habits of long ago.

President Monroe has finally succeeded in acquiring the two Floridas for the United States, but the other Spanish possessions in America have risen up and are about to declare their independence. Monroe's greatest fear is that the conservative European governments, who have formed the Holy Alliance, will either force these countries to return to the bosom of Spain or install sovereigns of their choosing there. This is what has motivated him to launch his famous declaration: "America to the Americans!" At this same time the Bourbon government of France has intervened in Spain in order to help King Ferdinand VII maintain his despotic authority in the face of liberal opposition. The American merchants, of course, are happy to see this new European war, which will allow them to extend ever greater commercial activity around the globe.

— "You should be careful about speculating on this war," Betsy tells her brothers. "Europe is not on the verge of another revolution. Believe me, people over there have suffered too much from past wars to allow this one to spread."

Henceforth, a little more respect is given to the "citizen of the world" she has become; she is admired, courted, her hand asked for in marriage. But she gives everyone the cold shoulder. Do they believe that she is so bored that the will let herself come to such a sad end? is all she replies when her father stresses the advantages of a brilliant alliance, vaunts the merits of a businessman who is rolling in money or of a young lawyer headed for a great future, when these men are interested in her. Thanks but no thanks! Now that she has tasted life in London and Paris, it is out of the question for her to moulder in Maryland; her place is in Europe!

In May she leaves to spend some time in Philadelphia, where her old friend Mme Toussard has little trouble persuading her to accompany her to Paris.

— "I'll be back a year from now," she says. "By that time Bo will have finished college and I will settle down with him in Baltimore. I promise."

Perhaps she means it when her ship weighs anchor and sails for Le Havre in this month of June 1825. However, fate, capricious fate, will decide otherwise. Nine years will pass before she again sets foot on her native soil.

23

*W*HO WOULD HAVE THOUGHT THAT LE HAVRE is such a lively place? But really, Betsy can hardly tear herself away. The British colony here in France is partying diligently, the sea air is delightfully fresh, the Norman countryside is beautiful, even in the rain. . . . Paris can wait. The ladies go for walks together, play whist, and gossip. The English tongues are just as sharp as those on the continent. It must be said that there is plenty to gossip about.

Lord Byron has died a few months earlier at Missolonghi in Greece, where he had gone to fight the Turks side by side with the Greek patriots. It is said that before he died he saw his old friend Thomas Moore in Venice and entrusted the manuscript of his memoirs to him. And Moore burned it!

"The memoirs probably smelled of sulphur, for Byron was a diabolical man," Betsy tells herself. But she would have liked to meet him just the same; he was without question the greatest poet of his time. To have missed Napoleon and Byron are the two greatest regrets of her life. And to think that Mary Caton, who had been lucky enough to meet Byron in London, had corresponded with him for years!

Mary Caton, here she is again. . . . The snob, the schemer, the stuck-up old thing. . . . And now she is about to marry, not Lord Wellington, who has gotten tired of her, but his brother, the Marquis of Wellesley, a sixty-five-year-old widower riddled with debts and crippled with rheumatism! But he is governor of Ireland, which makes up for quite a few drawbacks.

— "Will you come to the wedding, Betsy?"

— "Of course I will . . ."

Sidney Morgan soon writes to her: she must go to London for the wedding, which will be splendid, "the marriage of the century," and she is looking forward to the reunion with her American friend.

But the weeks go by and no invitation arrives. What is going on here? Have the Catons gotten wind of the sharp remarks Betsy makes about them whenever they are mentioned? Has her mail been opened and its contents communicated to the "Three Graces" and their mother? Or maybe the invitation has gone astray, she thinks. But no, for all around her in Le Havre many of her English lady friends have received theirs. So, what is this about? As the weeks go by and the great day draws near, Betsy has to admit, to her dismay, that she has been snubbed. "Come to think of it, it's just as well," she says to herself, deciding to make the best of a bad situation. "I didn't feel like crossing the Channel anyway. . . . And besides, my brother Edward is here, and I can't run out on him."

Thanks to a business trip, Edward has finally been able to escape from Baltimore; he has just ended his European circuit and will sail from Le Havre in the fall. Betsy spends a few days in perfect harmony with her favorite brother.

And then General Lafayette has arrived. Here too he is received with great ceremony. Returning from his triumphal tour of America, he is full of energy and radiates optimism. The very day after his arrival he has paid a friendly visit to "the beautiful Madame Bonaparte," the daughter of his old friend Patterson.

"Oh," he exclaims, "if you knew how pleased I am with your father's gift of his two black Virginia cows! I am taking them straight to my château at La Grange, and you must absolutely come to admire them!"

Princess Borghese has died earlier in the summer. Against all hope, she has left a small legacy of 20,000 francs to Bo. It is a modest nest egg, but at least it has the merit of officially integrating Bo into the Bonaparte family. "The princess had a kind heart after all," Betsy acknowledges in her own heart, as she remembers Pauline's capricious behavior and ambiguities in Rome four years earlier. Her rather exceptional gesture in favor of Bo, whom she privileges over most of her other nephews, seems to indicate some remorse toward him. But this legacy comes with one condition: the mother cannot receive this money for her son.

"There is nothing for it, Bo must go to Rome again, and he must also go to see his father, who in fact has asked for him," she writes to Mr. Patterson. "He must reestablish relations with his family; I do not want him to blame me one day for keeping him away from them. But to do this, he must ask the rector for a leave of absence from Harvard."

"And as for me," she thinks, "I will take this opportunity to spend the winter in Florence, which I briefly visited in the past, and for a very good reason! I won't be too far from Bo there. . . ."

The ex-king of Westphalia, for his part, seems intent above all to get his oldest son married. Since the projected union with Joseph's daughter has not worked out, well, he'll just have to find another match. Bo is bombarded with letters on this subject and complains bitterly about them to his grandfather: "What is this mania in this family to play the matchmakers all over the place!" he grouses. "How do you feel about this, grandfather? First of all, I feel very young. James Gallatin has just gotten married, but he is twenty-seven, but I am only twenty. And besides, I have become so used to hearing my mother denigrate the life of married couples and repeat over and over again that 'it is better to live alone than to be badly matched,' that I feel like enjoying my bachelor existence."

"How can anyone have such a stubborn mother?" he wonders to himself. "But then, I am really fond of her; and if she wants me to go, I'll go."

24

*T*HE SKIES ARE SOFT IN THIS EARLY TUSCAN win-
ter, mist is rising from the Arno, the hills on both sides of the valley are
crowned by cypresses, and vineyards tumble down their slopes. On the
horizon Siena with its palaces rises out of clay ravines and the harsh,
burnt earth — Siena, the marvel of the Trecento, which seems to be
forgotten in a desert, with its conch-shaped piazza del Campo, its monumental fountains, its spiraling streets, and its way of speaking the pur-
est Italian of all of Tuscany.

When Bo arrives there, the traditional August festivities surrounding the *Palio* have ended some weeks earlier, and the square has recovered its normal appearance. The ex-king of Westphalia has rented the
château of Lanciano, situated on a wooded hilltop not far from there,
because he wants to be close to his other son, also named Jérôme-Napoleon, who is presently a student at a Lazarist boarding school in town.
But Bo, who looks with curiosity at this landscape through the windows of his carriage as he tries to imagine this first encounter with his
father, would not be as lighthearted if he had read the letter the ex-king
had sent to him in America after he had already boarded his ship.

. . . My position is so complicated with respect to the queen
and the princes our children [he has written] that I do not
know how to balance them with your unusual position, for
although my wife, whose noble and generous heart is so well
known, would be ready to do a great deal for you, we would

find that the courts of Württemberg and Russia would oppose any action that might seem to invalidate the princess's marriage. You are a man now, my dear child, and the time has come for me to restore you to your proper position, without, however, prejudicing the situation of the queen and of the princes, my children, in any way whatsoever.

Nonetheless, the man who receives him in his study at the chateau of Lanciano is jovial and relaxed. Jérôme is very pleased with his grown-up son and tells him so. Queen Catherine, a fundamentally kind person, stifles any reservations she might have and warmly welcomes the newcomer. As for the three children, they are delighted to discover a big brother, especially little Mathilde, six years old at the time, who sucks her thumb as she looks at him in wide-eyed astonishment. All three listen to him in breathless wonder when he tells them about his voyage and his life in America. He has a strong Yankee accent that amuses them. King Jérôme looks pensive. In his mind he sees the port of Baltimore, South Street, and the banks of the Patapsco where he had enjoyed walking with his "dear Elisa." It was another life, another Jérôme, he thinks. It seems to him that a century has passed since then. So much has happened . . .

He cannot help feeling his throat tighten with muted emotion as he contemplates this son whose absence once caused him such cruel suffering. Would he have turned out differently if he had been raised at the court of Kassel?

Meanwhile he greatly enjoys walking with him in the Sienese countryside, where they watch wagons pulled by teams of white long-horned oxen, and showing him the marvels of Siena and San Gimignano, the city of many towers.

On weekends they go to pick up the other Jérôme at his boarding school. Sometimes Mathilde and her little brother Napoleon, nicknamed Plon-Plon, go along, accompanied by their governess. They are delighted to escape the supervision of their mother, who brings them up very strictly. Plon-Plon, who is only four, is given to tantrums and already promises to become an unpleasant person. Mathilde is more gentle, but she suffers under her mother's rigid and unloving upbringing. Queen Catherine is so much in love with her husband that she states without hesitation, "I would give up all of my children for Fifi's little finger!"

Yet Bo has known how to conquer this princess's heart. Though not formal, his manners are not as bad as Pauline had at one point reported to her brother. The years spent at Harvard have given him polish, and in Florence as well as Geneva the elegance of some of the grandest figures has rubbed off on him. At twenty-one, he is a hand-some and intelligent young man. At ease with himself, he observes what goes on around him with an attentive eye, but more detachment than his mother can muster.

If certain details of his father's life have not escaped him — such as a certain Countess Azzolino who follows him around and to whom good-natured Queen Catherine, willing to close her eyes to her husband's escapades, does not object — he tries not to judge him. Nor does he criticize his childish vanity and his manner of boasting at every turn about his rare military exploits. Relations between him and his father are cordial, and that is the most important thing. Jérôme the father is enjoying his eldest son's presence, even though he had awaited his ar-rival with considerable apprehension. Now he would be delighted to keep him by his side forever. When he questions Bo about this, the young man replies evasively:

— "I don't know. . . . This is not really my decision. . . . We would have to consult maman."

But deep down he knows perfectly well that he would a hundred times rather live in America.

IN LATE NOVEMBER THE WHOLE FAMILY, EXCEPT YOUNG JÉRÔME-NAPOLEON, who must stay at his boarding school in Siena, goes to Rome and moves into the Nunez palace, which Comte de Montfort (as ex-king Jérôme styles himself) has bought from Lucien. Immediately upon his arrival, Bo has rushed off to see his grandmother. My goodness, how feeble she has grown. She is but the shadow of her former self. Her black and clinging wool dress accentuates her thinness. In her pale and drawn face her long sharp nose and her jet-black pupils stand out even more. She is losing her eyesight and reaches out to touch the face of Bo who has knelt down by her side.

"My dear child . . . How I wish I could see you . . . I am told you have become a tall and handsome boy full of good health. I have heard from your cousin, Charles-Lucien, who is coming from America and has visited your grandfather in Baltimore: he was very graciously received and has spoken very well of your family."

And indeed, Lucien's son, who has married Joseph's oldest daughter Zénaïde, has been living at Point Breeze with his young bride since the year before. And Charlotte, who has married Napoleon-Louis, Louis's eldest son, is just now spending her honeymoon at the Villa Borghese.

Bo is delighted to see his cousin again, for he is very fond of her. He does not feel the slightest resentment toward her, unlike his mother, who cannot get over her disappointment at the failure of her matrimonial projects. To console herself, she tells all and sundry that Charlotte was not such a good match after all: her dowry was much smaller than one might have hoped, and as for her physical appearance . . . it is absolutely awful; she is a true dwarf, and her cousin is to be commended for agreeing to take her as his wife.

The ex-king of Holland has settled in Florence; his wife, Queen Hortense, sometimes leaves her château of Arenenberg to visit her mother-in-law, accompanied by her younger son Louis-Napoleon.

Bo soon takes a liking to this new cousin, who is only three years younger than he is. The two of them go riding in the Roman countryside, take walks at Tivoli or Frascati, and have unending political discussions: Louis-Napoleon is a fervent defender of liberalism and the cause of the Carbonari, who are beginning to cause a stir in the papal states.

The two young men have a wonderful time during the Roman carnival, which lasts for almost two months. Bo is fascinated to watch these thousands of masked people who roam the streets, throw confetti, and by late afternoon give way to horse races. In the evening there is dancing everywhere. Foreign ambassadors and Roman nobles vie for the reputation of having the best festivities, and the Montforts do not want to be left behind. Jérôme, who freely spends the allowances he receives from the king of Württemberg and the czar of Russia (Catherine's uncle), gives lavish receptions. His lifestyle is luxurious, and his household observes the strictest etiquette, as if he were still at the court in Kassel.

Once his cousin Louis-Napoleon has left, Bo is getting quite bored.

The reason is that aside from the social events, life in the Montfort household is anything but stimulating for the mind. One rises toward eleven, has breakfast between twelve and one, dinner between six and seven, and finally tea at eleven in the evening.

> I am extremely tired of this rhythm of life [he writes to his grandfather]. I rarely go to bed before half past one in the morning. My father does not see many people right now, but for most of the day the whole family assembles in the drawing room; it's just a matter of killing time. Nobody in this house is doing anything, and as far as I am concerned, I can neither read nor study. Fortunately I am not completely wasting my time, for I have the opportunity to visit the antiquities of Rome and to observe the ways of its inhabitants. My father's expenses are enormous and so far beyond his means that even if he wanted to, he would be unable to do anything for me . . .

Every afternoon Bo thus walks around the city on foot or has a *vetturino* take him to one of the villas in the surrounding country, such as Villa Adriana, which enchants him, Villa Mellini on Monte Mario, or Villa Medici, which affords a magnificent view over Rome. But he is beginning to count the weeks until his return to the United States. This time he is sure that he wants to settle in the United States and nowhere else. His father is a charming man, but his way of life does not suit him at all. And yet the Comte de Montfort has made a point of showing him all of his treasures: the sabre Napoleon carried at the battle of Marengo, which was given to Jérôme when he was an adolescent, or the keys to the city of Breslau — and a magnificent painting in which Horace Vernet had depicted this "victory" of Jérôme's hangs in the drawing room. In a large album that lies on a table next to a pile of French newspapers one can see the signatures, accompanied by drawings, of all the European painters who have passed through Rome and called on the ex-king of Westphalia.

Bo has paid another visit to his uncle Lucien (whom Plon-Plon and Mathilde call "the other papa" because he reminds them of their own father), who continues to live amidst his large family, as well as his grandmother, who is still looked after by the faithful Cesare Colonna and her reader Rosa Mellini. Zia Saveria, the old family nurse, has died.

The trouble is that in Rome one senses a rather heavy police presence, and the slightest move of any of the Bonapartes is closely watched. Pope Leo XII, who has succeeded Pius VII, is much less friendly than his predecessor, and gone too is Cardinal Consalvi. As time goes on, Bo is suffocating. Fortunately, his mother calls him to Florence. He starts out before Holy Week, even though his great-uncle Cardinal Fesch urges him to stay because he has gotten him a ticket to the Good Friday service in the Sistine Chapel: well, he will just have to miss Allegri's *Miserere* sung by castrati and the candles that are extinguished one by one until Michelangelo's famous frescoes are left in semi-darkness.

In Florence one breathes more easily. Grand Duke Leopold II, who has reigned there since 1815 (for at that time Tuscany had been given back to the House of Lorraine, enlarged by Piombino and the island of Elba), rules with a tolerant and kindly paternalism that pervades the entire atmosphere. Betsy is very excited to tell her son that she has been received with great benevolence at the grand-duke's court.

He honored me so much, and in the presence of so many people, that I felt like crying. But I was afraid that I would spoil my satin dress if I let the tears flow, and so I held back. I think that there is no more amiable court than that of Tuscany anywhere in the world. Now I am invited every week to the balls or concerts at court.

Bo looks at his mother and finds her bright-eyed and fresh-complected. Yet when she arrived she had complained that the air of Florence did not agree with her; she felt that it was almost as bad as that of Baltimore! It would appear that she has become accustomed to it. When all is said and done she recognizes that she is happier here than even in Paris because she has so many friends and a busy social life.

Discovering Florence in the springtime is an enchantment for Bo. During the day he saunters along the Arno by himself, visits churches and museums, admires the Medici palaces, and goes into raptures over the Gates of Paradise doors at the Baptistery. In the evening he accompanies his mother to balls or concerts.

"It's really too bad that I have such a grown-up son," she says with a laugh, "for I could easily pass for ten years younger than I am!"

Between the grand-ducal court, the Florentine nobility, and the embassies, there is a ball to go to almost every night. It's really exhausting! But Betsy considers it her "duty," she says, to drag her son into high society in hopes that he will wangle a good match. What she does not admit, although it can be clearly read in her shining eyes and her happy face, is that she simply loves it. Where is the sad young woman of Baltimore? She has molted, and it is as if she had slipped into a new skin. "If only she could come up with a good husband for herself, she has no idea how happy that would make me!" thinks Bo as he watches her. Meanwhile, he does as his mother wishes and bows and scrapes in Florentine drawing rooms. He is popular and charming, but none of these Russian and Italian countesses can make him forget his beloved Chesapeake and the house in Baltimore's South Street.

"Could I be like the fairytale goose who has hatched a little duckling?" Betsy wonders to herself.

Among the foreigners, the Russian colony is the most luxury-loving and extravagant group. Some of its members, such as old Count Demidoff and Princess Galitzin, shuttle between Florence, Aix-les-Bains, and Geneva. Caroline Galitzin, a snub-nosed blonde of Polish origin, shows little enthusiasm for accompanying her husband, Alexander — he is a close friend of the czar and the legal adviser to the synod — when he has to go to Saint Petersburg on business and prefers to stay in Italy or Geneva with her children. A cousin of Prince Galitzin is a missionary in the United States, somewhere in the Alleghenies. By a strange coincidence he has been ordained a priest in Baltimore. Count and Countess Chouvaloff, who have a whole string of children, are also very pleasant friends. Gregory Chouvaloff is a scion of an old noble family that has produced many statesmen. One of them was the favorite of Catherine the Great. Count Demidoff leads a sybaritic life in the Corsini palace, not far from the Cascines. He always employs a troupe of French actors who put on a play almost every night. His receptions are lavish, and Betsy never misses one of them. M. Demidoff has become very fond of her and invites her to lunch or dinner three times a week. These large gatherings take place either at the palace or at his superb villa at San Donato, outside of town. Demidoff's hospitality is so generous that he is always surrounded by a crowd of friends and hangers-on who profit from his largesse. A year earlier he has commissioned the famous Florentine sculptor Bartolini to build him a colossal marble mausoleum that is to be even more grandiose than that of the Grand Duke of Tuscany.

This work is barely completed when the unfortunate man suffers an embolism amidst a lavish festivity and is carried out in the throes of death as his bewildered guests line his path.

His eldest son Anatole, who has inherited his father's fortune, continues where he has left off, but Betsy finds it hard to come to terms with the loss of her dear old friend, Count Nicolas. "Florence is not the same since he is gone," she murmurs.

Bo has won over many girls, and a few older ladies as well, by his natural manner and his gentleness: this tall young man waiting hand and foot on his beautiful mother is a touching sight.

"Why don't you get him into a diplomatic career?" the Swedish ambassador suggests to Betsy. "With this family name, he would have every chance to be well received by our king.[1] Moreover, he is bilingual, which gives him an advantage over other diplomats, who only speak their own language correctly."

This advice has not fallen on deaf ears. That very evening Betsy has dashed off a letter to her father, asking him to talk to General Smith and to President John Quincy Adams (who has recently succeeded Monroe) so that they will think of her son if a position as secretary of a legation should become available. "It will be a great sacrifice for me to separate from my only son," she adds, "but parents must consider their children's best interest first. . . . Mrs. Caton has set a god example for me."

This "Mother of the *Gracchi*," who has not always stood well with Betsy, has just married her second daughter, Louisa, to the young Duke of Leeds.

"I surely won't be lucky enough to see my Bo do so well," Betsy sighs. "But I would rather have him become an old bachelor than see him fall stupidly in love with some little American bourgeoise with whom he would have scads of snot-nosed babies. No, I have no desire to play the grandmother under those conditions!"

Bo has gone back to America in mid-June, a little disappointed,

---

[1] The Napoleonic general Bernadotte, who became king of Sweden.

perhaps, that his mother is not coming along, but also rather glad to recover some freedom of movement. Actually, Betsy has promised to join him soon; she just has to go briefly to Paris, where she has invested the inheritance from Princess Borghese at four percent. Aunt Nancy, who is in charge of his finances in America, will pay him a monthly sum of $50, which should be sufficient, especially if he lives with his grandfather.

THE MONTHS GO BY, AND BETSY CAN'T FIND THE COURAGE TO FACE A voyage across the Atlantic and a return to the New World. She has so many friends in Florence, Italian, French, English, and especially Russian people. Slavic charm under a Tuscan sky — it is a highly charged combination! How can she possibly leave it?

Moreover, just then Italy is full of happy surprises. While Chateaubriand is French ambassador in Rome, Lamartine is chargé d'affaires in Florence. He is a brilliant man, surrounded by a halo of glory, who, having just published the *Nouvelles méditations poétiques,* sometimes reads from this work to small groups of friends and acquaintances. Everyone in Florence knows his famous poem *Le Lac,* which he had written in honor of Julie Charles at the lake near Le Bourget:

> O time, suspend your flight,
> and you, fortunate hours, stay your course . . .

Betsy has made these famous stanzas her own, especially at dusk, when, standing near the church of San Miniato, she contemplates Brunelleschi's dome, Giotto's campanile, the Palazzo Vecchio. Where else would she find so much beauty?

At an evening gathering in a Florentine salon, someone presents to her a blonde and chubby young woman with a fresh, pink face, with whom she talks poetry for hours, telling her about her infinite admiration for Byron, whose work she knows inside out. It turns out that the blonde contessa is Teresa Guiccioli, the last love of the "bel Inglese," the object of a passion fraught with thunderstorms and wild ups and downs. To Betsy's great amusement, Teresa describes to her the retinue of dogs, cats, falcons, ravens, and parrots that followed the poet wherever he went. "But it was not a peaceful existence," she concludes. "In these few years I tasted all the happiness and all the unhappiness this world has to offer."

And the corpulent blond man whom Betsy meets another evening is Alessandro Manzoni, the famous Milanese poet who had a few years earlier written the well-known *Ode for May 5* celebrating the memory of Napoleon. He has come here to refine his language by contact with Tuscan speech, to "wash it in the Arno," as he says, before he publishes his new book *I promessi sposi* (*The Betrothed*). And the man over there, with a long face and a pensive expression, is Salvatore Viali, a Corsican poet whose *Dionomachia,* published in 1823, has been a great success. A certain Henry Beyle — not very handsome, this one, with a trimmed beard framing his round face — scrutinizes the assembly with a searching eye. Extremely clever and passionate about music, he has just published a book on love and a *Life of Rossini*. He is now beginning to use the pseudonym Stendhal.

In this Florence, where a gentle wind of liberalism and *Risorgimento* blows among the intellectuals, Betsy is so happy with her life that the news she receives from America means almost nothing to her.

Everyone in Baltimore is fine, including the dog Wolf. Bo has gone once more to visit his uncle Joseph at Point Breeze: his daughter Zenaïde lives there now with her husband Charles-Lucien, who has returned from Italy, and her two little children, one of them a new baby. Comte de Survilliers has built for them in his park a pretty two-story villa with an Italian-style portico in front of the entrance. He calls it the "lake house" and it is connected to his own dwelling by an underground passage — which will cause the secret agents of the Bourbon government to spill a lot of ink, since they see it as evidence of sinister plots.

Zénaïde, a dark-haired beauty of aristocratic bearing who, though rather cold and not as artistic as her sister but a fine musician, plays the harp and translates Schiller, while her husband devotes a good part of his time to ornithology. A member of the Academy of Science of Philadelphia, of the Academy of Science of Baltimore, and of the College of Natural History of New York, he has just published a book on the birds of America, and a seagull of the Eastern Seaboard of the United States has been named the "Bonaparte seagull." He is a great friend of Jean-Jacques Audubon.[2] Bo has been received affectionately by everyone and has done his best to convey the latest news from Europe to his uncle.

In Baltimore, things continue to move forward: the tracks have just been laid for a railroad line to Ohio, to be called the Baltimore and Ohio Railroad. The first stone for the future railroad station has also been laid at Mount Clare. This rail line is designed to compete with shipping on the Erie canal, which advantages New York State. William Patterson and other Baltimore notables are financing this project. Old Mr. Carroll of Carrolton, grandfather of the Caton sisters, is already building a viaduct across the Gwynns Falls that will some day bear his name.

---

[2] American painter and ornithologist, and pupil of David. His colored prints of North American birds, published on 1830, have become famous throughout the world.

25

*A*MERICA IS FAR AWAY, AND TUSCANY AS seductive as ever. When summer comes, people walk in the shade of the Cascines, which are to Florence what Hyde Park and the Bois de Boulogne are to London and Paris. This is the place to meet all the best people, exchange greetings, engage in conversation — and also snub the undesirables. The half-darkness of dusk is the time to whisper secrets, pass messages from hand to hand, and spin intrigues.

If some evening Betsy does not engage in this ritual and skips her evening walk, she is immediately plied with worried questions by her Florentine friends, such as the Marquis del Douro, who has not remained indifferent to her proud beauty. "What is happening? I did not see you yesterday evening at the Cascines, were you unwell?"

Very British — despite the Hispanic sound of his name, which originated in one of his father's victories — this son of the Duke of Wellington has found it piquant to pay court to the ex-Madame Bonaparte, whom he finds charming. He floods her with flowers and sentimental notes like this one: "Will you come to visit a poor rabbit who has shut himself up in his warren from pure chagrin?"

Gregory Chouvaloff, for his part, sometimes escorts the young American to the theater or a concert when his wife Sophie is too tired and prefers to stay at home with her children. He is her attentive serving knight, a *sigisbeo,* as they say in Florence, and no one is shocked to see him by Betsy's side. At times his admiring friendship for her takes on amorous overtones, but the young woman soon straightens him out.

The Duc de Dino, Talleyrand's nephew, is another *sigisbeo* of the beautiful Madame Patterson, ex-Madame Bonaparte, as is Prince Borghese. A fine though recently thickened figure of a man with anthracite-grey eyes and a head of black, curly hair, Camillo Borghese has been a widower for three years and now spends most of his time in Florence.

"Could it be that he is carried away by the resemblance I was said to have to his late wife, Princess Pauline?" Betsy wonders, highly flattered by his attention. "But while I want to appear at all his parties, I do not want to be included among his mistresses. Actually, I don't find him attractive enough. I think he is clumsy and not very clever, and he has a piping voice that does not go well with his corpulence. But then, one never knows: if he had a mind to ask for my hand, I would think about it."

Prince Borghese, however, does not seem particularly inclined to remarry. But news travels fast, and Betsy soon receives a letter from Baltimore, from her aunt Nancy, who upbraids her: "Listen here, you are hiding things from us, my dear niece! Was I not told that Prince Borghese is ogling you? Well now, I dreamt last night that you were marrying him. Could this be a premonition?"

Betsy is amused. "Aunt Nancy mistakes her wishes for realities," she murmurs as she closes up the letter. "Bah, let her talk! And it's just as well that there is talk in Baltimore. I only hope that all of this will come to the ears of the Caton sisters! They would be green with envy if they could also read the fervent declarations I constantly receive from the son of the Duke of Wellington. Ah, my dear Mary, my queen has taken your pawn!"

She has done it to a few other ladies as well, for one morning finds the following epigram, slipped under her door by a jealous rival:

> Ah! who is that languishing fair?
> E bella, è bella, sicuro,
> In one hand a tabatière
> In the other the marquess of Douro.
> Pretty Patterson! Ply every charm,
> These charms will too soon be at zero.
> Get the hand, if you can, not the arm
> Of the heir of the Waterloo hero!

A bit of gnashing of teeth, here and there? She is quite pleased! One man observes her in silence. The blue eyes behind his wire-rimmed spectacles look amused. Tall and square, he holds himself very straight, almost rigid: this is Prince Gortchakoff, attaché at the Russian embassy.

Betsy has met him at the home of the Russian ambassador, who gives a reception every Sunday evening. She has noticed his energetic face, his high forehead surrounded by a halo of blond hair, and the intelligent curving of his mouth. At first this cold and reserved man had intimidated her. But one evening, as they were dancing a saltarelle, he whispered to her: "You are better than you want yourself to appear."

Betsy had been startled, her face turning crimson: had this unknown, with whom she had not yet exchanged more than a few words, laid bare her true nature?

"Why do you overwhelm yourself by leading this frenzied life? Just what are you looking for?" Gortchakoff had continued. For once Betsy was so troubled that, unable to find a stinging rejoinder, she could only stammer a few embarrassed words.

This was the beginning of a strong friendship between them; better yet, it was a kind of complicity, made of glances exchanged between them in society when someone seems overly burlesque or ceremonious, when their ears have heard too much insipid talk, made also of laughter about ridiculous situations. Their principal enemy is mediocrity. And while there are some clever people in the society they frequent, mediocrity is rampant. There are conceited fops who spout their opinions about everything, there are the rich parvenus with their overwhelming vulgarity, all gilding, frills, and furbelows.

Becoming bolder, Betsy relishes the pleasure of tearing apart this enemy. Oh, how cleverly she can make fun of her own kind! She is irresistible, and when she shows her pretty teeth in peals of laughter, one forgives her everything! "One had better be in the camp of your friends," observes Alexander Gortchakoff. "True," she admits, "but what a privilege to be counted among my friends, for I am capable of defending them to the death!" "Bah! you have a great many failings . . . but all in all, they are worth more than the platitudes of the others."

There is sweetness in this budding friendship, which does not want to call itself by another name, because Betsy has decided to strike it from her vocabulary. Gortchakoff is subtle enough not ever to pronounce it either. A patient man, he waits for this beautiful butterfly to burn itself in his flame. He knows how to risk a tender gesture when the moment is right, to enfold the young woman's hand in his own, send her an admiring look across a crowded drawing room, or hold her a little too tightly as they dance a waltz (and he is a wonderful dancer!), but he does not want to make her skittish.

And of course, he does not show any jealousy when he sees his beautiful friend at the theater in the company of some *sigisbeo* or other. Such a vulgar sentiment, jealousy! Betsy finds this disconcerting. Those blue eyes looking at her from behind those severe glasses and that enigmatic smile are keeping her ensnared much more securely than the smoldering glances of any Italian duke or prince. She has finally found an adversary worthy of her.

"I only want to be judged by my peers," she has confessed to him one day. These words have remained fixed in the Russian's mind. "You have no idea how much I admire your pride," he had murmured.

AT VARIOUS SOCIAL EVENTS, BETSY SOMETIMES MEETS THE EX-KING OF Holland, who has moved to Florence but still shuttles back and forth to Rome, where he goes to embrace his mother. Louis is absorbed by his writing. At the moment is working on refuting the assertions of Walter Scott, who has just published a *Life of Napoleon*. Acclaimed in *Ultra* circles and among the Anglo-Saxons, this book has enraged all those whose hearts once beat for the great man. Louis leads a very retiring life. Although he still treats Betsy with the utmost courtesy, she no longer sees in his eyes the little flame of affectionate connivance that had made him so attractive to her in the past.

Joseph's wife Julie, Comtesse de Survilliers, has also come to live in Florence, but she does not go into society much more than Louis. She has with her daughter Charlotte and her son-in-law Napoleon-Louis. His younger brother, Louis-Napoleon — with whom Bo had become friends — lives with his mother at Arenenberg and sometimes appears in Florence for a brief visit. Intelligent and pleasant, he is filled with generous projects, which he hides under a dreamy exterior. His mother, Queen Hortense, has begun to rent an apartment in the Ruspoli palace in Rome for a few months every year. It is located close to the Rinuccini Palace, so that she can be close to her mother-in-law, Madame Letizia. Betsy has had a fleeting glimpse of Hortense, a handsome woman of about forty, who, without being pretty, has charm and a subtle mind. But she is no longer so interested in rubbing shoulders with Napoleon's family . . .

There is no more talk of a princely marriage for Bo. This subject is dead in the water. Well, never mind, then! He will just have to stay a bachelor. The main thing is that he not marry an American. Alas! Betsy does not know yet what a cruel disappointment is taking shape in deep secrecy across the Atlantic!

26

"*I* CAN'T BELIEVE IT," SHE MURMURS WITH trembling lips as she puts back on a side table a letter she has just received from her brother Edward. She has read only the first paragraphs. Bo is married! It is true that this is not a complete surprise for her; her father and her brother had already warned her about this plan a few months earlier, but she had advised them that she was strictly opposed to it. And now they had simply disregarded her opinion; it is unbelievable! Yet she had explained to them that she had brought up Jérôme with the idea that he was of noble lineage and must not lose his standing by marrying some little bourgeoise. No one in America could be considered his social equal. She would have done better to give her son money for traveling in Africa or Siberia rather than seeing him do such a stupid thing!

What a terrible disappointment to find out how different her son is from her! She would have let herself be hacked to pieces rather than marry an American after she had been the sister-in-law of an emperor! "This sense of pride," she had remarked, "is the reason for the respect and the deference I enjoy in America and in Europe." And so she had tried to inculcate these principles in her son. Considering his birth, he should have harbored some ambition, more even than she herself. But one can never put oneself into another person's place! She had done everything in her power for him. . . . You just can't change people with the touch of a magic wand!

Edward tells her that he has done his very best to slow things down.

But his father and his brother George have put their shoulders to the wheel, afraid that Bo would let himself be influenced by his mother. No, really, Betsy keeps telling herself, it is just too cruel to be disappointed by a son for whom one has sacrificed everything since he was a child!

Fortunately, it appears that the young lady in question is not without fortune. That is one point in her favor. Bo might have done worse! . . . At least one can hope that the clauses of the marriage contract will be favorable to him. "I will write to my father asking him to give me the details on this point. I will use this opportunity to get everything off my chest and to tell him what I think of the underhanded way in which this matter has been handled."

It is true that Betsy has been the last person to be informed of this event. As early as April 1829 (and we are now in December), the Comte de Survilliers had received a letter from his nephew, asking him for advice.

My dear nephew [Joseph had evasively replied], I do not know what advice to give you. . . . I felt that your grandfather is a very sensible man, and it seems to me that you owe a great deal of deference and consideration to what he will believe is best for you. By this time you must know yourself and understand where your greatest chances for success and happiness lie.

As for the ex-king of Westphalia — notified by early November, along with the other Bonapartes in Rome and Florence —he had briefly made a show of being offended at being presented with a fait accompli, but was of course immensely relieved to see his eldest son finally taken care of. Ouf! he must have said to himself, one less thing to worry about!

. . . Since I was not consulted about an event of such importance to you, I assume that you have carefully thought it out; and since you do not need my consent, all I can do is to send you my fatherly blessing and wish you every happiness. . . . You must place yourself into a natural and positive position, for nothing in the world can compensate for a false position.

The most natural thing for you is therefore to stay frankly, truly, and without reservations, an American citizen. If you do this you will be better off in every respect than your brothers and sister.

Everyone in the Bonaparte family has sent fulsome letters of congratulations: Madame Mère, Louis, the Comtesse de Survilliers, and even Charlotte, who still has great affection for Bo.

My dear cousin [she writes], Maman allows me to add a few lines to this letter, and I am glad to have this opportunity, for I too was anxious to congratulate you and to assure both of you of my very best wishes. I hope that I will have the pleasure of meeting my new cousin, to whom I ask you to convey my tenderest feelings. I hope that you have not completely forgotten me, even though your correspondence has slowed down a bit.

Yes, everyone in the Bonaparte family is happy that the American Jérôme has finally opted for a way of life that seems to suit him perfectly. Only Betsy groans, curses her fate, and endlessly dwells on her rancor under the Florentine sky.

More news arrives from Baltimore. According to Edward, the young Susan May Williams whom Bo has married is not pretty, but graceful and well-made. An only child, she is very sure of herself and rather spoiled. "... But you should not have deployed all the resources of your vocabulary in your letter to our father," he concludes in a reproachful tone. A few weeks later, Bo sends a somewhat sheepish letter:

Please understand, Maman, that in my future life I can never get along without money. Yet as you know, the allowance from my father is very precarious, and grandfather has not, so far, promised to do anything for me. Contrary to your wishes, I have no desire to follow a diplomatic career. Business is what I like, and for that I need something to fall back on.

Does this mean Bo has not married purely for love? Or is he lying to spare his mother? If that was his intention, he has succeeded. For in a rather odd way, Betsy feels better about everything. "In any case," she thinks, "I hope he will not have a child right away. And it would even be better if he never did." As for that Susan May, she detests her. It is because of her that all her efforts have come to nothing. And how she has struggled to integrate Bo into the Bonaparte family! What she has suffered in the past to remain faithful to the name she has borne for ten years with such pride that it has been very hard to give it up. But he, her son, has the right to bear it as long as he lives. Jérôme-Napoleon Bonaparte. . . . At any European court, he could have asked for the hand of a princess of royal blood, or at the very least a duchess or a countess. . . . And here he is in the arms of a commoner! Instead of the brilliant diplomatic career of which she had dreamed for him, he will be content to be an obscure lawyer in Baltimore. It is exasperating! What has she done to deserve such a disappointment? She has been betrayed twice in her life, first by the father, now by the son!

But then, since they are getting along so nicely without her in Baltimore, she might as well stay in Europe. All these years she has deprived herself for her son; from now on she will freely spend her resources on herself, live in a superb apartment, keep a carriage and have servants like everyone else. Four thousand per year is a minimum!

In her most polite style she asks Nancy Spear to send on her dishes, her clothes, and her jewels from Baltimore, by the diplomatic mail. But Bo, to whom Betsy had entrusted the key to her jewelry case, has lost it. Of course, he had other things on his mind. And so the lock of the case had to be forced. As for the dishes, they were sent from America poorly packed and without any kind of packing list; on arrival many pieces were broken and others stolen. Fortunately, none of the jewels are missing, and Betsy is glad to see them, her turquoises, emeralds, diamonds, pearls, and white topazes. "Well now," she says to herself, "suppose I commissioned a Florentine jeweler to make me a tiara out of the diamonds from this brooch that was given to me by Princess Borghese, as well as the necklace and the long emerald earrings, the present Jérôme gave me that time in Lisbon. Such a piece could actually be used in three different ways and be worn also as a necklace or at the waist, attached to a belt. . . . And oh these white topazes! One would swear they are diamonds! There is nothing like them in all of Europe!" They make such a splash in Europe, these famous topazes, that Betsy has to order the same kind for her lady friends in Florence, who are delighted with them. And the tiara looks truly "royal," according to Princess Galitzin, who knows about such things.

While Betsy consoles herself as best she can by looking at her jewel case and managing her investments from a distance, and while she adds to the luster of Florentine drawing rooms by her grace and wit and also carries on a bit of a flirtation with the handsome Gortchakoff, things are moving at a rapid pace in Baltimore. In the fall of 1830 Bo has become the father of a boy who has also been given the name Jérôme-Napoleon. Noblesse oblige! Bo has quickly announced this birth to his mother and to all the Bonapartes in Italy, who have sent him letters overflowing with affection by return mail. The ex-king of Westphalia is the first to express his joy, followed by Louis, who takes the opportunity to report the news of all his family, including his mother who, he says, has had a bad fall at Villa Borghese and will be permanently immobilized. Nonetheless Madame Letizia does send a note ending with the words, ". . . never doubt my tender feelings for you as well as for your son." As for Cardinal Fesch, he continues to show the same solicitude from which he has never wavered over the last eight years, during which he has scrupulously seen to it that Comte de Montfort paid his son's allowance.

Joseph, for his part, has invited the young couple to Point Breeze and sometimes stays with his nephew in Baltimore when traveling. Everyone has applauded the birth of this new little Bonaparte, everyone, except Betsy.

For the last year she has exchanged only cold business letters with her son. She has asked Bo to send her monthly statements about the income from her investments. After all, they concern him too, for as a good mother she has not cut him off. Moreover, she has already made a will, in which she leaves him his rightful share. No one will be able to say that she has not done her duty to the end. But there are no more heart-to-heart exchanges between them. And Betsy haughtily ignores this grandson, who should have touched some grandmotherly chord in her. The child of Susan May Williams? For shame!

As is well known, 1830 is also a year of great effervescence in Europe. In Paris, Charles X has been overthrown in July and Louis-Philippe d'Orléans has come to the throne. Republicans and Bonapartists are suddenly full of renewed hope, and the wind of the French Revolution is once again blowing across Europe, particularly in Italy, where the Carbonari are agitating for unity and independence, to the great concern of legitimate sovereigns.

The Bourbons of Naples have asked the Holy See to tighten its surveillance of the members of the Bonaparte family. And rightly so, it turns out; for while Bo is enjoying his baby in Baltimore, his two cousins, the sons of Louis and Hortense, are pursuing dreams of political upheaval. Now that their hopes of returning to France have been dashed by King Louis-Philippe, who, for all his liberal ideas, refuses to revoke the sentence of exile recently imposed on the Bonaparte family, Louis-Napoleon and Napoleon-Louis have decided to place their considerable energy at the service of the Italian cause. In November 1830 they can be seen on the Corso in Rome parading on horses decked out in tricolored shabracks and accompanied, among others, by young Jérôme-Napoleon, the son of Jérôme and Catherine of Württemberg — the former pupil at the Lazarist school in Siena.

Someone was not pleased to be disturbed in the placid tranquillity of his existence in the Palazzo Nunez. This was the ex-king of Westphalia, of course, who asked the Holy See for help in hushing up the affair.

Young Jérôme-Napoleon agrees to return to the bosom of the family and to lie low, unlike his cousins, who go off to join their Carbonari friends in Bologna. By the spring there is an uprising in the Romagna and Modena proclaims Napoleon II — *l'Aiglon* [Eaglet] — king of Italy. The Austrian army intervenes and the two young Bonapartes are ordered to report to Ancona. The older brother, Napoleon-Louis, Charlotte's husband, dies at Foligno under mysterious circumstances, while his brother flees abroad. The upshot is that the Bonapartes living in Rome are ordered to leave the Papal States. Only Cardinal Fesch and Madame Mère are allowed to stay. The ex-queen of Naples, Caroline Murat, who with her children had resided in Rome for four years, now leaves for Florence, as does the Comte de Montfort with his family.

If Jérôme deplores the temerity of his nephews and the sad end to their epic endeavor, Betsy is dismayed to learn of her ex-husband's impending arrival in her own Florentine fiefdom.

"I shall soon have to say good-bye to you," she says to Prince Gortchakoff, with tears in her eyes. "I can't possibly live under the same sky with the Comte de Montfort. Can you imagine what it would be like for me to be in constant fear of meeting him at social gatherings, along with that fat German wife of his?"

"Actually," says Gortchakoff after an awkward silence, "I too have to tell you something I have put off for some time: I have been transferred to Rome. . . . I greatly fear that the time has come when we must part. But I do hope it will not be for very long!"

If Betsy had the courage, she would have said the words that are burning in her throat: "Prince Alexander, you will always be very dear to me. . . ." But she tightly closes her lips and swallows her tears. She knows that Gortchakoff is a confirmed bachelor, intent on advancing his career, a few years younger than herself, and at this point not interested in marriage. To be sure, he has tried many times to make her his mistress. But the American has been adamant in her resistance. "Why don't you employ your talents to convert the Marquis del Douro, that perpetual sighing lover, to your anti-erotic principles," he has scoffed. "Perhaps they would do him some good." Betsy, offended, had not answered. How could she explain to this handsome diplomat why she was so afraid of love? The only attachment she can accept is a distant and platonic love that can never bring disappointment.

There sometimes is a concatenation of evils that results so necessarily from a first cause that one must always go back to that cause to explain everything. . . ." If Prince Gortchakoff could have read these lines, written down in a little green notebook where Betsy jots down her best thoughts, the veil of mystery around his lovely friend would have been lifted in part.

"COME ON," PRINCESS GALITZIN CHEERFULLY TELLS HER, "I AM TAKING you with me to Geneva. Did I tell you that I bought a property at Genthod, some twenty kilometers from town? To begin with, though, we might go to take the waters at Aix-les-Bains."

Does this mean that her wonderful life in Florence has come to an end? But then there is a lively, cosmopolitan society on the shores of Lake Geneva, composed for the most part of Russians and Britons. So the change is not too abrupt, after all. The Chouvaloffs, in particular, have made it a habit to live in Aix and Geneva every year during the summer months. Gregory is delighted to be reunited with his lovely friend. He had felt a few twinges of jealousy as he watched the burgeoning of a tender friendship between her and Alexander, the blond diplomat.

"I too had hoped to bring enchantment to this face," he confesses one evening. But Betsy firmly puts him too in his place. "In any case, you know that you will always have a sincere friend in me; please don't forget that," the count had added. "No, I don't forget it, and I never will," Betsy had said to herself. "It is wonderful to have real friends."

The presence of Princess Galitzin not far from the city is a great comfort. When Betsy is weary of the social whirl, she is happy to visit Caroline at her château of Genthod. A small apartment there is always ready to receive her. She even has the privilege to help decorate it.

"That way," the princess has cheerfully told her, "you are sure to find everything to your taste. Anytime you feel like it, you can get away for three or four days in my company, and we can really relax: books, newspapers, no need to dress up, walks in the hills or by the lakeshore. . . . Peace and quiet to look forward to! The charabanc will wait for you at your door as soon as you send word that you are coming with the milk woman."

Betsy has taken lodgings in one of the city's best *pensions,* the Pension Donadieu, overlooking the Promenade Saint-Antoine. Here she has an agreeable view and the food is not too bad.

At his property of Chène, Sismondi is hard at work on a *Histoire des Français* in several volumes, which he has started after having published his highly successful *Histoire des républiques italiennes.* Jenny Sismondi has introduced Betsy to the more frivolous but extremely clever works of a young writer and visual artist by the name of Rodolphe Toepffer, who illustrates his own books. His *Voyages en Zigzag,* which relates his expeditions in the mountains with his pupils, is a masterpiece of humor and poetry, and his other books, *Les aventures du docteur Festus* and *Monsieur Jabot* make the two friends laugh till they cry.

"Do you realize that in order to make a living the author had to open a school in Geneva?" "Too bad it's too late! Ten years ago I would have been happy to entrust my son's education to such an entertaining teacher."

Prince Gortchakoff, having completed his mission in Rome, has returned to Tuscany; he just cannot leave Italy and sometimes writes nostalgic letters.

I am in a black mood, my dear ally, but I want to write to you anyway. Your letter of December makes up for the noise that is called conversation here and reminds me of some old times when my life was better filled. Alas! I am not about to see you in Florence, for the place is crawling with Bonapartes.

Come closer, my dear ally [Betsy replies], so I can whisper in your ear. . . . I have replaced your conversation with that of an old Frenchmen of the court of Louis XVI. What can I say, monarchy just suits me better than republican vulgarity: the republic has repelled me from the day I arrived in the world.

The Chouvaloffs have gone back to Florence. How sad for Betsy to have lost her two most fervent admirers. She feels herself getting old — a slow and steady feeling that seeps through every pore and chills her to the bone. And yet her beautiful face is still smooth, her chestnut hair is barely beginning to show a little gray, and she has gotten just a little plump.

"You are still a beauty!" Princess Galitzin assures her. "But I am no longer of an age to enjoy flirtations," Betsy sighs, "and without that stimulus I shall die of boredom!"

Nonetheless she has found a way to dazzle Prince Serge Galitzin, Caroline's brother-in-law, who had come to visit the month before. If she had encouraged him in any way, he would have proposed to her. But her heart is elsewhere.

Aunt Nancy, to whom her niece has complained about her low spirits, has not minced her words: "After all, you can always have a good time. And you are free to change scenery anytime you want to." Nor does she fail to point out to Betsy that she, Nancy, is more than ever tied down by the deteriorating health of old Mr. Patterson. She has had to give up her little annual trips to the federal capital in order to stay with him. "It is time for you to come home, my dear niece," she concludes, "believe me, your father is not doing well."

Not without hesitation, Betsy makes up her mind: *non più andrai . . . notte e giorno d'intorno girando*[1] she says to herself, quoting Mozart's *Figaro*. She will return to Baltimore traveling through France. She will allow herself just one brief stop in Paris to take care of some business and see some friends she still has there. But there is trouble: Paris is suffering a cholera epidemic. People (including the prime minister, Casimir Périer), are dying like flies, and it is certainly no time to take a chance with this epidemic. But Betsy asserts, "Bah, something tells me that I won't die of that disease."

However, she is prudent enough to wait a few months before setting out.

These plans are very disappointing to her friends in Florence, who had tried to persuade her to come there to say goodbye to them. They had hoped that she would at least opt for Rome if she absolutely wanted to avoid Tuscany. The only Bonapartes left in the Eternal city are Cardinal Fesch and Madame Mère, completely blind by this time; and Rome is so close to Florence that they could easily to go over and see her.

"Wouldn't that have been better than to brave the Parisian fog and the Phyrigian cholera? But I can see that you are determined to forsake your cisalpine friends," Gortchakoff writes to her.

"I confess that I don't understand you very well," Princess Galitzin tells her. "Don't you want to see the people who are so dear to you before you put an ocean between them and you?"

"The letters of Prince Gortchakoff are such a treat, his absence is so delicious, that I will not lay myself open to losing this flattering interest by getting close to him. . . ."

"*Happy is he who has never been born. For he has not known heartbreak and the faltering of the soul . . .*"

As her coach rumbles over the narrow route of Mont Cenis along a precipice from which she can see night falling over the gray roofs of a village nestled in the valley, Betsy sadly recites these lines from Chateaubriand. Without hurrying, and in small stages, she is making her way to Paris. But really, what does it matter where she goes? Nothing is in store for her anywhere . . .

---

[1] No longer will you go roving about day and night.

27

*P*ARIS IS A BIT OF A RESPITE BEFORE CROSSING the Atlantic. The city is a building site, where one still flounders in the mud on the Place de la Concorde or in the area around the Madeleine, where the Champs-Elysées are still a cutthroat neighborhood from which, far in the distance on the heights of Chaillot, one can just make out the unfinished skeleton of the Arc de Triomphe.

"Paris is so entertaining, Betsy says to herself as she rediscovers the charm of these narrow streets where coaches and carriages have a hard time getting by the big omnibuses that have recently been put into circulation, where lively crowds mill about, and where the showy elegance of the "lionesses," as fancy courtesans are called, can be seen side by side with the picturesque attire of modest people from the outlying districts.

Fashion has tightened women's waists, widened their skirts, and poured out floods of lace, flowers, and feathers, whereas men are tightly encased in narrow jackets that thrust out their torsos and show off colorful vests and shirts with very high collars.

This time Betsy is staying at a hotel in the rue de Provence, near the Chaussée d'Antin, which is still the neighborhood of businessmen and well-to-do foreigners. The aristocratic faubourg Saint-Germain will not see her again. Many of her old friends of the ancient aristocracy have died. And now that the bourgeois king has come to the throne, certain salons have closed their doors, their society has turned inward on itself or dispersed to its landed estates — not without grumbling about the end of the royal hunt ordered by Louis-Philippe.

As for the salons of the "Juste Milieu," the aristocrats shun them. But not far from the rue de Sèvres, Betsy has been pleased to make her way to the Abbaye-aux-Bois. Here Madame Récamier no longer occupies the top story, right under the eaves, where she had made her home ten years earlier; she now has treated herself to the luxury of a more spacious apartment on the second floor, with large windows looking out on the abbey's gardens. Her drawing room is still dominated by Gérard's large painting showing Madame de Staël as Corinne [her book's heroine] at Cape Misenum; the furnishings consist of no more than two bookcases, a sofa, a small desk, and a few chairs. In one corner stands a harp, on which Juliette sometimes plucks some chords when in her sweet voice she sings some romance of Boieldieu. She is still beautiful and gracious, despite her slightly graying hair; she is "at the same time twenty and sixty years old" and has about her a simplicity and a gentleness that warm her friends' hearts.

Having kissed her on the cheek, Juliette has held her American friend's hands in her own for a long time, questioning her solicitously about her stay in Italy. They might have met there, for she was just leaving when Betsy arrived; what a shame, she would have met Betsy's son! Right now, she has a neighbor who would be delighted to see her. It is the Duchesse d'Abrantès, who has just published the first volumes of her Memoirs, where she speaks very positively of Jérôme Bonaparte's first wife. She comes to see Juliette almost every afternoon, for she has taken a small apartment at the Abbaye-aux-Bois, which allows her to pursue her literary endeavors. These have now become her livelihood, for since the tragic death of her husband, she is in straightened circumstances.

But in fact, here she comes: the short, olive-skinned, and rather plump woman who enters the room is about forty years old, with intelligent eyes and a lively mouth under a long and thin nose. Her hair is jet-black with barely a few strands of gray, and her bearing is extremely dignified, despite the almost negligent simplicity of her outfit. She is Laure Junot, Duchesse d'Abrantès. She and Betsy, Juliette tells them, are old acquaintances, although they don't realize it, since Laure is in the presence of the model for the small portrait Jérôme Bonaparte, not yet King of Westphalia, once showed her in a Spanish art store.

Amused at first, the duchess soon begins to look more thoughtful.

She attentively watches the American, who talks with animation about her friends in Florence and passes over the disappointments caused by her family. Mobilizing all her talents as a psychologist, she tries to penetrate the American's true nature. She finds her interesting, but possessed of a cold beauty. Her dress of green faille silk with its large leg of mutton sleeves shows off her slender waist; the chignon placed high on her head and the long curls that frame her face, though often unbecoming on others, in this case enhance the classic purity of her profile. However, Laure notes that she has "a certain reticence in her smile, her glances, and her words" that might make a less attentive observer believe that she lacks sensitivity. "No doubt she has become too adept at controlling her feelings," the duchess concludes to herself. "I think she would be difficult to tame . . . but I am willing to try, because I like her."

And since she is just now working on the sequel to her *Mémoires du Consulat et de l'Empire* and on her *Mémoires sur la Restauration,* she might as well ask Mme Patterson for her testimony, since she and her son have had some contact with the Bonapartes in Rome. And perhaps she might even tell her about some scabrous anecdote from her life with Jérôme?

"Oh please! I think you have not been too kind to him in your *Mémoires,* and I would not want to add to that!

"You know," Laure says with a laugh, "Jérôme and I are the same age and we were childhood friends; I played with him in Ajaccio, and then I met him again a few years later in Paris, where both our mothers lived in the rue du Rocher. . . . He was a spoiled child, I always thought, and even Napoleon himself let his brother get away with too much."

Despite Betsy's reticence to disclose intimate details of her private life to the illustrious chronicler, she is only too glad to accept Laure's subsequent invitation to attend her salon on Mondays.

This, then, is a Parisian season begun under the best auspices: informal lectures in literary salons — at the Duchesse d'Abrantès's on Mondays, at Juliette Récamier's on Thursdays, and at the Baronne Hyde de Neuville's, wife of the former French ambassador to the United States, on Saturdays — interspersed with outings to the Bois de Boulogne, to the Tuileries, to Bagatelle, or to Saint-Cloud (sometimes in Juliette's company), where one goes by post chaise.

At Laure d'Abrantès's, Betsy has been intrigued by a heavy-set, dark-skinned, and mustachioed young man, who is exuberant, slightly vulgar and eccentric in his dress. He is Honoré de Balzac, a writer already famous for the many novels he has written, among them *La peau de chagrin,* and *Le Colonel Chabert,* published two years earlier. The world is unaware that he is gathering material for the future volumes of his *Comédie humaine.* The close friendship between him and the Duchesse d'Abrantès had had the character of a love affair for some years. It was at Honoré's instigation that Laure had embarked upon the writing of her memoirs. She is working on them without respite, spurred on by her friend's example. They have something else in common: both of them are pursued by a mob of creditors and have to deliver copy to their publishers as fast as they can.

Not content with composing her *Mémoires sur la Restauration,* soon to be followed by the *Histoire des salons de Paris,* Laure also writes for newspapers and revues; her name is constantly cited in summaries, and she is highly successful. Little by little, Betsy opens up to her. And Laure d'Abrantès, who is exactly her age, is pleased to discover a much more sensitive woman than first impressions would indicate. They compare their experiences in Italy and marvel in retrospect at the beauties of the Tuscan countryside or of the Eternal City. But few words are exchanged between them about the Bonaparte family. Laure understands that her new friend has been badly hurt and that, even though this name continues to exert an undeniable fascination for Betsy — the blood rushes to her face, and her hands tremble slightly, despite her characteristic self-control — it has never ceased to reopen an imperfectly healed wound.

"Will you go with me tomorrow to the opening of our dear friend Victor Hugo's new play, *Lucretia Borgia?*" Laure asks her one day. Victor Hugo is one of the regulars at Juliette Récamier's, where Betsy meets him every Thursday. At the Abbeye-aux-Bois she also sees the faithful Ballanche, the queen of Sweden, Gérard, Ingres, Delacroix, David d'Angers, Jean-Jacques Ampère, Alexander von Humboldt, whom she had known earlier, Béranger, "the bard of the streets," Sainte-Beuve, Lamartine, and above all Chateaubriand, "looking like the deserts of Arabia," as Lady Morgan had said. Leaving the mantlepiece against which he likes to lean, he sometimes agrees to read from his *Mémoires d'outre-tombe* from a manuscript he has brought along wrapped in a silk handkerchief.

One evening young Delphine Gay has come to recite her poems. Another time Lamartine has read a chapter of *Jocelyn*.

For Betsy, the happy experience of this literary spring under the fleeting clouds of the Parisian sky is sometimes marred by the arrival of mail from America. Aunt Nancy is nagging Betsy to come home as soon as possible: "Why do you dally so much on the banks of the Seine while your father is not well at all?" she inquires. It is true that Betsy has put off her departure again and again: she just can't resign herself to crossing the Atlantic. "Europe is my homeland," she thinks; "To me, America is an exile!"

"Well now," writes Princess Galitzin, "it looks as if Paris has recharged you; the liveliness of your mind has become more brilliant than ever since you are there." And Prince Gortchakoff, who continues to be a faithful correspondent, is furiously fighting off perfidious rumors about himself: "If they tell you that I am getting married, don't you believe it. That is a great folly at every age and in every position!" he asserts to reassure his friend. As for Count Chouvaloff, he openly sighs: "You will be something very special in America," he remarks enviously. "Ah, how I would like to be with you there!"

But Betsy is in no hurry to be "something special" to her compatriots; she wants just a few more evenings of informal lectures, a few more outings, a few more concerts. A young Italian composer, who is also a great violin virtuoso, is all the rage: his name is Niccolo Paganini. At one soirée given by the Austrian ambassador, Count Apponyi, Liszt plays one of Weber's piano concertos. And everyone rushes to the annual art exhibitions to admire the works of Corot, Ingres, Delacroix, Géricault, and the caricatures of Daumier and Gavarni.

With Juliette, or Laure, or Letizia Bonaparte-Wyse — she is Lucien's daughter who has married an Irishman and is living rather modestly in Paris — Betsy experiences some enchanting moments. She has also reestablished contact with an old friend from Geneva, Charlotte de Constant, widow of the great liberal writer Benjamin Constant.

This Charlotte, née von Hardenberg — she is a rather homely, boring, and dowdy German, but so sweet-tempered and feminine that people had sided with her at the time of Benjamin's liaison with Germaine de Staël — has a tumultuous life behind her. Twice divorced, she had secretly married Constant and exhibited an angelic patience in putting up with the moods, the rejections, and the sudden reversals of a husband who was better with biting epigrams than with kind words. He was a sensitive man, she explains, endowed with a most subtle mind . . . and she had loved him. There was between them "a shared intelligence that read each of the other's thoughts, responded to all of each other's emotions," as Benjamin had put it.

"I don't care," Betsy thinks to herself; "I could never have been a doormat to a man, or his slave. No, a thousand times no! . . . Unless, of course, he was a giant, but I have never met that man."

And her glance alights on the Vendôme column at the end of the rue Saint-Honoré, where she is walking with Charlotte de Constant. The government of Louis-Philippe has had the statue of the fallen Emperor replaced atop the monument. Coming from the rue de Castiglione, the last rays of the sunset cast their glow on Napoleon's effigy.

PARIS, GENEVA, FLORENCE. . . . SO MANY MARVELS KEPT DEEP IN HER HEART, a true interior museum through which she will wander later, for years to come, over there, on the other side of the Atlantic. The blue hills of Tuscany, the meandering Arno, the sun setting over Brunelleschi's dome, whispered words under the shade trees of the Cascines. . . . The sparkling blue gaze of Prince Gortchakoff, the velvety eyes of Count Chouvaloff. . . . And Geneva, calm and serene on the shores of its lake. . . . And Paris, many-sided and sprawling, where every nook and cranny is filled with phantoms . . .

Lost in her musings, she contemplates the imaginary lives that flit by in the wake of her ship. All the different Betsys she could have become: Russian, Italian, or French. But no, the die is cast: she has chosen to remain forever Elizabeth Patterson, the repudiated wife of a Bonaparte.

Part IV

LOST ILLUSIONS

Imperious destiny, your command is obeyed.
I no longer entreat you, I yield to your might.
I receive what you send as a burden to bear,
And have ceased to question your dismal decrees.
— FRIEDRICH VON SCHILLER, WALLENSTEIN

28

SOME TWENTY TRUNKS AND CRATES OF VARIOUS sizes are piled up in the front hall of the house on South Street. It looks like moving day! Betsy has had delicately inlaid French and Italian furniture sent from Europe, along with a profusion of bibelots and a set of Parisian porcelain dishes decorated with the effigies of different members of the Bonaparte family. The smiling faces of Jérôme and Napoleon look up from the bottom of plates and bowls decorated with garlands of laurel leaves or with golden bees all around their rims. Even the coffee set reflects Parisian scenes.

"My word, you must think you have come to live among the savages," exclaims Aunt Nancy as she opens a trunk filled with dresses in percale, taffeta, or silk pongee and boxes containing masses of silk bonnets, as well as felt, rice straw, or Italian straw hats. "Do you really believe that you can't find anything to wear here?"

"I decided to bring along a stock of clothes," Betsy declares as she pulls a lace bonnet out of a box and places it on her aunt's head. "Here you are, Aunt Nancy, I brought you a few for your personal use. This one looks lovely on you!"

"Dear me, how ugly my aunt has grown," she thinks to herself, looking at the old lady; "as poorly put together as ever, with her lips and nose stained yellow from taking snuff and chewing-tobacco. Really, how unfeminine!"

Betsy has decided to live for a few months at South Street, so that she can be near her father's bedside, since it is, after all, mainly for him that she has returned. And in any case, her house on Charles Street is occupied by Bo and his family.

William Patterson is but the shadow of his former self. Ghostly pale and with his eyes deeply sunk into their orbits, he wanders about the house supported by a cane and still dressed in the fashion of the Old Regime: black velvet knee pants, white stockings, swept-up hairdo.

Betsy's heart had grown heavy when she saw her father. This, then, was the dignified and authoritarian figure who used to make her tremble — a poor old man bent down by the years and so thin that the slightest breeze might topple him. Life is so cruel!

"I am happy to see you," the old man had stammered as he clasped her in his arms. "God be praised, you have finally returned to the fold! I had almost given up hope. Could it be that you have finally understood that family and home are the mainstays of happiness?"

Intent on avoiding all controversy, Betsy has been careful not to say too much about the rather frivolous life she has led in Florence. To the contrary, she has gone on and on about her literary friendships, the political conflicts that have shaken Europe, and the atmosphere in Paris since the advent of the July Monarchy.

"Here," William Patterson has told her, "we worry about the authoritarian politics of President Jackson. Having fired thousands of government officials and replaced them with his own supporters, he is now attacking the Bank of America. People are furious, and we may well have a revolution. In fact, there has already been an attempt on the President's life. So you see that we are not far behind Europe!

Betsy has waited a few days before contacting her son. But one evening he comes to see her, and her mother's heart leaps when this handsome young man with his firm face and intelligent eyes enters the room. He has filled out, acquired self-confidence. A brilliant lawyer, he is a credit to his grandfather. He does not have much trouble persuading his mother to come to lunch with him and his wife the next day.

As an added inducement, he adds, "this will also be a chance to meet your grandson."

Behind the Bonapartes' large white house adorned with a neo-classic portico on Charles Street stretches a lawn surrounded by flowers. There, sitting in the grass with his nanny, Betsy sees a pretty little boy of four with brown curls dressed in a white piqué dress, who laughs and holds out his arms to her as soon as she comes near. After a few seconds' hesitation, she picks him up and plants a kiss on his pink cheek. The child, at first laughing and struggling to get free, soon calms down and begins to play with his grandmother's necklace — three rows of white topazes — and prattles a few words into her ear.

And suddenly, in a hitherto unknown place in her heart, a flame is ignited. Her grandson! Her first grandson! And a little Bonaparte, too! The sweetest of all the little Bonapartes on earth, whether in Rome or in Florence! How could she have let four long years go by without trying to see him? She furtively wipes off a tear that runs down her cheek.

A tall and slender young woman approaches in a rustling of skirts. "Mother, here is Susan May, my wife. "Well, she isn't bad," Betsy says to herself, hoping that her daughter-in-law has not noticed her emotion.

"Welcome," Susan May says simply.

Betsy examines her in detail: a face which, without being pretty, is not lacking in charm. A distinct voice, great self-confidence. A large mouth, dark, intelligent-looking eyes, a strong chin. She must be a woman of character. . . . Just as well, this is what Bo needs.

The ties have been restored. Betsy once again has a family, and despite all her fears, there have been no scenes, no jolts. Now that she realizes this, Baltimore has a new charm, and this first autumn shows itself in bright colors. She is looking forward to many walks along the Patapsco and the Jones Falls, or through the meadows of Virginia, as long as she is allowed to take along the child.

Over the next few months Bo and his wife endeavor to distract Betsy and to show her new developments in the city. The Gothic style has made its appearance in Baltimore and new viaducts have been built over the rivers. One of them, which had been financed by William Patterson, bears his name. Henceforth, thanks to the train and the new locomotive, called the "Cricket," one can go to Washington in a mere two hours. The railroad's score is improving day by day, but four years ago, in a race between a horse and the first locomotive, the "Tom Thumb," the horse had won!

Bo is happy to be reunited with his mother. He is a good fellow, who loves nothing so much as a tranquil and uncomplicated family life.

How he wishes he could erase the lack of understanding that has accumulated on both sides over these six years. But Betsy is not about to forget the bitter tears she shed that day in Florence when she received a certain letter from her brother Edward.

Sometimes she sadly evokes the moments of intimacy she once shared with Bo, whether it was in Lancaster, South Street, Geneva, or Philadelphia. Her son has gone his own way; she must learn to live with that. But then it gives her a mischievous pleasure to notice that, for all the republican opinions exhibited by her son and daughter-in-law, the coaches and carriages of the Baltimore Bonapartes sport superb coats-of-arms on their doors, and the huge breakfronts in the dining room — with its silk wall-coverings — are filled to the brim with goblets, bowls, salad-servers and pitchers in massive silver, each with its cover topped by a crown.

"Well, well," she says to herself, "it looks as if Bo and Susan May are not as thoroughly democratic as they appear. But then, if in this respect my son has been a cruel disappointment to me, perhaps I will have better luck with my grandson!

One evening, as she returns home from a long visit at Charles Street, Aunt Nancy has waited up for her, looking stricken. "Your father . . ." she stammers, "your father is dead!"

Betsy quickly enters; old Mr. Patterson, dressed all in black, is stretched out on his bed under the high canopy with its heavy raw silk curtains that have guarded his sleep for more than sixty years. Death has conferred upon his face a strange majesty, tempered by a gentleness he never had in his lifetime. For a long moment Betsy stands perfectly still in the silent room, listening to her feelings with a lump in her throat. A dull pain weighs on her heart, but the tears don't come. "Oh Father," she thinks, "why was it so hard for us to love each other?"

John, Harry, George, and Edward have descended upon South Street with their families. Sisters-in-law, nieces and nephews are milling about, and the babies of the third generation; and later the Pattersons' friends and the notables of Baltimore come to call. Kisses on cheeks, handshakes, tears wiped away. . . . And soon, only too soon, comes the moment of truth, the reading of the will.

This document, the longest will to be seen up to that time, is a veritable volume. William Patterson had started working on it at the age of seventy-five. He used it to tell the story of his life, to elaborate on the philosophy that had informed it, and the advice it enabled him to give to his many descendants. "Work, merit, and sobriety are the surest paths to respect and consideration."

He had thought of everything: of the city of Baltimore, to which he bequeathed, in addition to bank securities, a huge piece of property on Hampstead Hill, which will eventually be made into a park that will bear his name. He forgot neither Aunt Nancy, who had devotedly taken care of him, nor his black slaves, who were to be freed at the age of thirty.

To his sons he bequeathed the bulk of his fortune and his business, *Patterson and Sons*. As for Betsy . . .

"The conduct of my daughter Betsy has always been disobedient; she has never consulted me about anything. Indeed, she has caused me a great deal more trouble than all my other children together. . . . It would therefore be neither fair nor reasonable if she were to receive the same share of my fortune as the others."

"Am I hearing this correctly?" Betsy wonders, while the solicitor drones on in his monotonous voice.

"Nonetheless she will receive the house on South Street, where she was born, those on Market Street, where a carpenter and a cabinet-maker live, as well as the new houses on Gay Street. At her death, all of this is to go to her son."

"So our father has disinherited me, hasn't he?" Betsy says to Edward who is taking her home after the meeting at the solicitor's.

"Why no, of course not. He just left you real estate, and he wants you to look after your interests yourself. He knew that you are perfectly capable of doing so. And then it also seems to me that he certainly has not forgotten your son in his bequests to his grandchildren."

It is true, he has always been very fond of Bo. But a speck of poison festers in Betsy's brain: her brothers have been greatly advantaged over her. . . . What an injustice! Her father is wronging her to the very grave.

She wants to flee, flee again. But where would she go?

Fortunately, there is little Jérôme; his innocent cheerfulness can dispel many a cloud. As her father had done with her, and later with

Bo, Betsy sometimes takes the child up on Federal Hill. From the top of the tower, they watch the arrival of ships through their field glasses. There is a great deal of movement on the Chesapeake. Amidst the profusion of steamships that serve to carry merchandise and passengers, a few superb sailing ships are still plying the waters. The two-masted clippers of the first generation have been succeeded by very long and slender four-masted boats rigged with square sails and completely lined in copper. Increasingly rapid and skippered by captains who push them to the outer limits of their capabilities, they are used not only for the trade with Europe, the Antilles, and Latin America, but also travel to China, from which they bring back tea. *Ann McKinn* and *Challenge* are some of their names.

One also sees long, flat boats equipped with winches and trawlers that are used for dredging for oysters; they are called *skipjacks*. Betsy loves oysters and sometimes makes fried oysters for her grandson. She often dons a cook's apron; in addition to Maryland recipes she prepares rather exotic ones she has brought back from Europe. Some of these call for tomatoes, a vegetable that at this time the Americans still consider poisonous.

She likes to entertain friends, but she does not have many in Baltimore. Some have died, others have moved elsewhere. The Gallatins are in New York; Albert has been approached for the post of secretary of the treasury, but has declined. James has become a distinguished figure as head of the National Bank. Henriette Rewbell divides her time between Baltimore and Paris. Her parents have died a few years earlier.

Betsy sometimes sees splendid carriages draw up to the door of wealthy Mrs. Caton. The ladies who alight are wearing showy clothes and are greeted by a bowing footman. "Mary . . . Louisa . . ." Betsy murmurs to herself when she recognizes her childhood playmates but soon turns her head so as not to show her jealousy. "The Duchess of Wellesley has come to visit her native city," run the headlines in the local papers. "The Duchess of Leeds will attend the races with her mother. . . ." What is the matter with these papers, that they take an interest in such trifles!

To make herself feel better, Betsy reads and re-reads the mail she receives from Europe. Princess Galitzin is in financial difficulties and writes that she is thinking of selling her property at Genthod. "It is too bad, for

I really enjoyed living there when Alexander was in Saint-Petersburg!"
The Chouvaloffs are still in Florence. As for Prince Gortchakoff, nobody
has heard from him. He might be in Stuttgart, where he seems to be
stuck in a mission that looks very much like a dismissal. Rumor has it
that he was married there.

Edward is upset to see his sister's determination to remain unmarried. He is the one brother whose company she enjoys. The others, she
claims, have betrayed her. George, who at the time had pushed for Bo's
marriage behind her back. Harry, the old boozer, who had cleaned out
the cellar of the South Street house as soon as his father was gone, and
who made off with all the bottles of Madeira and Kentucky bourbon.
"You would never have consumed all this stuff by yourself," he had told
his sister who was furious about this proceeding.

Despite her more than fifty years, Betsy is still so beautiful, with
her lively eyes, her fresh complexion, and her slender waist, that she is
not lacking for suitors. But she disdainfully rejects them all.

Yet one caller had made her heart beat faster. A tall, thin, somewhat
stiff gentleman of military bearing, about sixty years old and dressed in
a somber morning coat, had bowed deeply to her. "Allow me to introduce myself: I am Marshal Bertrand."

His hostess had looked puzzled, and so he had explained that he
was one of the officers who had accompanied the Emperor to Saint-
Helena. He had been present at his last moments. A wave of emotion
had swept over Betsy.

"You . . . you were at Saint-Helena?"

The marshal explains that he has not come to see her from idle
curiosity, but in response to a wish of the Emperor. He had sometimes
spoken of her. He was sorry for the suffering he might have caused her,
. . . for the shadow he had cast over her life. He had hoped that she
would forgive him. . . . But he had insisted that he had to act as he did
for reasons of state. He had been moved to learn that in spite of all of
this she had wished to remain faithful to his name and his image. "Alas,"
he had sighed, "those whom I have wronged have forgiven me, but
those I have showered with favors have often betrayed me."

As the years go by, word is received of the death of Madame Mère
and also of Queen Catherine, Jérôme's second wife. Bo suggests that

perhaps his mother should return to Europe? This would be the moment. His father must be rather lonely . . .

But Betsy knows otherwise! Of course, Jérôme has mourned Queen Catherine, who has always been a devoted wife to him. But she has learned from Princess Galitzin that he has a new mistress. She is a widow, Marquise Bartholini. What would she, Betsy, be doing over there?

BO'S FAVORITE COUSIN, LOUIS-NAPOLEON, SON OF THE EX-KING OF Holland, is causing quite a stir. In Strasbourg he has just attempted a coup d'état, which has failed. He and his accomplices have been jailed, but the government of Louis-Philippe has decided to reprieve him and send him into exile in the United States. Bo has just received a letter from him; his boat is stopping over at Rio de Janeiro. From there he will sail for Norfolk — as Jérôme had done in his day — and then make his way up the Chesapeake. He is asking for Bo's hospitality in Baltimore, where he will stop before going to Washington and eventually New York. Bo is delighted to see Louis-Napoleon, for they share some excellent memories of the time they spent together, riding their horses through the countryside around Rome and Florence. And yet they are of very different temperaments: whereas Louis-Napoleon, who since the death of Napoleon's son, the Duc de Reichstatt, considers himself the Bonapartist pretender and dreams of restoring the Napoleonic era, Bo aspires to nothing more than a quiet and smoothly running life in Baltimore. But he is a shrewd lawyer and can give good advice. As they had done at Villa Adriana or on the banks of the Tiber, the two cousins are having endless discussions about the fate of France and of her colonies (the conquest of Algeria is a very recent development), and about the upheavals that are shaking the world as they take walks in the park of "Chestnut Wood," the superb summer home Bo has built on the heights overlooking the city.

"I envy you, Cousin, for living in such exquisite surroundings," Louis-Napoleon says wistfully.

In his mind's eye he sees the white silhouette of Princess Mathilde, Bo's half-sister, with whom he was once in love, to the point that they almost became engaged. But since his ill-conceived escapade at Strasbourg, the entire Bonaparte family has turned on him, especially his uncles, who are furious. The Comte de Survilliers, who has left America in 1832 (returning only for short stays), now lives in London where, as the eldest of the Bonaparte brothers, he has once again become involved in politics. What a contrast to the healthy and tranquil life of a gentleman farmer he had led at Point Breeze. . . . But here he is, drawing up an official statement censuring that tumultuous nephew together with his brother Jérôme, Comte de Monfort, who is also in London at this point. In the end, Jérôme does not sign the statement, but he does forbid his daughter Mathilde to write to her cousin. And the marriage plans are off. It is a hard road for Louis.

The Baltimore reunion has been short. Soon Louis-Napoleon is off to Washington, and then to New York. While there he learns that his mother is dying of cancer at Arenenberg. Four months later he leaves America to go to her bedside — and on to a greater destiny.

Shortly after Hortense has died, Bo also learns of the death of his cousin Charlotte, which deeply saddens him. She had written to him from time to time and told him the latest news from Italy. He can still see her as a sensitive and charming girl in her sun-bonnet and her white dress, sitting in front of her easel with her palette in the magnificent park at Point Breeze.

Next it is Cardinal Fesch's turn to leave the world. And the family is surprised to learn that the old prelate, who had a particularly soft spot in his heart for Betsy's son, has made a special clause for him in his will, which advantages him over his other great-nephews: if he becomes the father of a daughter, this child will receive a dowry of fifty thousand livres; if not, this sum will go to Bo himself. He therefore has to pack his bags and go to Europe. He will take this opportunity to visit his family in Italy. Betsy, of course, feels that it would be terribly nice to accompany him as far as Paris, perhaps even Geneva.

If it were not so long, this journey would be like a bath in the fountain of youth. Bo is delighted to return to Rome and Florence, to the light of Italy, and to his family. His father, the Comte de Montfort, greets him with the same affection as before. He has had to cut back on his lifestyle, for now that Catherine has died he no longer receives a pension from the king of Württemberg or the czar of Russia. He has given up the Palazzo Orlandini as too costly and lives in a more modest house on the outskirts of Florence, the Villa Aldobrandini. He is still hoping to obtain the revocation of the law exiling all Bonapartes from France and bombards the French government with petitions. Rumor even has it that a marriage between Mathilde and one of Louis-Philippe's sons has been envisaged. But this project has been ruled out, and for the moment the pretty princess is quite smitten with Anatole Demidoff, son of the Nicolas Demidoff whose company Betsy had enjoyed so much in the past, both in Geneva and in Florence. Anatole has inherited his father's fabulous fortune and engages in a veritable cult of Napoleon. In his château of San Donato he has brought together numerous objects, paintings, and statues that celebrate the Empire: it is a miniature museum!

Jérôme-Napoleon, the eldest son of Jérôme and Catherine, and Bo's half-brother, serves in the Württemberg army, while Plon-Plon is finishing his schooling in Stuttgart. The ex-queen of Naples, Caroline Murat, has recently died, and Lucien is about to expire in Viterbo. As for Louis, who is becoming more and more of a bear denned in his villa on the outskirts of Florence, he has made an exception for his American nephew and has received him with open arms.

Meanwhile, Betsy has once again become a Parisian. To her great joy, she has found that the Chouvaloffs are living in the French capital to be near one of their married sons. How good it is to sit by the fire and resume the conversations they used to have, or to go to catch a few feeble rays of sunshine in the Tuileries or at the Champs-Elysees, to have hot chocolate in one of the many little shops there, and to listen to strolling Italian musicians who have come to play the melodies of Rossini or Paganini. Gregory Chouvaloff, with his graying temples, his trimmed mustache and his little goatee, is as attractive as ever. Sophie, his wife, has put on a little weight, but still has her gentle manner and her charming smile.

Prince Gortachakoff is finally heard from. The woman he has married in Vienna is a widow, the sister-in-law of his poet friend Aleksandr Sergeyevich Pushkin. He has a son. His career is taking off, although there have been a few difficulties. Nesselrode, the state councilor of Russia, fully aware of Gortchakoff's merits but filled with jealousy, had long kept him in positions of minor importance. Gortchakoff is a great lover of the arts. Princess Galitzin writes that she is in Florence, where Bo will surely meet her, as well as Lady Morgan, who has come there for a visit.

Charlotte de Constant is still a faithful friend, and Betsy sometimes has lunch at her house with a few friends. She has a piece of sad news for Betsy: Laure d'Abrantès has died the year before in the most abject poverty. Poor Laure! She was very talented, but she never knew how to take care of her resources. She spent freely as soon as she had a penny to her name and had made some disastrous investments. Among other things, she had helped finance plays that had turned out to be flops. She had ended her days in a veritable hovel. . . . But she had had a magnificent funeral, although her faithful friends — politician Vicompte François René de Chateaubriand, David d'Angers, and the writers Alexandre Dumas and Victor Hugo — had been unable to have a monument to her placed in the Père Lachaise cemetery. This failure was avenged by a poem Hugo dedicated to her memory:

> It's for us now to shield and defend
> Death from oblivion, its pale attendant companion.
> It's for us now to strew roses upon your ashes;
> For us to weave laurels to honor your name!

Juliette Récamier still conducts her salon. Literary critic Charles Augustin Sainte Beuve comes there to read from his works, and young Rachel, a rising star who is about to become the best tragic actress of her time, sometimes recites scenes from the French classics, *Esther* or *Polyeucte*. Juliette welcomes everyone with her customary affability, but is not quite able to hide from her friends that she will soon succumb to a terrible infirmity: she is beginning to lose her eyesight and already has trouble reading.

No, Paris no longer has the rosy hue it used to have. But even so, Betsy is still invited to a few balls here and there, even at the Tuileries, where hundreds of people are pushing and shoving. On such occasions Betsy sparkles with the last rays of her autumnal beauty. In her favorite black velvet dress that shows off her still superb neck and shoulders, and with a wreath of diamonds interwoven with black roses in her hair, she still attracts a good bit of attention.

"You are still beautiful!" Gregory Chouvaloff, wishing to reassure her, whispers in her ear.

But she no longer really cares and is beginning to think of going home. "I am getting old," she thinks with dismay. And, oddly enough, she realizes that she is actually looking forward to returning to Baltimore. How unusual. . . . But this time her grandson is waiting for her, and she is anxious to see him.

29

$\mathcal{J}$ÉRÔME-NAPOLEON II HAS GROWN INTO A FINE-looking little boy, tall and slender, with a proud and somewhat belligerent face; he secretly dreams of becoming a military man.

How proud Betsy is of him! Now that she has her own, and very attractive apartment in the South Street house, she often invites her grandson to have lunch or tea with her. After the meal they play a game of chess on the superb ivory chess board she has brought back from Italy. Set in her exclusive attitude, Betsy loves to persuade herself that she is in charge of the boy's schooling. This is her way of stealing some authority from her daughter-in-law, who does not seem to mind. Susan May has decided that her mother-in-law is a character, and that it is best not to cross her.

Baltimore is gradually acquiring more schools, universities, and new industries. The old flour mills along the Jones Falls have been turned into cotton mills. The first buildings with metal framing have gone up. Illustrious visitors come to the city: Charles Dickens lands there in 1842 and stays at the gigantic Hotel Barnum. Occasionally, one passes on the streets another writer, a very odd-looking man with an enormous forehead and a bitter mouth reminiscent of Baudelaire under a short moustache. He is already famous for his many poems and for his *Tales of the Grotesque and Arabesque,* which make shivers run down his fellow-citizens' backs. His name is Edgar Allan Poe.

Princess Mathilde, Bo's half-sister, is getting married. The lucky groom is Anatole Demidoff, son of Betsy's dear old friend Count Nicolas.

This match was already discussed at length when Bo visited his father in Italy. The young girl seems to be very much in love with her fiancé and has written a charming letter about it to her half-brother. By the same mail, Bo also receives a letter from her future husband, Anatole, reminding him that they have met years ago in Florence. To be sure, the more than tidy fortune of the Demidoffs is bound to be a major consideration for the Comte de Montfort. But Mathilde, who dreams of traveling, and particularly of Paris — where, as a member of the Bonaparte family, she had hitherto been *persona non grata* — expects wonderful adventures. Her fiancé is a very cultivated man, who counts many artists and writers among his friends. The young people have been introduced to each other by Jules Janin.

Yet this idyll, which seemed to begin under the best auspices, is to come to a sad end six years later. The years go by, and then one day it is learned that Mathilde has left her husband: in addition to cheating on her, he had treated her with great brutality and reportedly actually beaten her.

And there is another, even more sensational piece of news: Bo's cousin Louis-Napoleon, who had been imprisoned in the fortress of Ham following a second failed coup d'état, this one at Boulogne, has escaped, disguised as a mason, carrying a plank on his shoulder to conceal his face. He is said to be in England now, but the grand duke of Tuscany will not give him permission to go to Florence to see his dying father. King Louis? Yes, Louis, the perpetual hypochondriac, the misanthropist, but a man whom Betsy had liked anyway, and who had comforted her, once upon a time in Rome, when she was so upset about Pauline. . . . She has carefully kept the little poem he had sent her after she left:

> She's far from here . . . but her likeness
> Lingers where we must stay.
> We see it where flowers spread brightness,
> In the glow of a beautiful day . . .

Two years earlier, Joseph had preceded him in death. Thus the only one of the Bonaparte brothers left is Jérôme.

Jérôme-Napoleon II, following his military vocation, is a student at West Point. Betsy has trouble concealing her pride when she walks through the streets of Baltimore with this young man, so slender and elegant in his dark blue jacket, white pants, and short-vizored cap.

Sometimes she just can't stand it any longer: carrying a light bag, she climbs onto the train to New York, and then takes the Hudson steamer to West Point, where she takes lodgings in a boarding house a few miles from the military academy. This allows her to enjoy her grandson's company on weekends, invite him to a concert in town, or take him out to a fancy dinner for two.

She is a fond and generous grandmother, as she acknowledges with a smile. This is her only extravagance. Besides, she finds it amusing to observe all kinds of little intrigues that are being spun here. She has seen, for instance, a rich widow of forty who was so madly in love with a cadet that she was ready to give up everything in order to marry him! The young man had had enough sense to refuse this advantageous offer.

The news of the fall of Louis Philippe's government and the declaration of the French Republic in 1848 arrives like a bombshell. It turns out that one of the most visible figures of the provisional government is the poet Alphonse Lamartine. "How interesting," Betsy says to herself, remembering that she had met him years ago in Florence. "At that time he did not profess the same ideas as he does today. Who would have thought that he would be transformed into the bard of the Republic?"

As for Louis-Napoleon, he awaits his hour. He has left England and must already have arrived in France. By the end of the year it will be learned that the head of the Bonapartist faction has been elected president of the French Republic by a huge majority.

"Despite his oath to uphold the Constitution, nobody can persuade me that there are not some ulterior imperial motives behind this affair," Betsy asserts. "And as far as I am concerned, I am convinced that the Empire will come back some day. . . . And in that case, my grandson would have certain claims to the succession to the throne."

And so her Napoleonic dreams once again become as vivid as ever. As an added incentive, her grandson Jérôme-Napoleon seems to go along with them much more readily than Bo did in his younger days. This youngster is no stick-in-the-mud; he wants to fight and cover himself with glory. He is also very anxious to see France, his "second fatherland," he says, whose image has been purveyed to him through his grandmother's admiring descriptions. His grandfather, the ex-king of Westphalia, now lives in Paris. He and Countess Bartholini, whom he has secretly married, have moved to the rue d'Alger, very close to the *pension* where Betsy had lodged ten years earlier.

"This means that I can no longer go to Paris," she says, "for I would choke if I knew that I was living under the same sky as my ex-husband! But I do feel like traveling again these days, and so I shall content myself with going to London, where Lady Morgan wants to see me. She has recently been widowed and has left Dublin, which she finds sad and dreary; it's a city at the end of the world, she says. I also have an old friend from Baltimore, Harriet Stewart, who lives in Liverpool; I could visit her as well."

And so Betsy is once again packing her bags; filled with joyful excitement, she is surprised to hear herself sing. She is going to Europe . . . she will revive her European dream.

WHEN SHE RETURNS SHE LEARNS THAT SUSAN MAY IS PREGNANT AGAIN . . . after twenty years. A few months later Betsy becomes the grandmother of a little Charles, a big, round baby, twenty-one years younger than his brother. But for the moment she is not particularly interested in this newborn. Jérôme-Napoleon has a very special place in her heart and all her hopes are centered on him. Especially now that the situation in France is changing with breakneck speed. The Empire will come, the Empire is here!

The Baltimore Bonapartes follow the events from afar. Bo writes to his cousin Louis-Napoleon — now Napoleon III — to congratulate him. It is true that he has many enemies — in particular Victor Hugo, who always calls him "Napoleon the Small" — and that his liberal ideas of earlier years have yielded to the need to set up a strong regime, but he is nonetheless a unique politician, one who cares about his people's well-being.

"I think he will be a good sovereign" Betsy says. "But have you seen, Bo, that he has already established the order of succession to the throne? Since he is unmarried and childless, if he dies his successor will automatically be your father or his male descendants from his marriage to Catherine of Württemberg. That is to say that if King Jérôme were to die, his younger son, Plon-Plon, who is seventeen years younger than you, would become heir to the crown.[1] This is a new slap in the face for us. If you are passed over, it means that your birth is considered illegitimate, and that is something I cannot tolerate."

In order to calm his mother, Bo decides to go to Paris with his eldest son. Surely, the friendship his cousin Louis has always shown him was more than a matter of words. Jérôme-Napoleon would love to serve in the French army, and so he and Bo sail for France in May 1854.

Despite his phlegmatic disposition, Bo cannot quite conceal his worries. Between his father who, restored to his standing of Imperial Highness, is more haughty than ever and his cousin, the brand-new Emperor, how will he be received? He sees himself again on his long ride toward Siena, years ago, when his father was awaiting him at his château of Lanciano . . . a father whom he did not know at all. He is as excited today as he was then. But his son, Jérôme-Napoleon, just whistles a carefree little tune. "Life is really amusing," he thinks to himself. He is eager to see the coast of France emerge.

The Emperor, who had invited father and son to lunch at the chateau of Saint-Cloud, is charmed by his nephew. He has recently married a beautiful Spanish woman by the name of Eugénie de Montijo. The two of them, accompanied by their attendants, have moved to their summer quarters at the château of Saint-Cloud, where one breathes a better air amidst a magnificent park. Jérôme-Napoleon is endlessly impressed by the furniture he sees around him, the superb rugs and hangings, and the view from the windows: the heights of Sèvres and Meudon, and Paris beyond the Seine flowing along the edge of the park.

Empress Eugénie is taking a thorough look at this handsome, blond and blue-eyed boy, whose Yankee accent and fresh spontaneity greatly amuse her. As for Bo, he says to himself that this new Madame Bonaparte

[1] Jérôme-Napoleon, the eldest son of Jérôme and Catherine of Württemberg, had died in 1847 of a disease of the spinal cord.

is very beautiful. He has let his cousin know discreetly that he would like to acquire French nationality, to which he is entitled by his birth, and that the same privilege should be extended to his son, who would very much like to serve the French army with the grade of second lieutenant, the grade he holds in America. The Emperor states that he will be glad to study this question. He will do his utmost to give both of them satisfaction on this point, and is extremely touched by their solicitude for the interests of France. In the last several months, he continues, he has been pursuing, in agreement with England, a war against Russia, which is attempting to annex the Ottoman provinces. The outcome of the hostilities is still doubtful, but all those who wish to place their bravery at the service of the French armies are highly welcome. Bo's half-brother, Prince Napoleon (Plon-Plon), commands a division in the theater of war and has fought valiantly at the Alma River.

Bo has also presented his son to the ex-king of Westphalia, who occupies one wing of the Palais-Royal; the other wing is reserved for Plon-Plon, whenever he is in Paris. The Marquise Bartholini has gone back to Italy. King Jérôme, who has become an affable and smiling gentleman who does not have much hair left but looks most distinguished in his black frock-coat studded with decorations, has received them with open arms.

"Why not stay here at the Palace," he has proposed. "I will give orders to have an apartment prepared for you."

But Bo has declined. No need to complicate matters! He has found lodgings very close by, rue d'Alger, in a *pension* that perfectly suits his needs. His father has insisted, however, that they come to share his dinner every day; he would see to it that a place was always set for them at his table.

It is early summer in Paris, and the evenings flit by with light and frivolous entertainment. Offenbach's operas are becoming quite popular. At the lower end of the Champs Elysées, preparations are under way for the great World's Fair to be held the following year; its main attraction is to be the Palace of Industry. When they are not going to a concert, to the theater, or to a ball at Mabille, Bo and his son enter the gate of the Palais Royal and climb up to the east wing of the cour de l'Horloge to reach the apartments of King Jérôme, who is waiting for

them, always happy and full of smiles. Father and son have a great deal
to talk about. The old king tells about coming to Paris, and about
being given the position of governor of the Invalides, and then that of
President of the Senate, by Louis-Napoleon when he was President of
the Republic. At that time his son, Prince Napoleon [Plon-Plon], was a
member of the Constituent Assembly.

"If you saw your young brother, you would be struck by his resemblance to Emperor Napoleon I," Jérôme exclaims. "But in fact, the same
could almost be said of you too. . . . You and Plon-Plon have a very
similar physiognomy. . . . Here, I'll show you something that will amuse
you: it is a caricature recently published by a newspaper. It depicts my
nephew the Emperor saying to my son, Prince Napoleon, 'I have to
show myself to the people; let me borrow your face, will you?'"

Sometimes they attend a reception given by Princess Mathilde in
her superb town house on the rue de Courcelles or at her property of
Saint-Gratien. Since her separation from Anatole Demidoff, she has become a brilliant figure in Paris as the center of a coterie of artists and
literary men. Before the marriage of her cousin Louis-Napoleon she had
played an active role as his ally and adviser and had acted as hostess at
all receptions at the Tuileries or Saint-Cloud. She is a subtle, intelligent
woman of great dignity, who is proud to be a Bonaparte. At thirty-
three, though still beautiful, she is unfortunately becoming excessively
stout, a tendency she has inherited from her mother, Queen Catherine.
Her reunion with Bo is cordial, and then Mathilde too succumbs to the
charm of her Yankee nephew.

AT THE END OF AUGUST BO AND JÉRÔME-NAPOLEON LEARN THAT UPON
consultation with the Keeper of the Seal Abbatucci, the president of
the Senate, and the president of the privy council, a decree has been
passed: it stipulates that French citizenship shall be returned to Bo and
that henceforth he will be permitted to add to the name Patterson —
the only one he had the right to bear in France until now — that of
Bonaparte. He and his son are also granted a comfortable pension by
the Emperor, and moreover Jérôme-Napoleon is appointed second lieutenant in the 7th Dragoon regiment. They are overjoyed. Napoleon III
has kept his promise.

Bo's emotion runs high: after all these years the legitimacy of his parents' marriage has been recognized. This means that if the Emperor, who so far has no heir, should die, he, as the eldest of Jérôme's branch of the family — the only one eligible — would become the direct pretender to the throne. And while he is not ready for this eventuality himself, having no ambition whatsoever in this direction, he wants to be ready for his son.

A few days later, while Bo and Jérôme-Napoleon are still savoring their happiness, they receive the visit of an elderly military man of formal bearing. He is General Ricard, aide-de-camp at the Palais-Royal. Looking ill at ease, he clears his throat once or twice and finally declares, "His Majesty the King has asked me to inform you that it would be preferable if you no longer came to his table on the spur of the moment, without being expressly invited. He desires to take his meals elsewhere from time to time and does not wish to be tied down. But he will be delighted to receive you whenever you have made a date with him."

Jérôme-Napoleon looks up in wide-eyed amazement, wondering if he has heard right; he blanches. "General," he says, "Would you kindly explain to us what this means? The last time we saw my father he was brimming with affection for us and we made all kinds of plans together!"

"These are the orders I received," Ricard insists, "and this is all I can tell you."

"Very well then. The reply to my father is that we will bow to his orders."

But Bo is so upset about what he considers an outrage that he decides never again to set foot in the Palais-Royal. In the meantime, he will write a short note to the Emperor: sure of his friendship, he hopes to receive some explanation through him.

Alas, the Emperor's reply is only too clear: "I have received," it reads, "a letter from my uncle Jérôme, telling me that he would never agree to your remaining in France. I replied to him that since the French laws recognize you as his legitimate son, I was bound to recognize you as a kinsman, that it was up to you to judge whether your position in Paris was embarrassing, and that Plon-Plon, if he behaved properly, had nothing to fear from family rivalries. So you should try not to irritate your father and continue to pursue your chosen course. . . ."

It becomes clear that all this trouble comes from Prince Napoleon, Plon-Plon. And to think that in the past he wrote such amusing and affectionate letters to Bo! And that when they met in Siena, he hung on Bo's every word when he talked about his life in America! How can he be so jealous of him? Actually, it is quite understandable, he is afraid that Bo would usurp the crown if the Emperor were to die. Plon-Plon probably believes that this is a perfidious manoeuver on the part of the Emperor, with whom he has had political run-ins before. He has always been irked to see this cousin at the summit of honors. When he was a deputy and Louis-Napoleon presided over the Chamber, he sat at the extreme left, with the opposition, and was referred to as "the Prince of the Mountain."

Prince Napoleon had learned about his half-brother's and his nephew's arrival in Paris and about the decree in their favor when he was hospitalized in Constantinople for a tenacious dysentery. This trying illness, to which he succumbed in the midst of the Crimean War, was to give rise to some barbs from the opposition. These he did not deserve, for while Plon-Plon is the king of the grumblers, he is definitely no coward. But his horrendous temper causes havoc, and his family bears the brunt of it. Bo has no desire to encounter him; he has requested permission to return home and cut short his stay in Paris — despite the Emperor's advice to the contrary. As for his son, Jérôme-Napoleon II, he will soon join his French regiment in the Crimea.

But before long Plon-Plon returns from Constantinople, more aggressive than ever. "He has not exhausted his bellicose humors on the battlefield," sighs General Ricard, who has escorted him back from Marseilles. As soon as he arrives at the Palais-Royal he vents his cantankerous temper on his entourage, particularly on his father, even though the old king, claiming a migraine, is keeping to his own apartments.

"How could you receive your bastard in my absence?" he fumes.

"He too is my son," King Jérôme gently replies; he abhors scenes.

"If you grant him the same privileges as to your other children, you will cast doubts on your marriage to my mother, Queen Catherine! Just think how the opposition, and especially the royalist party, will jump at this opportunity for lots of talk! Pretty soon, Mathilde and I will be considered bastards. It is intolerable! I don't ever want to see the Pattersons here again, do you hear me!"

"Calm down, Napoleon. They both have already left. . . ."

Fortunately for him, Bo is already on the high seas when this stormy scene takes place; its content never reaches his ears.

But the terrible Plon-Plon is not about to let the matter rest there; he pesters his father until he writes another letter to the Emperor, one that treats his American son even more cruelly than the last:

> . . . the Pattersons are using my name without my consent, they bring into my family, without even consulting me, persons who have never belonged to it. They raise doubts, in the eyes of France, about the legitimacy of my children. . . . They cast aspersions on my honor and that of my late brother the Emperor by nullifying the solemn pledges we made to the king of Württemberg and the czar of Russia as conditions for my marriage to Princess Catherine. . . . I consider it my sacred duty to bring about, in my lifetime, a resolution to a question that is compromising my most cherished interests."

Old King Jérôme ends by requesting the calling of a family council to decide this painful matter.

Bo is glad to be back in Baltimore. Betsy and Susan May have besieged him with questions. Little Charles has burbled his first "Papa" into his ear. He is happy, and his quiet surroundings make it easy to forget the unpleasant circumstances surrounding his departure from France. In order to spare his mother, he has, of course, skipped over some of the details that seemed too painful to him and minimized the sudden deterioration of his relations with his father. But Betsy is not deceived. By certain signs she recognizes that her son has thrown an almost impalpable veil of deception over his story. His playful tone sounds false, and she is convinced that it hides a trauma. When she sees that after talking about his dinners with the ex-king of Westphalia at the Palais-Royal he vaguely gazes out the window, she feels certain that something else has happened there, something about which he does not want to talk.

She is cautious enough not to ask any more questions. But one day Bo seems to be more preoccupied than usual. She has come, as she often does, to spend Sunday at Chestnut Wood. It is a magnificent day. Through stands of poplars and beeches in the park one can see the sparkling Chesapeake far down below. On the lawn little Charles is chasing a gray squirrel amidst peals of laughter. Bo, looking very strained, wordlessly hands his mother a letter. It is from Chancellor Fould, and contains a proposition from Emperor Napoleon III.

Betsy puts on her reading glasses, and begins by looking with delight at the red seal bearing the imperial coat-of-arms. But she grows pale as she deciphers the lines of this long missive. The long and short of it is that, contrary to what had been declared in last year's decree, the Emperor wants to take away from her son and her grandsons the right to bear the name "Bonaparte," which at this very moment young Jérôme is covering with glory in the Crimea.[2] By means of compensation, the Emperor — who has a kind heart and is surely saddened by this business — is willing to create for them the title "Ducs de Sartène," which would become hereditary in their family. It is also pointed out to Bo that a number of important bastards in European history have borne the title of Duke in this manner, among them the illegitimate children of Louis XIV and Madame de Montespan or, closer to his own time, the Duc de Morny, the Emperor's half-brother.

"What an idea," she exclaims. "But why the name Sartène?"

Sartène is a town in the south of Corsica, one of the oldest on the island, her son explains. The first Bonapartes had come to live in this area in the remote past and the family still owns some land there. But what good would a ducal title do them in America? Why should they be made to give up a name that is their own and that Bo has born honorably since birth? To say nothing of his son.

FOLLOWING THE CAPTURE OF MALAKOFF AND THE FALL OF SEVASTOPOL, THE Crimean War has ended in early 1856. France and England have won. But Jérôme-Napoleon II has not returned to America: he has been acclaimed with the entire army upon the troops' return to France. Napo-

---

[2] He has just been decorated with the Légion d'Honneur.

leon III has warmly received his nephew at the Tuileries and decorated him with the order of the Turkish Medjidie which has been created to reward bravery in the Crimean War.

"You are a credit to us," he has murmured into his ear. He also keeps calling him "Prince Jérôme," which makes the young man very proud but causes Plon-Plon's anger to flare up worse than before.

These reports are received happily in Baltimore. The "Duc de Sartène" episode is almost forgotten, particularly since Bo has responded in the most lofty terms to the Grand Chancellor Achille Fould, who had transmitted the Emperor's offer. He had told him that he could not accept it and that he preferred to keep his name Bonaparte, quite simply because it is his own.

Young Jérôme-Napoleon writes enthusiastic letters from Paris, where the great powers are meeting for the signing of a peace treaty. France seems about to recover a certain moral prestige, due to the fact that, to everyone's surprise, it has not asked for any territorial compensation.

At the Tuileries, the young man tells his grandmother, he has been presented to Prince Gortchakoff who, together with Prince Orloff, represents Russia. He is quite a character, very cultivated, and also a great connoisseur of good food. He has hired the most famous chef in Paris, a man named Gruyère, for whom everyone envies him. When Jérôme-Napoleon met him, he had scrutinized him at length through his spectacles with a cold expression. Then his blue eyes had slightly clouded over. "Lieutenant Jérôme Bonaparte-Patterson?" he had asked. "Well now, this brings back old memories. Years ago in Florence I knew a Madame Bonaparte-Patterson, she was exquisite. . . ." They had had a long conversation. Jérôme-Napoleon had told him the latest news of his grandmother and the prince had assured him that he had not forgotten her. By a strange coincidence, the young man had fought against the prince's cousin, General Mikhail Gortchakoff, who commanded the Russian army at Sevastopol.

"Yes," Betsy thinks, much moved, "life sometimes brings strange surprises. How could I forget the friends of those days, whose sincere affection warmed my heart after suffering cruel disappointments!"

But after this brief clearing, more storms are about to break. During a visit to Paris of the king of Württemberg, Plon-Plon and Princess

Mathilde have called a family council, which has met behind closed doors at the Tuileries for more than a month to deal with the Bonaparte-Patterson dispute.

"Clearly, the authority of the decisions made by Napoleon I is being disregarded. It is therefore incumbent upon Napoleon III to call for a new decision," Prince Napoleon has stated.

At the end of the debate, the verdict has come down like the blade of a guillotine. While Bo and his descendants do have the right to continue to bear the Bonaparte name — which has been theirs since birth — they have no claims under French civil law, that is to say, no claims to Jérôme's property or to the throne.

Not that Bo had ever seriously thought about this. But he is chagrined about one thing: despite the rights it grants him, the decision asserts once again that in the eyes of the law his birth was illegitimate. This is very upsetting to him. He consoles himself by thinking that his half-brother is probably no more satisfied by this Solomonic decision than he is! And indeed, Prince Napoleon is in a constant fury. He has always had his troubles with Napoleon III, who refuses to comply with his never-ending demands, such as the request to be named governor of Algeria. Now the emperor has become the father of a strong, healthy son, which has increased his, Plon-Plon's, distance from the throne, and all of this is compounded by a new grudge against "the Pattersons," as he disparagingly calls them.

"You have got to break off all relations and all correspondence with your Baltimore bastards!" he screams at his father in the salons of the Palais-Royal.

Old King Jérôme drops his chin on his chest and says nothing. A tear runs down his emaciated cheek. It dries quickly. No sorrow lasts long for him.

Betsy has a steady correspondence with her grandson, lieutenant Jérôme-Napoleon. After the Crimea he has seen action in Italy, where he has acquired a reputation for outstanding bravery. "He is a true Bonaparte," she happily tells anyone who wants to hear it. She sends him large sums of money so that he can improve his daily fare and cut a fine figure when he is in Paris.

Her other grandson, Charles, is of a much calmer disposition. He will certainly not go in for a military career! Shorter and stockier than his brother and marked by piercing eyes in a face with irregular features, he already shows signs of a lively intelligence. Studious and thoughtful, he gives great satisfaction to his teachers at Saint Mary's school, where he has been sent at Betsy's urging, for it is important to her that her grandsons be raised in the Catholic religion.

"It is the religion of kings and queens!" she proudly exclaims. "I myself am sorry that I did not convert. But now it is too late."

Soon it is learned from Paris that Plon-Plon has married, not for love but for reason of state, Princess Clothilde, daughter of King Victor-Emmanuel of Savoy. The event has been celebrated with splendid festivities at the Palais-Royal.

"They say that the new bride is extraordinarily devout; this union with a fanatical anti-clerical, a cynical and debauched individual, is going to be quite a match," scoffs Bo, who now speaks very unkindly of his paternal relatives. "Well, anyway, at least this will be good for the Emperor's policy of alliances and his great plan to foster the unification of Italy!"

Then, one day, Bo has come to see his mother, looking somber.

"What is it?" Betsy immediately asks, sensing that he is bringing serious news. "My father is dead," he replies, handing her the newspaper.

Both are silent for a long moment. Betsy does not have the strength to make light of this. Bo, frowning deeply, bites his lip. Perhaps he regrets the harsh words he may have used in anger when speaking of his father. Poor Bo, he too is torn apart by contradictory feelings, caught in the web of an inextricable situation which, despite his best intentions and his peaceful disposition, has never made him look his best in the eyes of his father or, for different reasons, those of his mother.

"I . . . I don't know what to say. . . . I don't know what to think," Betsy murmurs, feeling nothing in herself but walls of silence, a memory darkened by heavy black clouds. "I believe he loved you," she adds after a moment. ". . . and me too, perhaps he loved me too, a long time ago."

That evening Bo does not go home to dinner. Seated by the fire, he listens to his mother as she evokes her memories. These are stories he has heard her tell a hundred times, but suddenly the frail bond between them has been tightened; once again, he feels like an adolescent.

A week later they read about the will of the ex-king of Westphalia in the newspapers. He has greatly advantaged Prince Napoleon (Mathilde is to receive only a tiny sum, for her share includes the — purely imaginary! — dowry she has supposedly received from her father at the time of her marriage) and the will makes no mention at all of the Baltimore Bonapartes.

"This beats everything!" says Bo, pale with suppressed anger. "I am denied the very right to an existence. My aunt Pauline and Cardinal Fesch, who were no more than distant relatives, were at least thoughtful enough to mention me in their wills. But my own father? I can't believe it!"

"Bo, you must go to France to claim your rights. We will hire a lawyer. This time I'll go with you."

"Don't even think of it, Mother! At your age, and with all your ailments."

"I am in very good health," Betsy replies, drawing herself up proudly, "and I am not suffering from any ailments."

"You will find yourself in an unpleasant situation, and you will be subject to emotions that will be bad for your heart."

"There is nothing wrong with my heart!"

"But really, I don't need this money; we are quite wealthy enough, and my business is doing well."

"Bo, this is a matter of honor, can't you see that?"

BETSY HAS HAD HER WAY. SHE HAS THROWN TOGETHER A FEW THINGS — making it clear that she would buy new clothes in Paris — and taken a ship to Le Havre in the company of her son.

"This is my last voyage to Europe," she keeps telling herself, hoping to recapture the excitement of earlier years.

Paris has shed its old skin and is no longer what it was. Under the aegis of Napoleon III Baron Haussman has cut wide swaths through the city, destroyed old dwellings and insalubrious neighborhoods in some places, built wide avenues, and developed parks and green spaces. The Bois de Boulogne and the Bois de Vincennes have been tidied up, cleared of underbrush, and enhanced by well-kept avenues. The ancient city wall surrounding the boulevards has been torn down and the city extends all the way to the fortifications.

Most of Betsy's friends are no longer there. But as a compensation she enjoys evenings spent alone with Bo; they make her feel thirty years younger! However, mother and son have a painful experience ahead of them. Betsy is ready to fight tooth and nail for her son's rights. Bo, less excitable, is talking to his attorney, a great courtroom performer and king of the Bar. He is the famous Berryer, the very man who had once defended Bo's cousin Louis-Napoleon after his attempted coup d'état at Strasbourg.

As he and his mother have claimed, from Baltimore, that the seals must not be removed unless they were present, they have incurred the wrath of the family council, which has informed them that under the terms of the decision handed down in 1856 they are not affected by the settlement of this succession. Thereupon Betsy and Bo have brought action against Prince Napoleon before the district court of the Department of Seine, demanding the liquidation and division of the succession. Princess Mathilde has prudently renounced her share, which amounted to very little anyway, in order to avoid conflict with her half-brother.

At his very first meeting with Berryer, Bo has expressed his indignation at being excluded from the family clan, which had until then always treated him as a true Bonaparte, and indeed with great affection. It is a most uncomfortable situation for him to find himself in a court of law, opposite a brother and a sister who in the past had signed their letters "your devoted brother," and "your affectionate sister," and who now treat him as a stranger. Berryer, for all his eloquence, is unable to prevent the court from upholding the decision of 1856: the Bonaparte-Patterson marriage is not valid, and Bo's birth is illegitimate.

This time Bo, stung to the quick, is the first to decide to appeal. The winter passes in long talks with the attorney. In Paris people are holding their breath. Everyone is passionately interested in this joust among the Bonapartes, whose prize might well be an imperial throne. Factions are being formed: one is either *for* or *against* the American Bonapartes. Tongues are being untied. Now that old King Jérôme is dead, one can talk about the life he led, unpack details of his numerous gallant adventures and recite the litany of his bastard children. The regime's adversaries, of course, are rubbing their hands: all of this is grist for their mill.

In June the case comes before the imperial tribunal of Paris. The courtroom is packed. Joyful chatter fills the air. The spectators identify the litigants from afar. Prince Napoleon, tall, heavyset, with a disdainful mouth and the profile of a Roman medal that strikingly recalls that of his uncle Napoleon I. And in the opposite corner of the room, an older man who resembles him like a brother and whose physiognomy also evokes that of the great Emperor.

Seated next to him is a very dignified old lady dressed in a short cape of black velvet. She is sitting up very straight with her head held high. Here for everyone to see are her finely chiseled features, the slender bridge of her nose, the smooth oval of her face, and her proud gaze. A murmur runs through the crowd: "Mon Dieu, she must have been devastating . . . she is still very beautiful!"

Berryer deploys all of his eloquence. He spins out this unfinished love story, retraces the despair of this young woman abandoned at the age of twenty when she was pregnant, tossed about on the high seas and chased away from every port in Europe. He evokes the dignified and energetic manner in which she has raised her son, for whom she has provided a solid education. He also talks about the respectability of her Baltimore family, her friendship with the "great Jefferson" and with General Lafayette, as well as the bravery of her grandson, who at this very moment is fighting for the independence of Italy after having distinguished himself in the Crimean War.

A hush has fallen over the audience. There is a lump in every throat. Berryer pushes on, drawing an even more precise portrait of Elizabeth that stresses the admiration she has always had for Napoleon I, despite the way he has treated her, and the veneration she has always had for his image, and which she has passed on to her grandchildren. In order not to compromise this "Bonapartian identity" she has even refused to remarry.

"Look at her," he says, "she has come from a far-away city across the Atlantic. She appears before this august court in order to assert her rights, defend her honor, and demand that her son be reinstated to the position to which he is entitled by his birth."

And then he turns to the precise legal details: No, in 1803 the First Consul (not being the eldest of the family) did not have exceptional powers over his young brother, nor had the dispositions of the new civil Code been enacted yet. Moreover, Madame Letizia's protest against the marriage of 22 February 1805 (which Napoleon had extorted from her) had been presented after the legal time-limit of one year. There had been nothing clandestine about the marriage, which was contracted in complete good faith, and the contract had been signed by illustrious witnesses. Furthermore, Jérôme Bonaparte-Patterson had been restored to French citizenship in 1854 and granted the right to bear the name of Bonaparte. Berryer also pointed out that when Prince Napoleon and his sister appealed to the family council, this very action was proof that they considered Patterson-Bonaparte a member of the imperial family.

The judges seem almost convinced and the audience, which has attentively followed the counsel's argument, leans in favor of Betsy and her son. But Berryer has a formidable opponent, an equally eloquent lawyer by the name of Allou.

"In 1805," he begins, "the Patterson family knew perfectly well that in getting married Jérôme Bonaparte rebelled against the laws of France. This marriage was a clandestine union, and Napoleon had a perfect right to declare it null and void. Louis XVIII acted in the same manner with respect to the duc de Berry, when he annulled his first marriage with an Englishwoman, Amy Brown; the two daughters issued from this marriage have been declared illegitimate. And what will happen, the lawyer adds, to Jérôme's second marriage to Catherine of Württemberg if the first union is recognized as valid? Such a recognition of the first union would cast aspersions on the second one and on the respectable princess who had joined her existence to that of the Emperor's brother. It would also be harmful to Princess Clothilde, daughter of King Victor-Emmanuel, who has joined her life to that of Prince Napoleon.

This turns out to be the final word. It does not take the imperial tribunal long to make its conclusions known: the son of Elizabeth Patterson has no claim to his father's succession; the Pattersons' claim is dismissed, and they are condemned to pay the court costs. A long silence follows the announcement of the verdict. Many in the audience contemplate the American Bonapartes with a great deal of sympathy. Others snicker. Plon-Plon can barely contain his exultation. Without saying a word, Bo and his mother have risen and left the courtroom, accompanied by their attorney.

Betsy is seething inside: that devil, lawyer Allou, has gone so far as to claim that she was twenty-two and Jérôme nineteen when he met her, as if to stress that she was older and therefore more responsible for this marriage. But it wasn't so!

Another page of her life has been turned.

Epilogue

O<small>N THEIR RETURN FROM</small> F<small>RANCE,</small> B<small>O AND HIS</small> mother are plunged into the Civil War. Abraham Lincoln has just been elected to the presidency. He is not a fervent supporter of the abolition of slavery, yet the Southern states, with their extended cotton and tobacco plantations that employ large numbers of slaves, have revolted and decided to secede from the union. This murderous war between the Northern Unionists and the Southern Confederates will end four years later with the defeat of the South.

In Maryland, passions run high and sometimes divide members of one and the same family. Thus Betsy shares the opinions of her son and her brother Edward, who lean toward the Northern side, whereas George, who runs the family's Springfield plantation, adamantly refuses to free the two hundred slaves who work there. But there has been trouble! One night, a Yankee patrol has come by to burn his harvest and steal his horses.

"Too bad for him," Betsy says with a shrug. "That will teach him to be so stubborn. If he wants to get himself massacred, that's his business!"

But George manages to get through the troubles. At the end of the war, he, Betsy, and Edward are the only surviving children of William Patterson: they have inherited their father's strong constitution, and this is a source of pride for them.

Bo is less robust, and his health is beginning to decline. He will soon experience the symptoms of an inexorable disease that will carry him off a few years later. In 1870 — the very year when the Empire crumbles in France — he will die of throat cancer at the age of sixty-five.

Betsy continues to correspond with her grandson. After Italy, he has gone to Africa. Between two campaigns he returns to Paris, where he is warmly received by the Emperor and his family. Empress Eugénie, still beautiful and gracious, often invites him to dine at the Tuileries or at Saint-Cloud. Loulou, the little Prince Imperial, a pretty, rosy-cheeked little child, admires him like a big brother and plays with his sabre and his epaulets amidst peals of laughter. On the other hand, there is one place he studiously avoids, and that is the Avenue Montaigne, where his uncle Plon-Plon has built himself a superb town house in the Pompeian style.

The young man's grandmother has long cherished the hope of seeing him marry a French girl, of noble family if possible, but he is in no hurry to get married. Meanwhile, she consoles herself about his absence by assisting Susan May, her daughter-in-law, in supervising the education of Charles, the family's Benjamin. A very gifted youngster, he is about to enter Harvard, where he will study law. But he has no interest in France, no curiosity about the European Bonapartes. All he wants to do is to stay in America and to get ahead there. Of a physical appearance very different from his older brother's, he is severe, moralistic, almost glacial, and feared for his caustic wit.

After the death of Bo, who has left his pretty residence of Chestnut Wood jointly to his two sons, Betsy will buy Jérôme-Napoleon's share, since he is still in Europe, and give it to Charles. At this point she decides to live in a modest family boarding house on Cathedral Street. Thanks to her skillful investments, she now has a considerable fortune that produces an yearly income of $100,000, of which she spends less than a tenth.

"What good would that do me?" she says, when friends express their surprise. "I have never liked to spend money on myself. Except perhaps for my clothes, when I was young and pretty. Now all of this will go to my grandchildren. I used to have everything but money," she sighs, "now money is all I have left."

She is over eighty now, and one can see her, still slender and straight, dressed in black and holding the inevitable red umbrella that protects her from rain and sun in one hand, and her small pearl-embroidered handbag in the other, making the rounds of her houses to collect rents or talking to a broker. Her miniature poodle, "Bibi Bonaparte," tags along. Betsy has become the best-known figure in Baltimore! People bow as she passes and greet her with respect — a respect most of her fellow citizens had denied her in her youth.

Some, both young and old, come to call on her. Having climbed up, huffing and puffing, the four flights of stairs leading to the tiny apartment she occupies in Miss Glynn's boarding house, they are intimidated in the presence of this old lady with the still lively eyes, who caresses Bibi Bonaparte while she evokes her youthful memories — or who, when she is in a sour mood, mutters incomprehensible words about the "Malapartes." Sometimes, too, her voice grows nostalgic or breaks when she pronounces the name of Prince Gortchakoff. He has been much in the news lately, for he has become state councilor of Russia and helped Czar Alexander II carry out his liberal reforms.

"Belle et Bonne," Lady Morgan, Sismondi, Juliette Récamier, Laure d'Abrantès, Princess Galitzin, the Chouvaloffs, Jérôme and Louis Bonaparte, Pauline, Madame Mère. . . . so many ghosts that haunt the walls of the fourth floor in the Glynn boarding house. In the bedroom and the modest drawing room of Betsy's apartment, she has placed pieces of furniture and prized objects that recall her past. Here is the large mahogany armoire of Provençal style, made in Louisiana, that was given to her long ago by her young husband, along with a writing table and a silver bowl engraved by Biennais, the best silversmith in Paris under the Consulate, and set in a small teak piece, the *French bidet* which at the time was unknown in America. Sèvres porcelain, center pieces, and silver dishes are displayed on an enormous credenza. The shelves are filled to overflowing with books that Betsy has sometimes annotated like a school girl. Among them are the *Mémoires du Roi Jérôme,* written by Baron du Casse, on whose pages she expresses her indignation by crossing out entire lines in a furious hand.

Steamer trunks of painted wood or encased in leather are lined up against the wall and contain treasures that she shows to her wide-eyed visitors: gowns, cashmere shawls, evening cloaks, high-heeled shoes, jewels, tiaras, collections of calling cards bearing the great names of

France, England, Italy, Switzerland, and Russia. Also among these treasures is Princess Borghese's famous evening cloak in pink satin, which
that lady had asked Betsy to return and then sent back to her a few days
later. The object dearest to her, although she does not show it to anyone, is the sheet of yellowed paper, fragment of an unfinished manuscript that had been found in the Emperor's coach at Waterloo: whenever she holds it in her hands, she feels as if she were approaching the
deceased great Emperor.

Betsy makes an effort to read for five hours a day in order to keep
her mind alert. She avidly peruses the papers and comments on the
news. This is how she learns about the unfortunate outcome for France
of the war of 1870 against Prussia. France suffers a tremendous defeat,
and the Second Empire collapses.

Jérôme-Napoleon, who has fought valiantly in that war as well and
has acquired the grade of colonel in the French army, will return to
America after his uncle's fall from power. There is one great disappointment for Betsy: he has not married in France and is about to do so in
America.[1] She is furious and does not speak to him for months on end.

But Napoleon III dies in 1873. And new hope sprouts in Elizabeth's
heart: some day the Empire will be restored and her grandson will have
a role to play in it, perhaps even become emperor himself. Why not? In
America rumor has it that Colonel Jérôme-Napoleon Bonaparte would
not be averse to exercising a co-regency with the Empress during the
minority of the Prince Imperial if the occasion arose. He himself does
not contradict these rumors. He had been very close to the imperial
couple and sincerely mourned the death of Napoleon III, who had held
him in high esteem. When the Empress and her son left France for their
exile at Chislehurst, he had served as their bodyguard. He is in correspondence with various members of the Bonaparte family, among them
Princess Mathilde, with whom he has become reconciled, and who has
opened her doors to him. Betsy clings to this vision of the future. A
smile spreads over her face when this subject is brought up in her presence. Everything is still possible . . .

When she is not reading a book or a newspaper, she busies herself
writing down her memories. She has also written, in deepest secrecy, a

---

[1] Jérôme-Napoleon married the grand-daughter of Daniel Webster.

work that means a great deal to her, and which she has entitled *Dialogue of the Dead*. It is a long poem in which the soul of her father exchanges bitter words with that of her husband; this is her attempt to exorcise the suffering these two men have inflicted on her, long ago.

She is slowly making her way toward the grave. "I am going to live to a hundred!" she sometimes exclaims. She stubbornly refuses to see a doctor when she falls ill. "They are charlatans," she says, "and they cost a fortune!" By sheer willpower, it seems, she always recovers, even when it looks as if the end had come. But one day, when she is ninety-four, she has to take to her bed. With her two grandsons keeping watch, she gradually declines and dies a gentle death on 4 April 1879.

She will be buried after a longer than normal delay in accordance with her instructions, for she was terrified of being buried alive. A simple hearse carries her body to Greenmount Cemetery, where she had acquired a grave site a few years earlier. It is not near the graves of the members of her family, who are all buried at Coldstream. "I have been alone in life," she had declared, "and I wish to be alone in death."

On her gravestone — a long slab of sculpted marble, modeled on that of Napoleon on Saint-Helena — these few words, chosen by herself, have been engraved: *After the fever of a stormy life she has found rest.*

Charles had just been admitted to the bar when his grandmother died. For a few years he will exercise his talents as a lawyer. But the day comes when Theodore Roosevelt, a classmate of his at Harvard, calls him to his side and offers him the position of Secretary of the Navy, and then that of Attorney General of the United States. Surely his success would have been a consolation to Betsy; if her grandsons could not play a major role in Europe, at least one of them has been in a position to do so in America.

Theodore Roosevelt appreciates not only Charles's intelligence but also his sense of humor. He sometimes jokingly compares him to the "Hound of the Baskervilles," saying that he has his gleaming eyes and his stinging tongue. At Roosevelt's side, he leads a long and valiant fight for honesty and plain morality in public life: he is the recognized leader of intelligent and respectable sentiment of the state.[2] He is known as a fearless trust-buster, and will grapple with Standard Oil, theHarriman Railroads, and the tobacco trust (in order to dissolve its monopoly in smoke he says humorously, with his typical whimsical smile). He will also create the Federal Bureau of Investigation, better known as the FBI.

Charles Joseph is a well-known personage in Baltimore, and is easily recognizable in the street with his long, swinging stride, swerving from one part of the sidewalk to the other, tapping with his cane every post or doorstep he passes, and moving his head from side to side.

After retiring from politics, he returns to his legal practice and devotes the last year of his life to Catholic charities. Married to Ellen Channing Day, he will die in 1921, without children.

As for Jérôme-Napoleon, he will have two children: a daughter who marries Count von Moltke-Huitfeldt, attaché in the Danish ministry of foreign affairs, and goes to live in Copenhagen, and a son, Jérôme-Napoleon. In 1913, when Albania has just proclaimed its independence, a delegation of Albanians comes to ask this Bonaparte to rule their country. He declines the offer. The last of the American Bonapartes, Jérôme-Napoleon dies in 1945, leaving no offspring.

So ends the dream of grandeur of a girl from Baltimore . . .

---

[2] Joseph Bucklin Bishop, *Charles Joseph Bonaparte: His Life and Public Services* (New York: Charles Scribner's Sons, 1922).

Sources

Manuscript Collections

Archives des Affaires étrangères: Correspondence politique des Etats-Unis, vols. 55–68: "Mémoires et documents, famille Bonaparte."

Archives departementales de la Corse, Ajaccio.

Archives of the Maryland Historical Society, Baltimore, Maryland.

Service historique de la Marine.

Works about the Bonaparte Family

"Les Bonaparte avant Napoléon." Series of articles in the *Petit Bastiais* in 1930 (1933).

Bernardy, Françoise de. *La reine Hortense*. Paris: Perrin, 1969.

Bertaut, Jules. *Le Roi Jérôme*. Paris: Albin Michel, 1954.

Bertin, Georges. *Joseph Bonaparte en Amérique*. Paris: Librairie de la Nouvelle Revue, 1893.

Bonaparte, Louis. *Les poésies du comte de St.-Leu*. Florence: G. Piatti, 1831.

Castillon du Perron, Marguerite. *La princesse Mathilde*. Paris: Amiot-Dumont, 1953.

Chastenet, G. *Pauline Bonaparte, la fidèle infidèle*. Paris: C. Lattès, 1986.

Du Casse, Albert, baron, ed. *Mémoires et correspondance du roi Jérôme et de la reine Catherine*. Paris: E. Dentu, 1861–66.

———. *Les rois frères de Napoléon*. Paris: Genner, Baillère & Cie, 1883.

Fleuriot de Langle, Paul. *La Paolina, soeur de Napoléon*. Paris: Colbert, 1944.

Guériot, Paul. *Napoléon III*. Paris: Payot, 1980.

Masson, Frédéric. *Napoléon et sa famille*. 13 vols. Paris: Ollendorf, 1898–1907.

Melchior-Bonnet, Bernardine. *Jérôme Bonaparte, ou l'envers de l'époée*. Paris: Perrin, 1979.

Mirtile, Marcel. *Napoléon d'Ajaccio*. Paris: Siboney, 1947.

Murat, Inès. *Napoléon et le rêve américain*. Paris: Fayard, 1976.

Nasica, T. (abbé). *Mémoires sur l'enfance et la jeunesse de Napoléon.* Paris: Ledoyen, 1852.

Pietri, François. *Lucien Bonaparte.* Paris: Plon, 1939.

Thierri, Augustin. *Madame Mère.* Paris: Albin Michel, 1939.

Turquan, Joseph. *Un joyeux souverain, le roi Jérôme.* Paris: Taillandier, 1903.

Diverse Memoirs and Souvenirs

Abrantès, Laure Saint-Martin Junot, duchesse de. *Mémoires . . . ou souvenirs historiques sur Napoléon, la Révolution, le Directoire, le Consulat, l'empire et la Restauration.* 3 vols. Bruxelles: Société belge de librairie, 1837.

Apponye, Rudolph, comte. *Vingt-cinq ans à Paris.* 4 vols. Publiés par Ernest Daudet. Paris: Plon-Nourrit, 1913–26.

Boigne, Charlotte Louise Eléanore Adélaïde. *Mémoires d'une tante.* 4 vols. Paris: Plon-Nourrit, 1908–9.

Bonaparte, Lucien. *Mémoires, écrites par lui-même.* Paris: Gosselin, 1836.

Hugo, Victor. *Choses vues.* 6th ed. Paris: J. Hetzel, 1887.

Hyde de Neuville, baron. *Mémoires et souvenirs.* 3 vols. Paris, Plon-Nourrit, 1888–1920.

Ricard, Joseph-Barthélémy de, general. *Autour des Bonaparte; fragments de mémoires.* Publiés par L.-Xavier de Ricard Paris: Savine, 1887.

General Studies

1. For the period until 1815

Adams, Henry. *History of the United States.* New York: Charles Scribner's Sons, 1921.

Poster, Augustus John. *Jeffersonian America.* San Marino, Calif.: R. Beale, 1954.

Kaplan, Laurence. *Jefferson and France.* New Haven: Yale University Press, 1967.

Quinn, Dorothy M. and Frank White Jr. "Jerome and Betsy Cross the Atlantic. Account of the passage by the Captain of the *Erin*." *Maryland Historical Magazine,* 48 (1953): 204–14.

Saffell, William T. R., *The Bonaparte-Patterson Marriage.* Philadelphia: private printing, 1873. This work is primarily based on Robert Patterson's correspondence with his family and other documents.

2. Period after 1815

Charles-Roux, François. *Rome, asile des Bonaparte.* Paris: Hachette, 1952.

Didier, Eugene Lemoine. *The Life and Letters of Madame Bonaparte.* New York: Charles Scribner's Sons, 1879. Based on Betsy's letters to her family and her European friends.

Gallatin, James. *The Diary of James Gallatin.* New York: Charles Scribner's Sons, 1912.

Méry, Joseph. *Nuits italiennes, contes nocturnes.* Paris: M. Lovy, 1886.

Mitchell, Sidney. *A Family Lawsuit.* New York: Farrar Strauss, 1958.

Oddie [O'Donoghue, Elinor-May]. *The Bonapartes in the New World.* London: E. Matthews & Marrot Ltd., 1932.

Suchet d'Albufera. "Récit du procès Bonaparte-Patterson." *Le Siècle* (February–July, 1861).

Weill, F. "Les Bonaparte de Florence." *Revue des Etudes napoléoniennes.*

Places where Betsy Bonaparte lived
United States

Beirne, Francis. *The Amiable Baltimoreans.* (New York: Dutton, 1951.

———. *Baltimore: A Picture History.* New York: Hastings House, 1958.

Dorsey, John R. and James Dilts. *A Guide to Baltimore Architecture.* Cambridge, Md.: Tidewater Publishers, 1973.

La Rochefoucauld-Liancourt, François Alexandre, duc de. *Journal d'un voyage en Amerique,* publié par Jean Marchand. Baltimore: The Johns Hopkins University Press, 1940.

Moreau de Saint-Méry, Médéric Louis Elie. *Voyage aux Etats-Unis (1793).* Introduction and notes by Stewart L. Minis. New Haven: Yale University Press, 1913.

Murat, Achille. *Esquisse morale et politique des Etats-Unis d'Amérique du Nord.* Paris: Crochard, 1832.

Philips, Edith. Les refugiés bonapartistes aux Etats-Unis. Paris: Editions de la vie universitaire, 1923.

Sioussat, Annie Middleton (Leakin). *Old Baltimore.* New York: Macmillan, 1931.

Wright, Frances. *Voyage au Etats-Unis (1818–1822).* Cambridge, Mass.: Harvard University Press, 1963.

France

Bertaut, Jules. *Le Faubourg Saint Germain sous la Restauration, 1835*. Paris: Les éditions de France, 1935.

Chateaubriand, François Auguste René de. *Memoires d'autre-tombe*. Nouvelle édition. Paris: Garnier fréres, 1910.

Morgan, Sydney (Owenson), Lady. *France*. 4th ed. London: Henry Colburn, 1818. Also: *France in 1829–30*. New York: J. & H. Harper, 1830.

Lenôtre. G. (Gosselin, Louis Léon Théodore.) *Paris qui disparaît*. Paris: B. Grasset, 1937.

Levaillant, Maurice. *Une amitié amoureuse: Mme de Staël et Mme Récamier*. Paris: Hachette, 1956.

Ormesson, Jean d'. *Mon dernier réve sera pour vous*. Paris: J. C. Lattés, 1984.

Stern, Jean. *Belle et Bonne, une fervente amie de Voltaire*. Paris: Hachette, 1938.

Véron, Louis Désiré. *Journal d'un bourgeois de Paris. Comprenant l'empire, la restauration, la monarchie de juilet, et la république jusqu'au rétablissement de l'empire*. 6 vols. Paris: J. de Gouet, 1835–1855.

England

Adburgham, Alison. *Women in Print*. London: Allen & Unwin, 1972.

Bernardy, Françoise de. *Un Falstaff royal, George IV d'Angleterre*. Paris: Librairie académique Perrin, 1970.

Langlade, Jacques de. *Brummel, ou le prince des dandys*. Paris: Presses de la Renaissance, 1894.

Martineau, Gilbert. *Lord Byron*. Paris: Taillandier, 1984.

Trevelyan, George Macaulay. *English Social History in the 19th Century*. London: Longmans Green, 1945.

Geneva

Andryane, Alexandre. *Souvenirs de Genéve*. Paris: W. Coquebert, 1839.

Courthion, Pierre. *Genéve ou le portrait de Toepffer*. Paris: Grasset, 1936.

Sayoux, Alexandre. "La haute bourgeoisie de Genéve entre le début du XVIIe et le milieu du XIXe siécle,"*Revue Historique*, 1937.

Toepffer, Rodolphe. *Aventures du Dr. Festus*. Paris: Dufrénoy, 1923.

————. *Aventures de M. Jabot.* Paris: Dufrénoy, 1923.

————. *Voyages en zig-zag.* Paris: Garnier, 1860.

Italy

Brillant, Maurice. *Le charme de Florence.* Paris: Blond et Cie, 1912.

Chateaubriand, François Auguste René de. *Memoires d'outre-tombe.* Paris: Garnier frères, 1910.

Faure, Gabriel. *Les jardins de Rome.* Grenoble: J. Rey, 1923.

Staël, Germaine de. *Corinne ou l'Italie.* 3 vols. 7th edition. Paris: Nicolle, 1818.

Stendhal (Henri Beyle). *Rome, Naples et Florence en 1817.* Paris: Julliard, 1964.

I have also made use of many books and articles on daily life in the above-named countries at various times, especially the Hachette series "Vieauotidienne," the series *Cercle Historia,* and *National Geographic Magazine.*

Index